YOUR HIDDEN SUPERPOWERS

HOW THE WHOLE TRUTH OF FAILURE CAN CHANGE OUR LIVES

BECCA NORTH

Published by Severn River Publishing.

First edition 2018.

CONTENTS

To my nieces and nephews—Sika, Cora, Yema, Billy, and Dylan,
When you are old enough to read this book, I hope it makes you
think and feel in ways that matter to you.

To Mom, Dad, Catherine, and Angie,
Thank you for being who you are. And thank you for your
unconditional love. Both mean so much.

To Grandma and Grandad,
The way you lived your lives—with courage, love, conviction
rooted in your values, integrity, a desire to seek challenges, and
a wonderful sense of adventure—inspires me.

"We delight in the beauty of the butterfly, but rarely admit the changes it has to go through to achieve that beauty."

— Dr. Maya Angelou

"I want you to first think about the virtue of failure.... If we are to profit from failure, to learn from it, then we are free to imagine, take on impossible things that we would otherwise avoid for fear of failure."

— Reverend Peter Gomes

"It is impossible to live without failing at something, unless you live so cautiously that you might as well not have lived at all—in which case, you fail by default."

— J. K. Rowling

"Last night, as I was sleeping, I dreamt... that I had a beehive here inside my heart. And the golden bees were making white combs and sweet honey from my old failures."

— ANTONIO MACHADO

"O my friends, there are resources in us on which we have not drawn."

— RALPH WALDO EMERSON

PREFACE

Like old photographs curled at the corners, favorite books, sports rivalries, fancy clocks and watches, family stories of triumph and tragedy, wartime letters, love itself, and sometimes hate, beliefs get passed down from one generation to another. Beliefs can get passed down within all kinds of groups, like families, communities, and society as a whole. The beliefs held by society today can be identified by finishing sentences that start with "Society tells us that," but where these beliefs began and why they stuck can be mysterious. They must have taken root at some point and then spread widely before leaping forward over time to us. What seems clearer to me is that in many cases, once these beliefs arrived to us, after the process of rooting and circulating and sticking had taken place, they were absorbed into the fabric of our society. They were such a part of us that they were no longer visible. They are now like unwritten rules, not explicitly stated but widely known. Because such beliefs are so ingrained in us, we often take them as "givens," assuming that they are true. It seems very possible though that some of these "givens" are not true. Even ones that were true at a particular time may not be true now, similar to how the lenses that helped me see clearly in sixth grade when I first got glasses would cloud my vision now. So, it seems worthwhile to test these beliefs, these lenses, from time to time: to take a fresh look at the unwritten rules. First, to bring old assumptions out of their storage places and hold them up to the light—to see what they actually are, to identify them and become aware of them, to make explicit what was implicit. And then to inspect them. To test them. To kick the tires on them, so to speak, and see if they hold up today. To see if they are accurate and help us see clearly.

Some of these society-wide beliefs probably don't matter at all. Whether they are true has no real impact. The notion that people shouldn't wear white after Labor Day seems to fall into that category.

Others, however, matter enormously. They affect the way we act in important ways; they influence the way we live. The truthfulness of these beliefs is vital. Our view of failure is one of these beliefs. It has a major impact on our lives. And, I thought to myself years ago, I am not sure that it is true. Questioning the prevailing view of failure is the motivation of this book. The book begins with a particular part of that big aim, a question that sparked the investigation, years ago, that ultimately led to this book: What *is* the relationship between failure and success? The answer, as you will see, reveals that the way we think about failure is misguided. It is only a slice of the truth. Yet this partial truth has a full-blown consequence. It suppresses our superpowers.

INTRODUCTION

" *The second day they put you in swimming. You have to do a swimming test in a seven-foot pool. And I came from the inner city of Chicago. I didn't know how to swim. So, I told him, I said, "Sir, I don't know how to swim." And he gave me a ten-pound rubber brick and said, "Swim as long and as far as you can." I said, "I can't swim." And they said, "Get in the pool." So the brick went down. I went down.*

— Coach Mike Krzyzewski ("Coach K"), on
failing his swim test at West Point

On a spring afternoon in 1991, near the end of ninth grade, I walked out of my high school library bearing a thrilling secret. On the outside, I was still trying to contain myself, probably wearing a slightly tamped-down smile, but on the inside, I was about to burst with excitement about my subversive discovery. I hadn't witnessed or engaged in any illicit, detention-worthy behavior as you might suppose. This

3

"secret" was in a book on a shelf in the library. I came across it while doing research for a paper for my English class. Here is what I read: when William Shakespeare was in school, he experienced failures but hid them because they made him feel self-conscious, and he didn't want his peers to know. At first, I was stunned and confused: Shakespeare failed? My mind went into slow motion as it sunk in: Shakespeare, as in *the* William Shakespeare, failed. This new knowledge exhilarated and comforted me because it flew in the face of an assumption I had taken for granted my entire life: extremely successful people do not fail. More recently, a Shakespeare scholar told me that we know too little about Shakespeare's early life to answer questions about any school failures, so there seems to be no support whatsoever for what I remember reading. Regardless, this "secret" had a lasting impact on me. It planted a seed of interest —one that would bloom years later—in the hidden role that failure plays in people's lives.

That seed of interest bloomed in the spring of 2004 when I saw a certain billboard. Seriously. On the left side of the billboard was a big picture of Abraham Lincoln, and on the right were the words: "Failed, failed, failed. And then…" And underneath those words was "persistence." As a lover of history and a history major in college, the billboard grabbed my attention and prompted me to go back to my history books to see exactly when and how Lincoln failed. Consider this timeline of defeats leading up to his presidency. It doesn't include all his failures, but it provides a sense of how intimately he knew defeat.

1832—Lost election to Illinois state legislature
1848—Lost election to US House of Representatives
1854—Ran for US Senate and lost
1858—Ran for US Senate and lost
1860—Elected president of the United States

Lincoln not only experienced many failures, he experienced many big failures. We are not talking about a long list of everyday mistakes.

Over time, I began to realize that other people who have shaped history with their profound success also have failed in big ways. Winston Churchill, for example, was fired as first lord of the Admiralty, the equivalent of secretary of the navy in the United States, during World War I for involving Britain in a disastrous, failed military campaign in Gallipoli. Later, he lost a string of parliamentary elections before he became prime minister and courageously led Britain to victory over Germany and the Axis powers in World War II. Ulysses S. Grant is another example. He was a failed farmer, a failed businessman, and an alcoholic before he became head of the Union army, led the Union to victory in the Civil War, and was elected president of the United States. I started to wonder: Was it just a coincidence that these individuals who had shaped history with their success also had experienced major failures? Or was there some connection between their failures and the tremendous success that followed? In other words, was it possible that failing fueled greater success?

A few years after seeing the Lincoln billboard, that question lingered in my mind. I was a doctoral student in psychology at the University of Texas and wondered if failure could foster greater psychological success, or flourishing. And if so, how could we respond to failure in a way that would be associated with greater subsequent flourishing? I decided to investigate that question for my dissertation, and over the next two and a half years, I designed studies for my dissertation, collected and analyzed data, and wrote up the results. I was very excited by what I found. (The findings are discussed in part 3, Turning the Dust of Our Shoes to Gems.) And my excitement fueled my desire to understand the relationship between failure and success more fully. I decided to investigate further by taking a more creative, personal approach. I wanted to interview people who inspire me from a broad range of careers—writers, businesspeople, political leaders, sports figures, educators, scientists, entertainers, etc.—about what role, if any, failure had played in their success. And I wanted to integrate the research and insights from the interviews—the science and stories—to write a book investigating the relationship between failure and success. That idea grew into this book.

Part of what draws me to this topic is that it touches on one of our most vital, personal questions: How can I reach my full potential? And it involves one of our most intimidating, shame-inducing fears: failure. Then it links the two together—what we yearn for most deeply and what we fear most—in a counterintuitive, somewhat unnerving, but also freeing way. Failure, rather than blocking us from what we want in life, may actually be a vehicle that helps us get there. Failures may not only help in the unfolding of our full potential—they may in fact be needed.

The Interviews

In the summer of 2010, right after I graduated with my PhD in psychology, I started contacting people for interviews. I contacted *a lot* of people. And I got *a lot* of rejections. A lot. Some rejections came in the form of no response. Some were generic form letters. Some were curt, even unkind. A couple were heartwarming, seriously heartwarming. They were personalized, thoughtful, and encouraging rejections—the kind (and I didn't even know this kind existed until I got them) that make you want to get rejected again. Thank you to the teams of J. K. Rowling and the late Steve Jobs for the most uplifting rejections I may have ever received. I also received acceptances from individuals who have had a major impact on the world through their work in a range of fields—poetry and literature, politics, sports, education, business, social media, technology, and, more generally, leadership.

The process of deciding whom I wanted to interview was simple. My main criterion was completely subjective: "people who inspire me," which can be roughly translated as people whose remarkable success has had a meaningful impact on the world. Other than that, I only had a couple of guidelines. I hoped to talk with people from a wide range of careers whom many other people would know—public-figure types. I wanted to learn about the relationship between failure and success in these individuals' lives by going to the source. I wanted to know if they had failed, what they considered to be their biggest failures, and what role, if any, they felt failure had played in their success.

Ultimately, I interviewed Dr. Maya Angelou, US Senator Cory Booker, Carl Hayden (former head of the State University of New York), Mayor Pam Iorio (former mayor of Tampa and current president and CEO of Big Brothers Big Sisters of America), Coach Mike Krzyzewski ("Coach K"; head coach of men's basketball at Duke University and former head of the US men's team, whose story of his swim test at West Point is continued in chapter 2); Libby Leffler Hoaglin (senior manager of strategic partnerships at Facebook at the time of the interview and named "Most Important Woman Under 30 in Tech" by *Business Insider* in 2013; currently vice president of membership of a finance company called SoFi, which, according to its website, is "a new kind of finance company taking a radical approach to lending and wealth management"); and Dr. James McPherson (Pulitzer Prize–winning historian who spoke about the role of failure in Abraham Lincoln's success).

The interviews were in person, in depth, and refreshingly

candid. Even though these seven individuals inspired me before I met them, they inspired me even more when we talked. The interviews are woven into the fabric of this entire book and offer powerful insights, emotional richness, wisdom, and humanity beyond what I could have imagined.

Science and Stories: The Substance of the Book

This book draws on my scientific research but also on a broader kind of research. Like a historian or journalist, I pull from a range of sources, including the in-person interviews, scientific research of other experts, literature, philosophy, speeches, biographies, and popular culture, to discern underlying patterns. Whereas scientific research sheds light on what is true on average but not necessarily for any one individual, stories reveal what is true for one individual but not necessarily for others. Therefore, these two kinds of evidence complement each other in homing in on truth. Together, science and stories make up the substance of the book.

By using this approach, I argue that the deepest, most resonant, universal truths of being human are not found in traditional ways of thinking, like intellectual vs. emotional or science vs. art, nor do they obey conventional boundaries of academic fields: history, literature, philosophy, psychology. They transcend these boundaries and are best glimpsed through multiple lenses. The deepest, most far-reaching truths are found at the intersection of conventional categories, and that is precisely where this book lies.

While working on this book, some people asked me whether it was a self-help book. In a sense, it is. I hope that people find it useful in a personally meaningful way. But it is not a "how-to" book. It is not prescriptive and does not aim to be definitive. It is an ideas book. While drawing from a sweeping range and unique combination of sources, this book ultimately offers my perspective, my voice, to the ongoing society-wide conversation.

The Architecture of the Book

The book begins by considering the way we think about failure and the impact that our view of failure has on the way we lead our lives. Consider for a moment how you think about failure. What is your relationship with it? If failure were a person, how would you describe your feelings toward it? How would you feel if it asked to stop by your house? If you saw it in an aisle of the grocery store, what would you do? We tend to think of failure as *bad*, completely bad, like an enemy. We tend to want it out of our lives, never to show its face. At the very least, we want it around as little as possible. And this way of thinking makes a lot of sense given that failure has a readily apparent dark side. It's painful and embarrassing. Oftentimes it's humiliating. And it's scary. Failure can be threatening not only because of its immediate consequences but also because we fear that it might signal even worse outcomes in the future. If you perform poorly on a test in college, you might worry that it means you will be a failure in the real world. If you get fired from a job or overlooked for a promotion, you might be afraid that you will never achieve your goals in the future. The view that failure is bad does reflect part of the truth of failure. But it also hides part of the truth—a big part. Failure has a powerful light side, but it gets overlooked, obscured, and oftentimes completely hidden.

Part 1: The Light exposes the potent bright side of failure—illuminating unseen dimensions and cranking up the light on less visible, overlooked parts. Part 1 starts with the question that is fundamental to the book: What is the relationship between failure and success? Once established, this fundamental connection raises another question: What is the pathway —or pathways—from failure to greater success? In other words, what are the benefits of failure that fuel success? Part 1 digs beneath the relationship between failure and success to expose many pathways and then spotlights a particular hidden pathway that is extremely powerful and especially relevant in today's world. Uncovering this "secret pathway" is a driving force in part 1.

In *Part 2: The Dark*, we take an unflinching yet tender look at the dark side of failure. Failure has a dark side: pain and humiliation. Counterintuitively, acknowledging failure's downside can help us extract failure's benefits, whereas refusing to acknowledge it blocks us from the benefits. Part 2 reveals that feeling pain after failure is universal; even people we might assume would not hurt after failure, like those who report not caring what others think of them or extremely accomplished public figures, feel pain when they fail.

Part 3: Turning the Dust of Our Shoes to Gems turns to this question: How can I respond well to failure? Failure creates tinder—raw material for something better—but if we don't convert the tinder, it becomes waste. Part 3 puts forth an approach for converting the waste to treasure. The poet and philosopher Ralph Waldo Emerson wrote that if a person "harvests his losses," then he "turns the dust of his shoes to gems." So how can we turn the dust of our shoes to gems? Part 3 taps into cutting-edge research addressing a new line of questioning about responding well to failure: How can we grow from failure? In other words, how can we respond to failure in a way that allows us not just to bounce back or recover from it, but to grow? This question drives part 3, and the answer is surprising, counterintuitive, and conventional-wisdom defying; it shatters current assumptions we have about responding well to failure.

Part 4: Hidden Magic envisions how changing the way we think about failure would change the way we lead our lives. And it imagines the impact that such a shift in how we live would have on us as individuals and as a society. The answers are quite simple and revolutionary. Whereas the question "can failure foster greater success?" is foundational to the book, there are underlying questions in the book that emerge at different moments and come together in part 4. These questions, at the heart of the book, are among the biggest questions we have for our lives: How can I reach my full potential? How can I find the courage to live a life that is true to myself? How can I cultivate greater happiness? How can I change the world? And like a deep root connecting all these questions: How can I feel freer? The questions are diverse but the answers converge, and they are deeply and inextricably linked in a counterintuitive way to one of our most overwhelming fears: failure.

Ultimately, this book aims to shift how we view failure by exposing more of the whole truth of failure. It aims to shift our view in a way that is registered not only in the mind but also in the gut—rewriting the story we tell ourselves about failure. Changing our view of failure would change our lives—and our world—beyond what we can imagine. How? It would change how we lead our lives, in ways that would feel bolder and freer. In the last part of the book, I put forth a vision of what this new, more audacious way of living would look like. Such a shift in how we live would empower and nourish us. It would yield profound benefits for us as individuals and as a society by exposing hidden resources within us—unleashing innovations, breakthroughs, joy, meaning, and magic yet to be discovered.

What Is Failure?

It is worth pausing to clarify a definition: What exactly is failure? There is subjectivity in what people call a failure, but the dictionary definition provides some clarity: *fail* means "to be unsuccessful in what is attempted." Whenever we go after a goal and don't reach it, that is failing. If you want to stay at your job and you get fired, that's a failure. If you interview for a job that you want and don't get it, that's a failure. Going for a promotion and being passed up is a failure. Failing also can mean doing something poorly or inadequately, like delivering an ineffective presentation or performing "The Star-Spangled Banner" off-key. In social situations, failure often is in the form of rejection. When you want to date someone and the person says no, that is a failure. If you want a relationship to continue and it dissolves, that is a failure. This does not mean that you are a failure, it means that this particular effort was a failure. There certainly is a spectrum in terms of magnitude of failures: a swing and a miss at a softball game is typically minor, whereas getting fired from a job is usually major. The failures discussed in this book hover near the "big" end of the spectrum.

We tend to dislike the word *failure*. It can feel imbued with harshness, judgment, and pain, and so we tend to avoid using it. We might argue, for example, that if a particular failure leads to something better, it is not a failure. This either–or interpretation, however—either it was a failure or it led to something better and therefore was not a failure—overlooks failure's straightforward definition. Failing has to do with whether you reached the goal you were aiming for; it does not speak to what followed from the outcome. When a failure leads to something better, I would suggest that this is a both–and scenario—it was both a failure and led to something positive. Often when we avoid the word *failure*, we intend to remove its power: to render this scary word impotent. Ironically, avoiding it may increase its power, whereas using it may sap its power. So, in this book, I use the word *failure*, and when I do, I am drawing on the "you-tried-to-reach-some-goal-and-you-didn't" definition.

On a practical note, to allow for a more fluid reading experience, I use no footnotes, but all references are in the notes section at the back of the book, organized by chapter. Also, you will notice that many stories include substantial quotations. This is especially true for the interviews. My aim was to draw on people's own telling of their stories as much as possible, and in the case of the interviews, to provide a felt sense of what it was like to be in the room with each person. The portions of the interviews that are in this book are from longer conversations; interviews were on average about one and a half hours and ranged from approximately forty-five minutes to three hours. I selected what I felt were the most essential, poignant, and, in some cases, humorous parts.

Now is the time to take a fresh, frank look at failure.

1

THE WAY WE THINK ABOUT FAILURE

In January 2012, Bronnie Ware, who worked in palliative care for many years, wrote an article called "Top 5 Regrets of the Dying." She had cared for patients in the last weeks of their lives, and in talking with them, she often heard about their biggest regrets. She noticed recurring themes and wrote the article to share the most common ones. The number one regret? "I wish I'd had the courage to live a life true to myself, not the life others expected of me." The top regret of people facing death illuminates a deep conflict inside many of us: How can *I* find the courage to live a life that is true to myself rather than one that others expect of me? The desire to live that kind of life is one of the deepest yearnings we have. And it is extremely hard to do. Discovering what that looks like—what it really means—and then finding the courage to do it is difficult. This book offers an answer to that deep-seated question: the amount of courage we can muster to live in an authentic way is intimately tied to the way we think about failure.

The way we think about failure affects our lives powerfully, often in ways we don't see. The way that most of us currently view failure—the prevailing view—is that failure is bad. This view of failure holds us back. It limits our imaginations and shrinks our ambitions. It paralyzes our courage to pursue our boldest goals. It serves as a barrier that blocks us from accessing the entirety of our resources and tapping our full potential, and it prevents us from experiencing our full capacity for meaning and joy. And this view of failure is highly skewed. It is one-sided. It is only a slice of the truth based on a single story about failure.

If the way we think about failure had no real impact on our lives, our faulty view of it would not be a problem. But that's not the case. The way we think drives the way we act, and the way we think about failure drives the way we act in big ways. It shapes the way we lead our lives.

Seeing failure as bad leads us to invest enormous time and energy into not failing: avoiding failure. Avoiding failure actually becomes a main life goal. We don't usually say that explicitly, but the way we approach life can reflect it. This type of approach can take on various forms in everyday life. It can mean having some version of these unwritten rules govern your decisions: don't mess this up, don't get this wrong, don't look dumb, avoid any chance of rejection, don't make a mistake, don't embarrass yourself. It can mean always trying to avoid disapproval or rejection, or conversely, being preoccupied with obtaining approval or praise. In this approach to living, preoccupation with outrunning failure is always on the scene, guiding our decisions. Fear of failure looms, and it can show up in a host of guises: fear of being judged as inadequate, appearing stupid, being rejected, humiliating yourself, not making others proud. The omnipresent fear of failure demands attention and contracts the scope of what we dare to do. It restricts our goals to areas that involve a high probability of success. It leads us to take fewer risks, to play it safer, hoping to maintain a spotless record or winning streak. And it nudges us to ignore our deepest passions out of a fear that if we fail in those efforts, that pain would hurt the most. With the specter of failure looming, we stay well within the bounds of our capacity. In important ways, our view of failure leads to an impoverished way of living.

This way of leading our lives is alluring though because in the short term, it can shield us from pain, embarrassment, and humiliation. And given the belief that failure is all bad, this approach makes sense. Who would even want to flirt with failure if it only has disastrous consequences?

But this way of living also has costs—big costs—for us as individuals and as a society. By leading us to stay well within the bounds of what is possible, it leaves a wealth of untapped potential within us. By holding us back, it draws on a limited range of our resources, leaving vital parts of us dormant. It steals from us in a couple of other ways too. It leads us to hide failure when it does happen, out of shame, and hiding failure blocks us from reaping its rewards. And, to the extent that we succeed in minimizing failure, we miss out on what failure offers. By leaving us sitting on top of powerful, untouched resources, this way of living prevents us from realizing our full potential.

To get a fuller sense of the costs of this way of living, consider an analogy of learning a new language while living abroad. If you have ever tried to learn another language while living amongst native speakers, you know that the beginning phase can be hard and humbling. This was definitely the case for me when I went to Chile for a summer exchange program after my sophomore year in high school. I had taken two years of high school Spanish, so I had a solid grasp of the fundamentals, but my knowledge of the language was still quite limited. And I had little experience speaking Spanish with native speakers or really anyone outside my class. The first several days were hard, especially for my ego. While eating dinner with my host family or going out with my host sister and her friends, I often felt lost. I couldn't keep up with the conversation. I remember my host father telling jokes, and I had no idea what he was saying. I didn't even know that he had told a joke until everyone started laughing and looked at me to see if I was laughing too. At that point, I would start laughing—trying hard to keep up with the flow of the group. When I spoke up, I often would mangle phrases, use the wrong verb tenses, and inadvertently slip in English phrases, like "I mean… I mean." Sometimes when I would talk, people would laugh. It didn't even feel like they were trying to be mean. Typically, they found some mispronunciation endearing or an incorrect word choice amusing. Nonetheless, it was hard. And at times, with my elementary comprehension and speaking abilities, I didn't just feel like a beginning Spanish speaker, I felt dumb and socially awkward. As a result, I felt a strong desire to avoid these gaffes. That desire made me want to engage less and maximize time with my three-year-old host brother, who I felt was more or less on my level of language ability. Giving over to this understandable urge would mean avoiding feeling embarrassed, stupid, and sometimes hurt by my communication fumbles in the short term. But in the longer term, it also would have meant forgoing growth in my language abilities and friendships; it would have diminished my entire experience. The impact is very similar when we give in to the urge to place high priority on avoiding failure in our lives. The benefits are alluring, but the costs are profound.

Going toward Comfort

Years ago, a close friend from high school and I drove to Lost Maples State Natural Area in the Texas Hill Country, a few hours from my home in Austin, to hike. On a country road about fifteen miles from Lost Maples, my car ground to a halt. It felt like we hit a thick layer of molasses. When I pulled over to the side of the road, I saw that the front right tire had shredded. It had blown out completely. We called AAA emergency roadside assistance for help putting on the spare tire, but shortly after we called, two motorcyclists passing by offered to help, and we took them up on their offer. After the spare tire was in place, we drove to a gas station to ask if there was a tire shop on this side of the park. The answer was no, so we decided to go to Lost Maples and hike and get a new tire afterward. Right before entering Lost Maples, we stopped at a local country store outside the park for drinks and snacks. The two motorcyclists were inside. We had a short conversation with them and thanked them again for their help. When we walked back to the car, we saw that the spare tire had deflated almost entirely. We were laughing at the absurdity of our unlikely situation—two flat tires in less than a half hour. But we were also a little scared. We didn't know exactly how far away the closest tire store was, but it wasn't close, and we weren't sure how much farther we could travel with a nearly flat spare tire. The motorcyclists were still in the store, so we went back inside to see if they had any guidance, and they pointed us to a particular product—some spray-foam situation—that temporarily inflates the tire and patches the leak. We bought it. It worked and we drove the short distance to Lost Maples and had a lovely hike. As we got on the road after the hike, though, we were both on edge. We knew that we would be in trouble if the temporary fix on the spare tire didn't last until we could get to a tire shop. Even if the temporary fix stayed on, spare tires aren't designed to last that long—maybe sixty miles or so—and there weren't many towns nearby. There also weren't many cars on the road in this rural area, and neither of us had consistent cell phone service to call for help if we needed it. As these realities sunk in, we passed signs warning us of steep hills for the next several miles. I can't remember the exact language, but they were almost farcically daunting. They weren't signs I had seen before, and I haven't seen them since. I was doing a running estimation in my head of the likelihood that we could walk the miles of steep hills if the tire gave out. We were both fairly fit, but it was hot, and the hike and Texas summer heat had already worn us out. After forty-five minutes or so of driving in scared silence, we drove by a road sign with two towns on it. My friend snapped a picture of it.

"Comfort 7?" We erupted in nervous laughter. The idea that

someone could assure us that comfort was coming in seven miles was precisely what we wanted at that moment. About thirty minutes after passing this sign, we arrived at a tire shop, got a new tire, and that was the end of our scare. But the episode made me think more deeply about the allure of comfort.

First, I thought about how wonderful it would be to have a sign like that in difficult times—a sign that not only assured me that comfort was coming but told me how far away it was. There have been times in my life when I would have done the freaking crab walk for seven miles if someone could have promised me comfort when I arrived. But on a broader level, the experience made me reflect on how the desire for comfort plays a central role in our lives. Going toward comfort and away from discomfort or pain describes the way many of us tend to lead our lives. This unspoken mantra can characterize how we make small and big decisions, how we live our moments as well as our months and years.

And this approach has real benefits. It motivates us to tend to our emotional and physical needs and to seek protection and salves in distressing times. It steers us away from situations that could be dangerous or harmful and motivates us to take action when we get sick or injured. It protects us.

But our tendency to be comfort seeking and pain avoiding has costs. It leads us to pay extra attention—to give extra air time, so to speak—to failure's real but not defining downside. It means that failure's downside monopolizes our attention, and we see failure in a one-dimensional way. We see it as bad. And when we—who as human beings tend to be comfort seeking and pain avoiding—see failure as bad, it makes us want to place top priority on avoiding failure.

So, the current way we view failure has severe consequences. And here's the other thing: it is not accurate. It reflects only a slice of the truth.

* * *

When I met with Pulitzer Prize–winning historian Dr. James McPherson in his office in Princeton, New Jersey, on a fall afternoon in 2010, the big question on my mind was: What is the relationship between failure and success? I went there to talk with him about what role failure played in the success of Abraham Lincoln. Consider what I discovered.

PART I

THE LIGHT

2

FAILURE AND SUCCESS

I n October of 2010, I flew from my home in Austin, Texas, to New Jersey to interview Dr. James McPherson, Professor Emeritus of American History at Princeton University and expert on the Civil War. That spring was when I had decided that I wanted to interview people who inspire me about what role failure played in their success. Abraham Lincoln was high on my list, and Dr. McPherson was the Lincoln scholar I hoped to interview. When he agreed in the summer of 2010, my first interview was set.

Although Lincoln's many failures are well documented, it can be hard to register them, to really feel their weight, in light of his subsequent success. It can be easy to discount them or even forget them because they seem incongruous with the image of our national hero. But imagine for a moment that you were a friend of Lincoln's in 1859. Over the course of ten-plus years, he has run for a major political office three times and lost every time. He lost in two consecutive elections for the US Senate and his last run for the US House of Representatives. He never won an election for the Senate, but now he is telling you he wants to run for president. What would you feel as he spoke? It would be understandable if you would be sighing in frustration, rolling your eyes, or cringing in embarrassment for your friend. Many people at the time must have wondered privately what it was going to take for Lincoln to understand that he wasn't cut out for such a high level of leadership.

When I asked Dr. McPherson what he thought Lincoln considered to be his biggest, most painful failure, he said losing the election for US Senate in 1854. It was the first of two times that Lincoln ran for US Senate and was defeated. He ran as a candidate of the anti-Nebraska Coalition, a precursor to the Republican Party, that opposed the Kansas-Nebraska Act opening the Kansas Territory to slavery. The Illinois Democratic Party at the time was in favor of opening the territory to slavery. Lincoln ran against two men: the Democratic Party candidate and an antislavery former Democrat. At the time, US senators were elected by state legislatures, and in this election, there were many rounds of voting. After about seven rounds, Lincoln had a plurality of votes but fell short of a majority by five or six votes. On the next round, it appeared that a contingent of antislavery former Democrats were going to swing their votes to the Democratic Party candidate who supported opening the Kansas Territory to slavery. Lincoln didn't want that to happen, so to prevent it, he withdrew from the race, thereby releasing his votes to the antislavery former Democrat, Lyman Trumbull, who won the election.

The defeat hit Lincoln hard. "Lincoln clearly was hurt," Dr. McPherson said. *Hurt* is the word McPherson used most frequently to describe how Lincoln felt after the loss. The hardest part seemed to be the politicking that forced him to yield his votes: "The manipulation of politics is what cut him off at the knees there. I think that probably hurt him."

McPherson added that after the defeat, Lincoln reportedly said that "it was like the boy who had stubbed his toe... he was too big to cry, but it hurt too much to smile." Many apocryphal quotations are attributed to Lincoln, McPherson mentioned, so it is hard to know if he actually said that. "But clearly he felt that way; there is no question about that."

Still, Lincoln's failure provided opportunities. "Even though he lost in '54, and I think the loss hurt, I think it was a step toward bigger things for him," said McPherson. In the short term, the loss enabled him to build a stronger following. "By giving up his own ambition in 1854," McPherson explained, "I think he created a feeling among Illinois Republicans that they owed him one now because he had given up his ambitions in order to make sure that this new party—it wasn't even yet called the Republican Party in Illinois, the anti-Nebraska Coalition—achieved success. The next time a chance came around, which was 1858, the next time Illinois had to elect another senator, he was the guy that was going to get the nomination because of what had happened in '54, and so the party backed him unanimously."

Then he lost again. The campaigning he did that year, though, created another opportunity: a chance to prove himself on a bigger stage. Lincoln engaged in a series of seven debates with his opponent, Stephen Douglas, who was considered the most prominent politician in the country. Lincoln went toe-to-toe with Douglas, fighting him "almost to a draw," showing that he was a formidable political contender. Through his performance in the debates, Lincoln garnered a broader regional reputation: "Here's somebody who had fought the foremost politician in the country almost to a standstill and almost had beat him, so that was another step toward national prominence for Lincoln." The experience seemed to shift the way Lincoln thought about himself as well. McPherson said that this shift was revealed in a letter Lincoln wrote in 1859: "Earlier in response to suggestions along that line [whether he wanted to run for president], he had said he didn't think he was qualified for the presidency and what he really would like to achieve was election to senator from Illinois, which of course, he had tried twice, but in 1859 he wrote to a political friend, saying, 'The taste *is* in my mouth a little.' So by that stage, I think he was beginning to take seriously the prospect that he might become the Republican nominee."

Lincoln's performance in the debates with Douglas, McPherson said, is likely what earned him an invitation in late 1859 from a Republican club in New York City to give a lecture on politics at Cooper Union, a college in New York. His Cooper Union speech was an enormous success, and McPherson believes that it probably changed the way Lincoln saw himself even more than the debates with Douglas, and it earned him a national reputation: "I think... what gave him an even greater boost was the success of his Cooper Union speech in New York City in February 1860 and the New England speaking tour that he made just after that when he was widely praised. Up until that time, he was pretty much unknown in the northeast, which was really the power center of American politics at that time. This made him widely known and widely admired in the northeast for the first time. I think that probably, not only did it boost his candidacy, but I think it probably also convinced him that he was a viable candidate, even more so than back when he had said, 'The taste is in my mouth.'" McPherson said that Lincoln believed and historians agree that the speech was "a launching pad for him." Later in our talk, McPherson underscored its importance, saying that the speech "really was the major launching pad toward the nomination" for presidential candidate of the Republican Party.

So, briefly, what was it about that speech? What did he say, and why was it so impactful? McPherson explained:

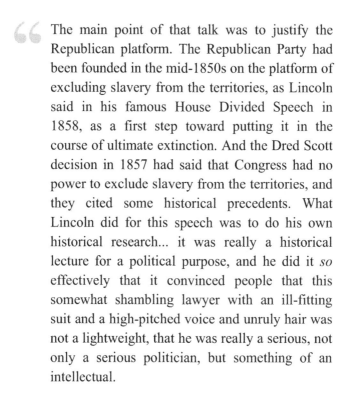

The main point of that talk was to justify the Republican platform. The Republican Party had been founded in the mid-1850s on the platform of excluding slavery from the territories, as Lincoln said in his famous House Divided Speech in 1858, as a first step toward putting it in the course of ultimate extinction. And the Dred Scott decision in 1857 had said that Congress had no power to exclude slavery from the territories, and they cited some historical precedents. What Lincoln did for this speech was to do his own historical research... it was really a historical lecture for a political purpose, and he did it *so* effectively that it convinced people that this somewhat shambling lawyer with an ill-fitting suit and a high-pitched voice and unruly hair was not a lightweight, that he was really a serious, not only a serious politician, but something of an intellectual.

I commented that it sounded like the argument Lincoln put forth in this speech was "kind of a new argument," and McPherson said:

It wasn't a new argument so much as it was providing proof that the framers of the Constitution and the founders of the country... had intended to give Congress that power [to exclude slavery from the territories] as opposed to the ruling by the Supreme Court in 1857 [the

Dred Scott decision] that they [the framers of the Constitution and the founders of the country] had not [given Congress that power]. It was really a challenge to the Supreme Court and its interpretation of the Constitution, and [it] supported the position of what had now become the majority party in the north, the Republicans.

The speech was distributed widely: "All four or five of the major New York daily papers reported that speech in full, and then it was published in pamphlet form and scattered by the hundreds of thousands over the country, so it had a huge impact."

Just before delivering the Cooper Union speech, Lincoln had his picture taken at the New York studio of the photographer Matthew Brady. McPherson said that it "was quite a flattering photograph of Lincoln, who, you know... was not the best-looking man in the world." As McPherson told me, Lincoln later said "that Brady's photograph [below] and my Cooper Union speech made me president."

Lincoln's most painful failure appeared to create a ripple of opportunities that eventually led to his presidency. It is, of course, impossible to know to what extent his failures caused his subsequent success. Would he still have become president if he had won the Senate seat in 1854? Would he have been the transformative leader that he was? We cannot know what his trajectory would have been like had he not experienced his failures. But from Dr. McPherson's perspective, Lincoln used his loss in 1854 and his other failures as fodder for reaching bigger goals in the long term: "Lincoln used every failure as a means of bouncing back and generating a desire to succeed next time."

Assumptions about the Relationship between Failure and Success

At stake in all my interviews were two common assumptions about the relationship between failure and success. Here, I am talking about straight-up, standard, short-term success. These assumptions are worth examining because they wield significant power. We tend not to even know at a conscious level that they are there. We may not overtly endorse them, but these two assumptions shape how we view failure. One of my main motivations in the interviews was to test these assumptions, to see if they carry weight.

Assumption #1: Extremely Successful People Do Not Fail

I mentioned previously that reading that Shakespeare had failed shocked me because it challenged a longstanding assumption I had: that extremely successful people do not fail. Since then, I have realized that this assumption was not unique to me. It is common. We tend to think that people become successful because they don't fail. We suppose that our heroes are individuals for whom success is apparent from the start, those whose success is universally agreed on and comes without much struggle. We imagine that their lives are a continuous upward trajectory—that they leap from victory to greater victory. Everyone approves of them. Every sign along the way says "yes, you can do it," and they do. They have no doubt or fear, no shortcomings or setbacks, and no naysayers—just clarity, confidence, flawlessness, and smooth sailing. Okay, that was a little over the top, but you get the idea. We see our heroes in idealized ways.

And this assumption causes a problem. It creates moats. Let me explain. First, viewing individuals who inspire us as flawless creates a moat around them. It makes us feel that they are on an island, and we are on the opposite shore, and there is no getting across. We know the reality of ourselves—that we have made mistakes and had setbacks, that we have shortcomings and doubts—so it makes us feel like our heroes are categorically different from us and that there is no bridge from us to them. Second, and perhaps more importantly, this assumption creates a moat between us and the fullest, brightest version of ourselves—the person we hope we are growing into. In other words, it places a moat between who we are now and who we hope to be. It makes the idea of becoming that person seem impossible. Why? Because the assumption feels defeating. It leads us to believe that our failures disqualify us from unfolding into the hoped-for, fullest version of ourselves.

And this assumption sprouts from a broader assumption about the relationship between failure and success that also needs to be reassessed: that failure stymies success.

Assumption #2: Failure Stymies Success

We tend to think that failure and success are opposites. And in the immediate sense, they are. You can't win and lose a game. You can't get promoted and demoted at the same time. You can't pass and fail an exam. But we also assume that failure and success are opposites in a broader sense—that the more failures you have, the less likely you are to experience success in the long run, and the fewer failures you have, the more likely you are to experience success over time. In short, we assume that failure thwarts success—that failure has a withering, rather than a blossoming, effect.

This assumption is a moat-maker too. It too makes us feel that our failures—those we have had and will have—remove the bridge between who we are now and who we hope we are becoming. It makes us feel that we are disqualified from becoming the fullest, brightest version of our selves.

And here's the thing: if these two assumptions were true, these moats would just be hard, annoying realities of life. But they may not be true. My interview with Dr. McPherson about Abraham Lincoln punctured both assumptions. I was eager to hear more.

Coach Mike Krzyzewski

Ever since my family moved to Durham, North Carolina, when I was entering seventh grade, I have been a fan of Duke basketball and have admired Coach Mike Krzyzewski—"Coach K." Coach K is head coach of men's basketball at Duke University and the winningest coach in Division I men's college basketball history with more than 1,100 career wins. As head coach at Duke, he has won five National Championships (1991, 1992, 2001, 2010, 2015) and has led the team to twelve Final Four appearances. Coach K was head coach of the US men's national basketball team from 2005 to 2016 and led the team to gold medals in the 2008, 2012, and 2016 Summer Olympics. He was inducted into the Naismith Memorial Basketball Hall of Fame in 2001 and named Sportsman of the Year by *Sports Illustrated* in 2011, the same year that Pat Summitt, the legendary basketball coach at the University of Tennessee, was named *SI* Sportswoman of the Year; they appeared on the cover of the magazine together. In March 2014, *Fortune* magazine named Coach K one of "the world's 50 greatest leaders." (He tied for the #20 spot.)

When I interviewed Coach K in his office at Duke University in Durham in November 2011, I asked if there was a moment in his life when he realized he wanted to be a head men's basketball coach. He said, "Well, not about being a *head* men's basketball coach," and then he told me the story of when he knew he wanted to coach.

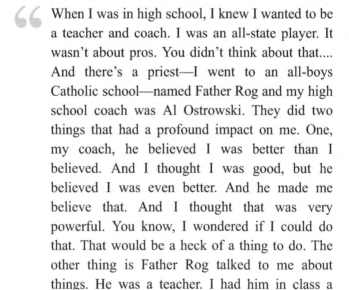

When I was in high school, I knew I wanted to be a teacher and coach. I was an all-state player. It wasn't about pros. You didn't think about that.... And there's a priest—I went to an all-boys Catholic school—named Father Rog and my high school coach was Al Ostrowski. They did two things that had a profound impact on me. One, my coach, he believed I was better than I believed. And I thought I was good, but he believed I was even better. And he made me believe that. And I thought that was very powerful. You know, I wondered if I could do that. That would be a heck of a thing to do. The other thing is Father Rog talked to me about things. He was a teacher. I had him in class a couple times, but often out of class, he put things in perspective in my faith in a way that no one had ever done up to that point, and I just felt that here are two men in teaching and in coaching that they kind of...

He paused and I said, "changed your life." And he said, "changed my life, at least steered my life in a very positive direction." Then he continued the story.

 So I knew I wanted to coach when I was in high school. And I wanted to teach. Then when I went to West Point, I wasn't sure that I could do that. But then being an army officer is really like being a coach and a teacher, and I tried to do that during my military career. Plus, I played and coached a lot of basketball in my military career. But after my five years of military service were up... I was done and I went to be a graduate assistant and not make nearly as much money and put my family in a little bit of a precarious situation, but for me it was easy. That's what I'm going to do. Since I was sixteen, I've had a clear understanding of what I wanted to be. Not necessarily at the level I wanted to be at. It's just worked out that I'm at this level. Which isn't necessarily a better level than high school. I think I would have had great fulfillment there too. But it worked out and I was the lucky guy.... My buddies in high school and my grade school buddies, they're always jealous; they said, "You've never worked a day in your life because you've done what you loved." And, they're right.

When I have spoken with people about interviewing Coach K about failure, many have said incredulously, "What does Coach K know about failure?" But when we met, he talked openly about failing. Before asking him about failures, I asked him about his most meaningful success, which I will share later, but in discussing success, he brought up failures he encountered at West Point. He said they played a vital role in his education and have a lasting impact today.

When I went to West Point, they made you fail. I mean, they put you in many situations where you would fail, and there I learned that failure would never be a destination. You would stop there every once in a while, but you wouldn't stay there, and then how you didn't stay there would determine how good you were going to be. And that you would not be able to do it alone, that you would always be better if you had a teacher, a coach, a teammate, or group. That you would succeed better if you collaborated with one person or more but if you acted as one, and so things like two's better than one. If two can play as one, that type of thing, imagine what five guys playing as one could do? All those things. I didn't know the wording of those things when I went to West Point, but the teaching I had there is one of the reasons that I don't use failure as a destination. And people talk about reference points in their careers, and I think many people look at reference points as times of achievement —I graduated from here, I did this. My reference points are not those. My reference points are tough losses, and then I never want to revisit them. That type of thing.

I asked for an example of how West Point made him fail, and he said, "I could give you hundreds of examples," and then he told a story, the beginning of which I shared in the introduction of this book.

> The second day they put you in swimming. You have to do a swimming test in a seven-foot pool. And I came from the inner city of Chicago. I didn't know how to swim. So, I told him, I said, "Sir, I don't know how to swim." And he gave me a ten-pound rubber brick and said, "Swim as long and as far as you can." I said, "I can't swim." And they said, "Get in the pool." So the brick went down. I went down. They picked up the brick and then they picked me up.

I said: "No! In that order?"

"Oh yeah," he said, while adding that they weren't going to let him drown, and then continued the story.

> Then I was in what's called "Rock Squad" swimming for a whole year, three mornings a week with about thirty other guys. And I had been this golden boy. I had only done things that I could do well. I didn't think of it that way, but it's just my life worked out that way, and all the things I did, I did pretty well. And then, I didn't know how to—I wasn't an Eagle Scout or Boy Scout, so I didn't know how to tie knots, and I

never knew how to march. I never fired a gun. I didn't put up a tent.... You got pulverized and then you always, not always but on many times, think of quitting. But then that would have been a destination. And I think I would have quit if it wasn't for the fact that I was part of the Krzyzewski family. Not that we had accomplished a lot, but my family worked hard and they didn't quit. So I could never face them. So if I was just by myself, I would have been weak, and I would have taken another direction, but because of being on a good team, and having the proper mindset, I never stopped there, and that doesn't mean I was some heroic figure or anything. I think when you have that backing and you have that mindset, then you'll find a way to work through it. And so that's one of the great lessons I learned at West Point. I've used it throughout my career as a coach.

I said, "And you started building it there," and he replied: "Yeah. There's no question. Or having it built for me."

When I asked about his most challenging failure, Coach K named two: his "two lowest points." The first one stretched out over three years—his first years as coach at Duke—and culminated in the last game of the third year.

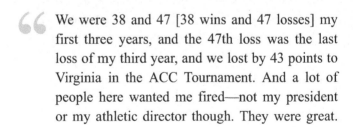

We were 38 and 47 [38 wins and 47 losses] my first three years, and the 47th loss was the last loss of my third year, and we lost by 43 points to Virginia in the ACC Tournament. And a lot of people here wanted me fired—not my president or my athletic director though. They were great.

And after that game—it was in the Omni in Atlanta—when I walked out, I felt a little bit like a leper because you knew Duke fans, and, you know, it's like, we should get rid of this guy.

So we went to a Denny's, some of my family and coaches, and some of the support staff, and one of the guys... raised a glass of iced tea and said, "Here's to forgetting about tonight," and I said, "Wait a minute." I pushed his hand and I picked up a Diet Coke, or whatever it was, and I said, "Here's to never forgetting about tonight." And, uh—but that was a low point.... There are defeats, but that was a defeat that could have changed the course—first of all, I might not have a job, so—it was a bunch of defeats, but that one manifested itself into a night where it got me angry, more angry, and even more determined while I still had the support of my athletic director and my president. That's one of the reasons I think I've stayed at Duke all these years, because at that moment they were committed to me, and reciprocal commitment is a nice thing.

The next low point started with a bad back and unfolded into something bigger.

But, in the '94–'95 season, I had a bad setback. It was health produced. I had a bad back, then nerve damage down my left leg where I had a dropped foot, and we had already started practice, and I had to get my back operated on. And... we lost the National Championship in '94 to Arkansas in

Charlotte, and so this was the next year, and we had a good team. And when I had to get my back operated on, they said I'd be out for about a month, and I said: "I'll be out for two days."

And by that time, I had—it was hard for anybody to tell me what I shouldn't do or what I should do. Not that I even—I mean, they wouldn't even approach me.

As Coach K made this last comment, he motioned with his hand like you would to shoo away a fly and then said: "You know what I mean?" I said, "Yeah." He continued, "It's not like —" and I said "yeah" again. What I understood him to be saying is that at this time, it was not that people were approaching him and he dismissed them but that people had even stopped approaching because he had dismissed them so many times. His success had insulated him.

 So even when I started doing this, no one said, "Okay, that's it. We said you're not coaching." So, I didn't—it was *my* fault, but I didn't get—I somehow created a wall around me where—that wasn't good for a leader to have.

So about a month and a half later, we're 9 and 3 or 9 and 4. I mean, I could hardly walk, and I was just exhausted. And I was burned out. And, I went to—my wife made me go to see a doctor, and they put me in the hospital right away, and they told me that I couldn't coach for the rest of the year, and uh, that was a dark moment. Because I had no feeling, you know. I mean, I had a bad back and everything, but I had no emotion.

I had literally been emotioned out. And so that wasn't one moment. That was a period of time. And I was able to get help from my family and Dr. Brodie and to try to start *feeling* again. Like how do I, how can I, *feel*? Because my feelings are what I think help me the most. And it took me a few—I reviewed tapes. I watched myself when I was bold or when I was coaching to try to remember... and then over a few months I was able—I offered my resignation during that time, just because as an army officer, I knew I shouldn't lead my team. And my AD [athletic director] said, "You take as much time as you want off." And by the next season, I was ready to go. So those are probably the two lowest points.

Coach K then brought up a third low point that related to coaching the US men's national team. In his entire time as coach, the team lost only one game—to Greece in the 2006 World Championships. It was his first summer as coach. He said that the program and team culture hadn't been developed yet, and it was a difficult loss. "After that game, it made me feel like jumping off a building because you're coaching for your country." Jerry Colangelo, who ran the program and is former owner of the Phoenix Suns, told Coach K: "Look, we have to do this better." Coach K apologized and Colangelo responded, "There's nothing to be sorry about. We will build it." And they did: "We ended up building something very good. But, again, that was a low point, and for each one of my low points, being part of a team or being with good people, not being alone, was the difference. And that's what I try to tell all of our guys. Those moments, don't be by your-self. Be part of something bigger than you or what could become bigger than you. So those would probably be the three."

By this point, Coach K already had spoken some about how he responds to setbacks, but I asked if he could say a bit more. He said: "Right now, as a result of having setbacks... there's that moment when you say, 'I can't believe this is happening.' And what I found is I immediately... as I've gotten older—[I say,] 'Okay, where's the opportunity?' We're going to be good. How will we *now* be good?... And saying, 'I'm not staying there.' Like, that's there. We're going to be with what *is*.... I think trying not to stay there too long. That's been helpful for me, and I probably stayed there in my younger days too long." He emphasized that for him, there's no one-size-fits-all approach to responding to setbacks, because each one is different and each team is different. The response has to be tailored to the situation.

If we lose a game here and it's because we didn't work hard or we didn't prepare as well, we'll— we go through a cleansing.... Now, in saying that, if we played our butts off, and somebody beat us, I might not do anything.... There's not just, 'Okay, we lose. We do this.' You have to figure out what the level of your team is, the maturity level. How much *can* they take?... You have to approach it in a different way. Each team, each player is different. So I don't have—that's one of the things about leadership. I mean, there are people who write books about it and the number of steps or these things happen.... I think those are good guidelines, but you don't become a leader that way. You've got to know you. You've got to know the people you have the privilege of leading. The context that you're leading in. And then be bold enough to make decisions based on how much you've developed your team and gotten to know your group.

And some would say, "Well, you're pushing them too hard." "How would you know? You're not in my group. I may not be pushing them hard enough." [Others may say,] "You know, why *don't* you push them?" I say, "I am."... Then you suffer the consequences of those decisions. Which every leader does. And takes responsibility for the consequences, whether they be winning consequences or losing consequences. But you don't stand pat or you don't just repeat things over and over.

When Coach K finished that sentence, I said: "So that boldness and courage is probably a big part of—" and he said: "Yeah, well, it's just—it's kind of what you have to do. Otherwise, you should let someone else lead. I mean, that's one of the beauties of leadership is, leadership is a new job every, it's an exciting job every day. And there's always *something* coming at you."

When I asked Coach K whether he saw a connection between his setbacks and his success, he said: "I think in all those things, you learn from them. I think you have to learn from a loss or setback, and why it occurred." Then he talked about specific benefits that emerged from certain setbacks, starting with the one in the '94–'95 season, which transformed his coaching: "I changed the way I coached and the way I run my program after '94–'95 because it wasn't good enough." He continued, "If I had a…" and looked around his office. He went to his desk and grabbed a pad of paper with a Duke Basketball logo at the top. It looked like something that might be used in practice. When he sat back down, I said, "Am I going to get a diagram? This is wonderful." He said, "No, it's not a play but..." and started drawing. He drew a large spot near the middle of the page and put *X*'s circling around it. As he drew, he described how he led before the '94–'95 setback. "Basically, a leader has a group. Okay. And everyone looks at the leader as a central part of that group. And, basically, how I led was I developed relationships with each one—or tried to—with each one of these people. It's a wheel, you know, it rolls." He drew lines from the center spot to each *X* on the perimeter of the circle to illustrate. (A picture of the drawing is on the next page.) "The one flaw, and it's a major flaw, in leadership of this kind is, What if you don't have the leader? Who—? Well, the wheel collapses. That's what happened. And our team collapsed. We were 13 and 18 after going to the [National] Championship game. And anyway, it wasn't the right thing to do. So afterwards what I tried to do is still develop those relationships, but I tried to develop a relationship between that person and that person and that person and..." As he spoke, he drew lines between the *X*'s on the perimeter of the circle, lines that did not pass through the center, and continued with what he was saying.

In other words, I empowered—I don't like the word *delegate*. Delegate to me in some way means that it's a job not worthy of me, and I don't think that's right. Every job that everyone does, whether it be Celestina, who cleans our offices, Felipe, who cleans our locker room, or Gerry [executive administrative assistant to Coach K] or whoever, every one of those jobs is important, and so the word *empower*—I would want all these people to be empowered. That it's not *my* team. It's *their* team.

And so over the last sixteen years—fifteen, sixteen years—that's what we've built and it's a much better model. Our infrastructure—I know if I got sick today, we'd still win. We might win better. I don't know! I believe our infrastructure is so strong, and my people love it, they will do anything, and they believe it's theirs. And I *thought* that's what I was—I didn't know what the hell I was doing. I was leading the best way I knew how. But after going through this, I saw, I mean I saw that.

45

Coach K said that the old system was not all bad: "The old system got seven Final Fours in nine years." It was not sustainable though: "But the old system was so predicated on *my*, on *me*, hitting all the areas. And really, probably didn't take advantage of all the strengths we had. But it certainly didn't prepare my people to do things on their own as well."

Other opportunities emerged from the '94–'95 setback. "I thought of succession," Coach K said. "I said, At some time I'm going to leave here. What would I want for the next person? And so, I said, I would want a program that's completely endowed." And he and others since have raised money to endow coaches' positions and players' scholarships, and to build new practice facilities. "None of that stuff would have happened if I didn't get knocked back," Coach K said, "and the other thing, though, is that if someone didn't help me to come back."

The specific benefit that came from the USA basketball team's defeat to Greece, Coach K said, was catching a glimpse of a budding team culture of "collective responsibility" that a victory would not have provided.

 When you lose like that, we lost to Greece, you think everything is wrong. And in the press conference right after the game, they have the two coaches and a player from each team in front of all these reporters from all over the world. And the player from the losing team talks first. That's the way they do it. And Carmelo Anthony was there, and he had a chance to say, "We stunk," or "Coach didn't do this," or "LeBron," you know, and to point fingers. And instead he said, "Our team played—we played hard. The Greece team was fantastic." And he gave a lot of credit.

And we took a lot of heat... from the American press—also as a college coach, coaching the US team, like, "A college coach should have never done that," and stuff like that. Never, over the next few months, did you hear anybody from that team say a negative thing about anybody. Well, I learned from that that although we didn't win, our culture was being established because they totally embraced collective responsibility. We win together and we lose together.

The next summer when we had to qualify for the 2008 Olympics, it's the very first thing I told the group, and I said—we're there and I said, "You showed collective responsibility in a loss." And I'm getting chills thinking of this. "The only way you'll have to show it again in the future is after we win, but it'll be because we had it when we lost that we knew that we had something special." So, yeah, you learn from all those things.

It seems important to note here, as Coach K did in the interview, that his biggest setbacks, particularly the first two he spoke of, were not brief moments like blips on a screen. They were extended periods of time. The first spanned three years: "The loss to Virginia was not the one loss, it was the culmination of three years." The second spanned months: "When I got sick, I mean, I just—that was a long period of time to get well." And they were painful. But they made him better in the long run—serving as a catalyst for transformation, fostering learning, growing his determination, and offering a valuable perspective that success could not have granted.

So what was his most personally meaningful success? He prefaced his answer by saying, "In order to win champion*ships*, you have to have won a champion*ship*."

And so there's a first championship that you win.... 1986, our team won the regular season championship of the ACC. And to me, that's still as important a championship—not only that we won our first, but the kids who did it were really the blueprint of the type of youngsters I wanted then to recruit for Duke. They had only won eleven games as freshmen—Dawkins, Bilas, Alarie, Henderson. Amaker joined in the next year. And then that senior year in '86, they won thirty-seven games and were within a basket of winning the National Championship. We lost in the National Championship game that year. But when they won in Cameron [Indoor Stadium, where Duke plays]—we beat North Carolina on senior night—that was as good a feeling as I've ever had. Just because it showed that through commitment and having the right type of guys, and we had our noses rubbed in dirt, you know, when we only won eleven games and lost, you know, we were defeated. We had setbacks that we got *stronger* as a result of.... So to me, that was the most important thing.

Carl Hayden

Over the course of several decades, Carl Hayden has been a leader in education policy in the state of New York at all levels—from K–12 to university. When I spoke with Mr.

Hayden in his home office in Elmira, New York, in August 2012, he had recently retired from his latest post in education policy in the state of New York—chairman of the Board of Trustees of the State University of New York (i.e., head of SUNY). SUNY is the largest comprehensive higher education system in the United States, with sixty-four colleges and universities. The position of head of SUNY, which Mr. Hayden held from 2007 to 2011, is appointed by the governor of New York. Hayden served in this position under the leadership of a few governors and during a recession, and according to an NBC news report from December 2011, he was a fierce advocate for SUNY: "...Hayden led the SUNY board through years of budget cuts from Govs. Spitzer, Patterson, and Cuomo, each time fighting for greater funding for the 64-campus system." The same NBC news report referred to him as "one of the state's most veteran education policymakers." Before becoming head of SUNY, Hayden was chancellor of the New York State Board of Regents, a government organization that shapes school policy for New York public schools. The Board of Regents oversees the New York State Education Department as well as other education-related institutions. Hayden was elected to the Board of Regents by the state legislature in 1990, and in 1995, he was elected chancellor of the board by his colleagues. He served as chancellor of the Board of Regents, also called "schools chancellor" more informally, until 2002 when his term ended, having been reelected twice. In this role, Hayden was a driving force behind initiatives to improve learning and accountability in New York schools with a focus on addressing the achievement gap. The 2011 NBC news report, which reflected on Hayden's career, commented that "as schools chancellor, Hayden led the Board of Regents through an era of conflict in raising standards and greater accountability at schools." And when Hayden left the Board of

Regents, he was voted chancellor emeritus by his colleagues, a rare distinction.

Mr. Hayden, a lawyer, first became involved in education policy at the local level—specifically the Elmira City School District—to have an impact on his own children's lives. "As the kids entered school, it became pretty obvious that if I really wanted to make a difference in their lives, I ought to get active in the educational system. So I ran for a local school board and became the president of that school board, and that began a series of steps that culminated in these other positions."

When I asked Mr. Hayden what his most personally meaningful success was, he said it was marrying his wife, and then he spoke about success in his work:

 I'm not sure that I would identify an event as something I would say was the greatest success. I think rather it was changing the perspective of some of the policymakers to refocus the educational enterprise on expectations. What was happening in New York was that we really were on a slippery slope. We had a dual diploma. You could get a Regents diploma or you could get a local diploma. And the Regents diploma was a very rigorous diploma.... The local diploma was a low-standard route to a low-standard credential based on a low-standard examination. And what was happening was that increasingly over time, more and more families were urging their kids to take the low-standard route to graduation because their grades would be better. And so the selling point was: well, you'll have a better chance at college because your grades will be higher. So I just thought that gave the schools a pass, because what it meant was that if you were a teacher or an administrator and you had a kid who was encountering difficulty in any particular subject, you would simply move the kid over to the easy track and end of problem.... You were kind of reconciling the kid to a future that wasn't terribly promising, but you didn't have to do any lifting to get him out of school. So I think changing the mindset... that really started turning the system.

What came of the mindset change of education policymakers? Under Hayden's leadership as schools chancellor, they did away with the two-tiered education system, the dual diploma that Hayden described previously: "No more easy way/hard way." The system became just one track with the Regents diploma because, Hayden said, "Everyone ought to have access to the richness of the Regents track."

Mr. Hayden named another personally meaningful success, also from his time as schools chancellor. It had to do with the achievement gap in New York public schools. "The other thing I would identify was obliging the system to come to grips with the educational gap, with the really indefensible disparity in achievement between affluent kids—usually white or Asian— and kids of color. We used to bury it and *we* decided to publish it. We decided to issue a report card that talked about how we were doing with *all* of our kids in *all* of the disciplines and to further break it down by race and ethnicity so that you really could see the extent of the problem. So we put our dirty laundry out on the line for everyone to see. And then we decided to aggressively attack the problem by providing additional resources to those schools that dealt with minority populations and putting in place programs that would attract better teachers and allow them to operate within lower class sizes and a number of other strategies."

Mr. Hayden added a third success—one from much earlier in his career, in the early 1980s, when he was president of the Board of Education for the Elmira City School District. He started by providing context. The neighborhood school for kids who lived on the hill where he and his family live is the Thomas K. Beecher School. Mainly white people live on the hill, and Beecher is below on the valley floor in a neighborhood where most of the African Americans and Latinos in Elmira live. "And when I became board president," Hayden said, "all of the kids who lived on this hill, for whom Beecher would be the neighborhood school, were being bussed across town to an all-white school." Under Hayden's leadership, they reintegrated Beecher. He and the board "redrew all the boundaries for the various neighborhood schools, and returned all the kids who were living up here to where they should have been all along so that what happened was that we reintegrated the Thomas K. Beecher School." As a result, white students, including his own, started going to Beecher. Hayden said that his decision to reintegrate Beecher was controversial at the time: "Cindy [his wife] and I took a lot of criticism from people who said, 'You're running an experiment with your own kids.' And I said, 'Well, I suppose you could look at it that way, but we really don't see it as an experiment. We see it as an opportunity... and we just think it's the right thing to do.' So that I would take to be a great success."

When I asked Mr. Hayden about his biggest failure, he said: "I have a number of failures from which to choose, and some of them are, I think, not best described as failures but just kind of adverse life circumstances." He spoke first of adverse life circumstances before talking about "more literal failures": "My father abandoned us when I was, I think, three, and I only recall seeing him one time after that in which he drove into this little town in which we were living in upstate New York about seventy miles from here and tried to get me in a car.... And I always felt a huge sense of loss at not having a father." Hayden said that for reasons he doesn't understand, that loss "created a bright perspective" in him; it granted him an optimistic disposition. "I can't tell you why I ended up looking at the bright side," he said, but "somewhere along the way I got a sense that what had happened to me was just hugely unfair and bad fortune, and that if there was any justice in the world, that something good would happen that would make up for it." His mother remarried when he was eight, and her husband, Bill Hayden, who adopted Mr. Hayden and his sister, "was a very frustrated, sort of taciturn guy but very demanding." Hayden said that the two male figures in his life while he was growing up were both quite tough: "I had two men in my life, one [was] Bill Hayden and one the coach of all the sports in this little school I attended, who were both very demanding and neither of whom was given to praise at all, so that if you did something well, nothing was said; if you didn't do something well, a great deal was said. So silence was essentially approbation." Then Hayden remarked: "And in a way, that worked for me. And made me strive harder, because I was always wanting to meet their expectations."

After discussing adverse life events, Hayden said: "Now on to more literal failures," and he talked about academic struggles. In college, he was on academic probation at more than one point.

 So off to Hamilton [College] I go and I'm struggling academically. I'm an odd student. In those things in which I'm confident, I'm pretty darn good, and in those things in which I'm not,

I'm pretty darn bad. I had trouble with language. I had trouble with calculus. And I got on academic probation my sophomore year and got myself off, and then I got a warning that I was at risk of failing. And... I had a big mountain to climb.

In his first year at college, Hayden played soccer and basketball, and after struggling academically, he gave up soccer. It was a major sacrifice for him because he loved soccer and had started on the team: "It broke my heart." When he finished his junior year, he was back in serious academic trouble—in "tremendous peril" academically. He needed a cumulative average of 75 to graduate and had a combination of D's and C minuses, so he had a lot of ground to make up. And he sacrificed more.

 I gave up basketball. Broke my heart. And I spent that entire year in a chair in my room, working. And I didn't know if I would succeed because I had so much to make up.... So, I went right down to the wire, and I can't tell you as we're talking whether I actually did it or not, but I suspect that I was allowed to graduate because I got credit for my effort and for what every member of the faculty knew was my sacrifice in giving up the things I loved so much.

Hayden said that his academic struggles in college had something to do with not dealing well with the freedom college offers.

 How do you deal with getting to choose from an

unlimited array of possibilities every day with no adult to say no, you can't? And I didn't have any money, so I wasn't going out drinking with all these guys, but I would go watch television, I would go shoot the fat, I would play bridge with my mates, I would find ways to screw around, and then I would go study from like ten o'clock till three o'clock and then I would try to get up at seven thirty for an eight o'clock class and I would sleep through . . . Nobody could wake me up. They would send delegations of kids to my room, and they just couldn't wake me up. And I was just doing everything wrong.

After graduating from college, Mr. Hayden was in the navy for four years and then went to Cornell Law School. He struggled in law school too.

No way in the world I should be admitted to the Cornell Law School based on my Hamilton record. Out of the question. But... the dean of Hamilton College was the roommate of the associate dean and the dean of admissions of the Cornell Law School when they were both at Hamilton together in whatever year. So Dean Tolles said to Ernie Warren: "Ah, he's not the sharpest knife in the drawer, but he's a good kid, and he showed some grit. Give him a shot. And, he'll be good on your touch football team." I think that is exactly the way it went down.

So, I'm at the Cornell Law School in my second week, and there is a professor named Gray Thoron. Gray Thoron is Harvard College undergraduate, Harvard Law School, bow tie, blue blood, just the total antithesis of everything that I am. And he gets up, and he's—I think it's a New York practice class. He said: "I've developed an unerring instrument for ascertaining the probability of success for each of you. So we're going to take this practice examination today, and it will really tell you with an uncanny degree of accuracy how you're likely to fare at the Cornell Law School." So, he passes out this exam, and I fill it out, turn it in, and the next thing that happens is I get a note from him to see him in his office. And he said: "You're in the wrong place. You can't succeed here. And you would be very well advised to make other plans as promptly as you can." Second week. Second week, and his unerring exam. Well, there's more than just a little irony because later on down the road I end up being the president of the Law Student Association and then later on holding all these positions, and there would be a number of circumstances in which he would be coming forward to seek something from the Board of Regents or he would want my participation in some event that the law school was running, and I never—I would always joke with my mates, of course, about it, but I never told him what a horse's ass he was.... There was that.

And I did struggle, and it wasn't for want of effort. I was working. It was just very hard for me. And, in fact, I got another one of these letters from Ernie Warren, the guy who was responsible for my getting in... : "You might want to consider something else." All right, so, you know, once again... but it's kind of like, all right, I thought I was grinding, now I'm really going to grind... work even harder. And of course there you don't have the allure of athletics and that sort of thing, so you can really cloister yourself. And that's what I did.

Hayden ended up graduating from Cornell Law School and became a trial lawyer, which, in addition to his work in education policy, was his career. Hayden said that he had victories and defeats as a trial lawyer too, as one would suspect: "[I] had a good career as a lawyer. I wouldn't characterize myself as a great lawyer. When you're in the trial lawyering business you win some and you lose some and it's difficult. I mean, really it is.... I mean, to stand in front of a jury and have them tell you what they thought of your case is hard. Because no matter how hard you try, you take it personally.... But I was admitted to the American College of Trial Lawyers, which is a lofty thing in our profession, because you don't apply; you get chosen." Mr. Hayden wrapped up his comments about his biggest setbacks by saying: "So, that's it. It isn't like—nobody burned an 'A' in my head. I didn't fall off a building. I just—I had the knocks that go with not having things come easily."

He already had spoken about how he responded to some setbacks, but I asked if he wanted to add anything about how he tends to respond to them. He replied: "I really love to have fun, and my response to reversals has historically been to become ascetic. So I just deprive myself of the things that I most enjoy.... I have consistently removed from my daily routine the things that I would do for enjoyment as the price for my past failings. You could call that putting your nose to the stone. There are lots of different ways to describe it. But it's just an exercise in self-discipline based upon an acknowledgment that you have failed the basic tests of self-discipline, and that's why you're in the position you're in!" He later elaborated on what it feels like to have setbacks too: "When you have something terrible happen to you, there's a—just this awful feeling, this sting-y sort of feeling."

When I asked Mr. Hayden if he saw a relationship between his failures and success, he said: "Yes... the failures create habits of mind and rules for self-governance that increase the likelihood that you will succeed." He went on to say that his academic struggles showed him how hard he would have to work in order to succeed, and they made him more disciplined in a way that fueled his success in the long term: "If I had been able to do Hamilton tra-la-la and the Cornell Law School tra-la-la, I'd more likely be the Great Gatsby than who I am, and I would have taken some pleasurable route and gone off and done something vastly self-indulgent. But the fact that none of it proved to be easy and that I had to make really serious accommodations in order to just get the exit credential made a big difference in the path that I ultimately chose."

US Senator Cory Booker

On a weekend afternoon in August 2010, while I was on the Princeton University website looking for information relating to this book, I stumbled upon a lecture series that Cory Booker, then mayor of Newark, New Jersey, now US senator from New Jersey, had given at Princeton. The lecture series took place over the course of three evenings, one each night, and the title of the series intrigued me immediately: The Unfinished Journey of America's Spirit. The title of each of the three lectures drew me in further: "The Past: A Testimony to the Impossible," "The Present: Through Cynicism, Negativity, and Self-Doubt," and

"The Future: Humble Hopes and Insane Idealism." As someone interested in psychology and history, these titles were like waving red meat in front of a dog; they were so compelling to me. Videos of the lectures—about four hours in total—were on the website, and even though I was intrigued, my first thought was, "Why did they upload four hours of lectures? Who would sit and watch a lecture online for four hours?" You can see where this is going. I planned to watch ten or fifteen minutes, and four hours later, I found myself on the same spot on my couch, moved by Mayor Booker's insights, vision, and authenticity. As I learned more about his leadership, my admiration grew.

As mayor of Newark from 2006 to 2013, Mayor Booker led a major revitalization of the city. When he left office, Newark was experiencing its biggest period of growth since the 1960s. New hotels were being built downtown for the first time in forty years and new office towers for the first time in twenty years. In his time as mayor, crime in Newark decreased significantly, including fewer incidents of shootings, theft, aggravated assault, rape, and murder. And many new parks were created, resulting in the largest expansion of parks and recreation area in more than a century. Mayor Booker made improving public schools a priority, including securing a $100 million grant from Mark Zuckerberg to improve education in Newark. He pioneered many innovative programs, like the Newark Prisoner Re-entry Initiative aimed to get former inmates back to work, a program that has decreased recidivism. I interviewed then mayor Booker in his office in Newark's City Hall on February 17, 2011. In 2013, Mayor Booker was elected as a US senator from New Jersey in a special election. He was reelected in November 2014 and currently holds this position.

When I asked then mayor Booker what he considered his most personally meaningful success, he said:

Well, understand, the job that I'm in now, there are tough days. Days you gain ground, days you lose ground. So you may get things done like build a dozen-plus parks, but then you also have days when you make mistakes.... So a job like this doesn't give you this feeling of like you've got an Academy Award, you've created the body of work and you are a success. This is the kind of thing where every day you get up and you take hits and you stumble and you're able to do some good things, but you never have this sense of triumph. Because, you know, last night a three-year-old died in a fire. Today, I went to a wake for a man that was murdered outside this bar, and so you may reduce crime and we should be proud of the progress we've made, but when a weeping widow is clutching onto you and asking for help and to do something about the crime, you know that there's still so much work to do. So I feel every day senses of success as well as senses of not failure necessarily, but, dear God, I've got to do so much more. I've got to work so much more. So your question, What's the biggest success so far? I don't know if I think about it in terms of one thing really sticking out.

For me, what is successful is that feeling like you're leveraging the best of yourself to make a difference in the lives of other people. So I feel very successful in the sense that I get to get up every day and it's a really wonderful thing when your professional world is completely resonant with your moral compass and your highest aspirations and your most righteous hopes for your life. So it's a tough job, but I feel so blessed that I've been afforded the ability to be in a position where I could just give every ounce of my being and all the skills I have and the ones I'm learning on this job to push things forward.

When he finished talking, I commented: "So that part feels like the most meaningful to you?" And he added a bit more.

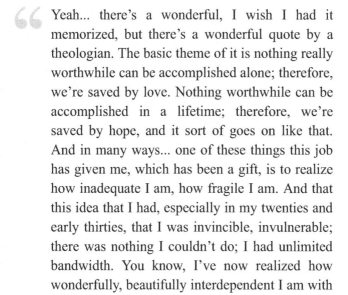

Yeah... there's a wonderful, I wish I had it memorized, but there's a wonderful quote by a theologian. The basic theme of it is nothing really worthwhile can be accomplished alone; therefore, we're saved by love. Nothing worthwhile can be accomplished in a lifetime; therefore, we're saved by hope, and it sort of goes on like that. And in many ways... one of these things this job has given me, which has been a gift, is to realize how inadequate I am, how fragile I am. And that this idea that I had, especially in my twenties and early thirties, that I was invincible, invulnerable; there was nothing I couldn't do; I had unlimited bandwidth. You know, I've now realized how wonderfully, beautifully interdependent I am with others and how much you need other people. And there's a surrender in that, but there's also, in that surrender, you gain a lot more power and fulfillment.

When I asked then mayor Booker about his most painful failure, he already had brought up his failed attempt for mayor of Newark in 2002, remarking: "That's the failure. That's one of the failures." But when I posed the question of his most painful failure, he said that his mind immediately skipped back to seventh grade.

 You know, it's so funny you say that, and in my mind, I just jumped away from recent history, and I'm thinking about the seventh grade when I—it was one of the most humiliating experiences of my life. My young life!—when I was running for my first office ever, which was president of my seventh grade class.... So one of the requirements to run for this office, you had to pick a vice president. I remember I picked a guy... because I thought he was smart and whatever, not necessarily popularity. And I was trying to do everything with this sense of nobleness that I had gotten, and then there was a speech to give, and that was the big thing. The whole class was going to get together for a speech—all my peers, really my universe in a sense of peers. And I worked the whole night on the speech, which in seventh grade probably meant that I went to bed late —like ten.

And I got up to give the speech, and I never really knew it until that moment that I was terrified about speaking in front of people. It was like a real fear, and I completely froze, and I couldn't get a word out. My hands were shaking on the speech. It was just horrible. People didn't know whether to laugh at me or feel for me, and I still remember the teachers trying to make me feel better, trying to get me to speak, and I just couldn't get it out.

He said it was "humiliating" and also a catalyst for growth.

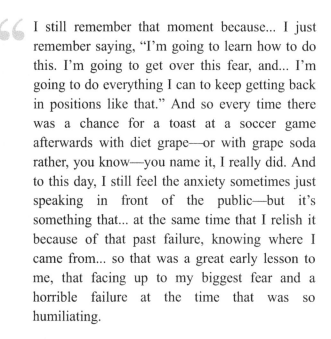

> I still remember that moment because... I just remember saying, "I'm going to learn how to do this. I'm going to get over this fear, and... I'm going to do everything I can to keep getting back in positions like that." And so every time there was a chance for a toast at a soccer game afterwards with diet grape—or with grape soda rather, you know—you name it, I really did. And to this day, I still feel the anxiety sometimes just speaking in front of the public—but it's something that... at the same time that I relish it because of that past failure, knowing where I came from... so that was a great early lesson to me, that facing up to my biggest fear and a horrible failure at the time that was so humiliating.

It seems that for Senator Booker, who is a moving public speaker, his painful failure evolved into a powerful strength.

When I asked then mayor Booker about how he responds to failures, he first spoke about how he responded to his failed bid for mayor of Newark in 2002, his first run for mayor, and then more broadly about how he responds to setbacks. His feelings about the 2002 defeat were captured in a documentary, *Street Fight*, made about that campaign, he said.

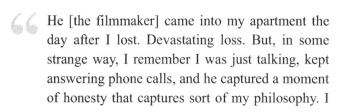

> He [the filmmaker] came into my apartment the day after I lost. Devastating loss. But, in some strange way, I remember I was just talking, kept answering phone calls, and he captured a moment of honesty that captures sort of my philosophy. I

said to him, "Gosh, I've never had something bad happen to me"—I don't think I said the word *failure*—"that hasn't resulted in something really good." And so that's really my life, is that I feel that every failure brings with it such opportunity. So, in some ways, I don't welcome them nor do I want to fail, but I feel very blessed that that has been this consistent pattern that the times of biggest disappointment... I can clearly see patterns where everything quote, unquote "bad" turned out to be something extraordinarily good. And so, when things are really, really down, I think to myself, "There must be some opportunity here that I'm just not seeing." And some of it is just lessons of spirit, you know. I've messed up before in this job, even in the five years I've been mayor, and there is a growth in maturity to forgive yourself, which is a very hard thing to do, to learn to do, to be really good at. To just forgive yourself. That you're not perfect and you're going to do really dumb things sometimes.

One opportunity that came from his defeat in 2002 was starting the nonprofit Newark Now, which serves Newarkers through a variety of programs, like free tax filing services. He was quick to say that starting Newark Now was a collaborative effort. "But to say that I even started it—it's like I had the idea. I brought people together. I got it launched, but it's sort of... I feel like the beaver sitting on top of the Hoover Dam and saying, 'Yeah, I had the idea.'" While Mayor Booker and I met in his office in City Hall, people from Newark Now were offering free tax service for residents downstairs. Booker said that he never would have started the nonprofit if he had not lost the election. He also was offered an opportunity to form a law firm with others and be a partner in it. He took the opportunity and gained valuable experience; it was his first experience in the private sector and enabled him to pay off law school loans. If he had won in 2002, he would have become mayor while in debt. He summed up the opportunities provided by the loss by saying: "As bad as it was to lose and the harsh impact it had on the lives of many people, there is some wisdom. I mean, I was a guy much more ready to lead in 2006 than I was in 2002."

Mayor Booker briefly mentioned a third big failure: the premature ending of his college football career. Without going into detail, he said his football career at Stanford University ended a year earlier than he thought it would, and it was "a huge disappointment." But it allowed him to study as a Rhodes Scholar at Oxford University, which he would not have done if he had been able to keep playing football.

Senator Booker's biggest failures, although "humiliating" and "devastating," offered opportunities that he would not have had otherwise. As he put it, "I can clearly see patterns where everything 'bad' turned out to be something extraordinarily good."

Mayor Pam Iorio

When Mayor Pam Iorio and I spoke in April 2011, she had left office just a few weeks before because of eight-year term limits for mayors in Tampa. She stepped down with an approval rating of 87 percent. That was in the middle of a recession. Iorio is the second woman to be mayor of Tampa. During her time in office, crime in Tampa decreased by 61.5 percent. Under her leadership, Tampa went from being a city with one of the highest crime rates for its size to a city with one of the lowest crime rates for its size. She also led a major revitalization of

East Tampa, a relatively impoverished, predominately African American area that historically had been neglected by city leadership. To her, the project that symbolized her work in East Tampa was the "widening of 40th Street that runs through East Tampa." She carried out a $103 million project to improve this main thoroughfare. Although 40th Street is a "major artery" in East Tampa, it had been a winding, dangerous road for a long time. Every mayor since the 1960s had promised to fix it, to widen 40th Street, but no one had followed through. In her last week in office, the final ribbon was cut on this massive project. She also improved other aspects of the city's infrastructure, initiating major sewer and water projects, and she enhanced recreational and cultural opportunities. Two museums and a waterfront park were completed during her administration. Mayor Iorio, a Democrat, earned bipartisan praise for her achievements. In April 2013, the largely Republican Hillsborough County Commission gave former Mayor Iorio the Ellsworth G. Simmons Good Government Award, awarded to groups or individuals who improve government through leadership and vision.

Mayor Iorio decided to run for mayor of Tampa when she was a graduate student in history. In her studies, she focused on the civil rights movement in Tampa and learned more about the discrimination and neglect that people in East Tampa had experienced from the government. She asked herself if she had done enough, if she had contributed enough to her community, and concluded that she had not. That is when she started thinking about running for mayor, and she decided that if she ever became mayor, East Tampa would be a priority.

Looking at the record of her attempts to run for public office, it appears that Mayor Iorio has never experienced professional setbacks. She was first elected for public office, as county commissioner, at the age of twenty-six. She has run for public office seven times: twice as county commissioner, three times as supervisor of elections, and twice as mayor. She won every time.

When we talked, however, she told me about her most challenging, if not readily visible, setbacks. You would think that a mayor who ended eight years of leadership with an approval rating of 87 percent would have received support from most community leaders during her campaign, but that was not the case. When I asked Mayor Iorio about her most painful failure, she told me a story about when she first decided to run for mayor. She and a close friend, Fran, had put together a list of twenty top leaders in the community whom Ms. Iorio wanted to talk to about her campaign.

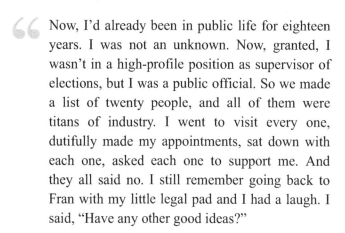

Now, I'd already been in public life for eighteen years. I was not an unknown. Now, granted, I wasn't in a high-profile position as supervisor of elections, but I was a public official. So we made a list of twenty people, and all of them were titans of industry. I went to visit every one, dutifully made my appointments, sat down with each one, asked each one to support me. And they all said no. I still remember going back to Fran with my little legal pad and I had a laugh. I said, "Have any other good ideas?"

The rejections had a significant impact on her.

It's motivating. To me, it's always been motivating because I might visit someone in their office in the bank building and they might say, "Oh, I'm just sorry. I can't support." But when I go to the shopping—when I go to Target—they want me to run. I've always thought what's really important is what the voters want, not what some small subsection wants. What do the voters want?

The voters kept telling me they wanted me. So if I went to Publix [grocery store], I went to Target, I went wherever, they were saying, "I'm all for you." So I had to kind of take it with a grain of salt that people who are kind of the who's who list weren't willing to support me.

And the voters of Tampa clearly did want her, even though the "who's who list" did not. They elected her and kept her in office for the longest amount of time possible for a mayor in Tampa. Mayor Iorio offered another takeaway from her story.

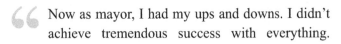 You're always going to run into adversity. You're always going to apply for the bank loan that doesn't come through, apply for the jobs where you get rejected, send your books to numerous publishers and get rejection letters. Try for ten colleges and have nine reject you. That is called life. That just tells you that you're nothing special. That's the way life is. I've had more than my share of that. But in my own unusual way of looking at things, when the door is shut to me, it motivates me more. I tend to get more motivated. I say, "Okay, well, then what's the alternative way?"

She also spoke of facing setbacks once in office.

Now as mayor, I had my ups and downs. I didn't achieve tremendous success with everything.

Some ideas didn't pan out. Sometimes the city council would say no to an idea, but you know, it's all—I feel that you just take those setbacks as what they are. They're part of life. They're not here or there. I mean, if you let a setback or a "no" define you, then you probably will not be very successful. But if you just view it as a part of the process called life, then you just pick yourself up the next day and say, "Now what's the alternative way for me to achieve my goal?" Or, maybe that goal wasn't all that important for me as mayor. That was just a subissue, and I let that go, and now let me focus on something else.

While in office, Mayor Iorio made a "big push" for a light-rail mass transit system in Tampa, but it was voted down by the citizens of Tampa. She had spoken for years about the need for light rail, and by the time the plan was finished and the referendum was put to voters, it was 2010. The plan entailed a penny sales tax increase at a time when the economy was in poor condition, and most people were focused on just trying to make mortgage payments. The referendum was voted down by a margin of 58 percent to 42 percent. Mayor Iorio knew it wouldn't pass at the time of the vote. "I was out there giving a lot of speeches, and I could tell that the support for it was going down, not going up, because the economy was so poor." She had been the chief spokesperson, so it was a personal setback. But, she said, the effort resulted in tremendous learning that provided a foundation for an improved public transportation system that she believes will be realized in the future: "One day we are going to have light rail... when it happens, the fact that we took a referendum in 2010 will be one of the reasons why it was successful—because we learned from it, learned what not to do, learned... more about voter sentiment, learned about ourselves, learned about the message."

When I asked Mayor Iorio how she responds to setbacks, I asked whether she experiences a period of time when she feels bad about the setback or if she quickly gets to a place of feeling more motivated. She said:

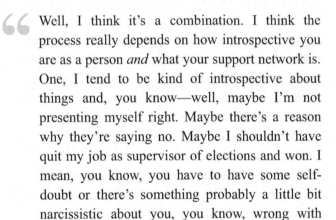

Well, I think it's a combination. I think the process really depends on how introspective you are as a person *and* what your support network is. One, I tend to be kind of introspective about things and, you know—well, maybe I'm not presenting myself right. Maybe there's a reason why they're saying no. Maybe I shouldn't have quit my job as supervisor of elections and won. I mean, you know, you have to have some self-doubt or there's something probably a little bit narcissistic about you, you know, wrong with you. So, I have lots of—lots of self-doubt.

And the other thing is, Who's your support network? Who's around you?... I think your ability to deal with failure or adversity has a lot to do with, What's your support network? Now, I've always been very fortunate to have a very strong and positive support network, and I've been fortunate to be kind of an introspective person who's willing to look at my deficiencies very openly, my faults.... So you just have to dig deep... and you have to rely on your network that you have that can say, you really did make a mistake there, or you're not presenting yourself well, or you're going down a road that's not attainable. You're thinking, you're being slightly delusional here, or whatever it may be. You have to have some of that in your life.

Later in our conversation, she elaborated on the process of responding to failure.

Whether you're the mayor or whether you're a cancer doctor or whether you're a NASA scientist, as long as you are willing to acknowledge and learn from your mistakes, that is absolutely critical. If a mistake becomes someone else's fault and not you, and if you're not willing to look in a steely-eye way at why that mistake occurred and to learn from it, you know you have to... but if it's always someone else's fault, you don't learn from it. In politics, there tends to be a lot of that "it wasn't me, it was —" you know?... If you're a serious person about life, you learn from your mistakes.

...To the degree that you are in self-evaluation mode and learn and grow from it [failure], then it's just a part of human life because we all do make mistakes. Sometimes I'm astonished at the mistakes I make even now when I'm supposed to be so much older and wiser, right? But I continually make mistakes, not as many, maybe not severe ones, but I make my share of mistakes.

When I asked Mayor Iorio if she saw any connection between her setbacks and subsequent success, she said, "Yes, absolutely," and then elaborated on her response.

You go through the grief, but you emerge stronger on the other end. And you do emerge stronger.... I look back at myself as a twenty-five-year-old running for the county commission, and I'm just a better person today. I'm fifty-one, and today I am wiser. I'm more empathetic. I understand people better. I understand grief. I understand adversity. I understand the strength that people have within them. I have through my life experiences—*many of them negative,* many of them negative—grown to be a better person than I was when I was first starting out in politics.... They've made me better equipped for the next fifty years of my life or whatever I have, you know, so I feel better equipped to march forward for the next many years.... So what can you say other than the fact that I think adversity and failures in many respects make you stronger, and they make you better equipped to deal with future challenges.... There is something about that —going through life's process, particularly the adversity, that if done right, if done through an analytical prism, makes you a better person, I think. Yeah—more equipped to handle what challenges come your way.

Rethinking the Relationship between Failure and Success

What I gathered from the interviews flew in the face of both assumptions about the relationship between failure and success. Consider the old assumptions in light of the new evidence. *Assumption #1: Extremely Successful People Do Not Fail.* Everyone I interviewed had experienced setbacks, rejections, low points, and defeats; they all had failed. *Assumption #2: Failure Stymies Success.* Everyone indicated that their failures propelled subsequent success. The interviews level both assumptions.

No one I interviewed said failing was pleasant. In fact, they all said it was painful. They used words like "hurt," "humiliating," "angry," and "emotioned out" to the point of having "no feeling" to describe how they felt after major failures. But another word kept cropping up: "opportunity." Failure provided opportunities that fostered subsequent success. The opportunities themselves varied. Some were similar and others were quite different. Often, the people I interviewed talked about more than one failure and noted that different opportunities came from each failure. One theme was the same for everyone: failure, rather than being a mere nuisance to endure or maneuver around, was a vehicle, or a stepping stone, to get somewhere better in the long run; failure fostered greater success.

What I gathered from the interviews dealt a serious blow to the two assumptions, and as a result, the people I interviewed have built part of a bridge over those moats. They are not the only ones to challenge these conventional assumptions. There are other bridge-builders too. In recent years, the idea that failure can foster greater success has been bubbling up in society.

The chef and restaurateur Thomas Keller embodies the idea that failing can pave the way to greater success. Days before I defended my dissertation in an oral presentation to professors, I was at the grocery store and walked by a *Wine Spectator* magazine with a headline on the cover that leapt out at me.

Thomas Keller
His Rise from Failure to Create America's Greatest Restaurant

I was intrigued, obviously. When I flipped to the article inside and read the title, "The Phoenix and the French Laundry: Thomas Keller's Rise from the Ashes of Failure to Create America's Greatest Restaurant," I wondered what the "ashes of failure" really were. Maybe they were minor stumbles that were magnified because they were taken by someone who is now so successful. But no, he pretty much fell on his face—more than once too.

At the time, I only knew Keller's name and that his restaurant The French Laundry in the California wine country was supposed to be one of the best. Keller owns eight restaurants, including two that have been awarded three-star Michelin ratings, The French Laundry and Per Se in New York. (Only fourteen restaurants in the United States currently have three stars in the Michelin Guide.) The French Laundry also won the "Best Restaurant in the World" award from *Restaurant* magazine for two consecutive years. And Keller has won numerous awards as a chef, including "Best Chef in America" from the James Beard Foundation in 1997.

When he was raising money to start The French Laundry, a major challenge was persuading people to invest in him because he had failed more than he had succeeded. Before opening The French Laundry in 1994, his most recent failure was getting fired as executive chef at Checkers Hotel in Los Angeles in 1992. Before that, his professional path was marked by other failures. He failed in his first effort to open a restaurant in Palm Beach in 1978. Later, he went to Paris looking to be an apprentice to a chef. He made phone calls, sent letters, and knocked on doors, but as he said, "The responses came back, no, no, no." After many rejections, he landed a position at a top restaurant in Paris. Then after Paris, Keller went to New York City, where he was hired and then fired as chef at the restaurant La Reserve. Next, he started a restaurant, Rakel, in

New York. It fell into a deep debt and shut down in less than five years.

While discussing getting fired as executive chef at Checkers Hotel, Keller said: "I am grateful they fired me. If they hadn't, I wouldn't be here today." Since The French Laundry opened, Keller's success as a chef and restaurateur has grown exponentially. He and his restaurants have received several of the top honors available in the industry, and he credits his previous failures with paving the way to his success.

Dr. Brené Brown, researcher and storyteller, gave a TED Talk in March 2012 about her research on shame. She articulated brilliantly how shame leads to silence and silence perpetuates misconceptions. The shame we have about failing, she said, leads to silence about failure, and the silence perpetuates myths about failure. In about a minute, she leveled both assumptions about the relationship between failure and success.

> You know what the big secret about TED is? I can't wait to tell people this. I guess I'm doing it right now. Um, this is like the failure conference. [*Laughter, then applause.*] No, it is. You know, this place is amazing because very few people here are afraid to fail. And no one that gets on this stage so far that I've seen has not failed. I have failed miserably. Many times. I don't think the world understands that. Because of shame.

Consider what Mark Zuckerberg, cofounder and CEO of Facebook, said about failure when he was a guest on *The Oprah Winfrey Show* on September 24, 2010. He told Oprah in the discussion after the show that he celebrates failures at Facebook. To show how, he told a story about an incident that had occurred the previous day. An engineer at Facebook took a risk in testing out a new feature and ended up paralyzing the entire Facebook website for a couple of hours. In Zuckerberg's words, "He pushed some code to the site, and it broke the whole site." If you were on Facebook at the time, you might remember this incident. When it happened, it was the longest time the website had been down in more than four years. Zuckerberg said that he took the issue seriously since it inconvenienced Facebook users, but after the problem was fixed, he ordered pizzas and bought beer for employees to celebrate the failure. He said that although many companies would fire someone for that kind of mistake, he celebrated. Why? In his words: "We want people to keep on taking risks and trying to do crazy stuff—right?— because that's what pushes the world forward."

Recently, Facebook has experienced major setbacks. It will be interesting to see whether progress emerges from them. I imagine it will take time to know. This could be a defining moment for the company, and it reminds me of a story I read about an interview with John T. Chambers, who was CEO of Cisco Systems at the time, in 2009. To provide a bit more context, Chambers stepped down as CEO of Cisco in 2015, having been CEO since 1995, and he held senior leadership positions at Cisco prior to being CEO. In this interview, he talked about a lesson he learned from Jack Welch, longtime chairman and CEO of General Electric. Chambers told the interviewer:

 It was in 1998, and at that time we were one of the most valuable companies in the world. I said, "Jack, what does it take to have a great company?" And he said, "It takes major setbacks and overcoming those."

I hesitated for a minute, and I said, "Well, we did that in '93 and then we did it again in '97

with the Asian financial crisis." And he said, "No, John. I mean a near-death experience." I didn't understand exactly what he meant.

Then, in 2001, we had a near-death experience. We went from the most valuable company in the world to a company where they questioned the leadership. And in 2003, he called me up and said, "John, you now have a great company." I said, "Jack, it doesn't feel like it." But he was right.

The idea that failure can foster greater success is not just on television and in newspapers, in a glossy magazine, and in a TED Talk; it seems to be surfacing in a range of settings. A few years ago, I saw this idea written on a bathroom wall in a coffee shop in Seattle while on vacation with my family. The message was written above the toilet paper in black permanent marker: "If you can't make mistakes, you can't have sucess [*sic*]."

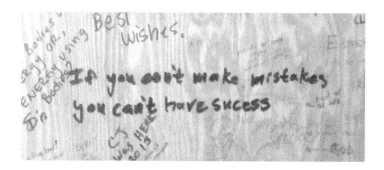

We couldn't decide if the misspelling of *success* was intentional or accidental. Either way, the message is clear. The words on this bathroom wall are different from those of Mark Zuckerberg, Thomas Keller, and Brené Brown, but the underlying idea is the same. And the same idea was articulated in the interviews:

failure can fuel greater success. Taken together, these accounts —from a historian, political leaders, an education policymaker, a coach, an entrepreneur, a restaurateur, an anonymous bathroom-wall writer, and a researcher/storyteller—pierce old assumptions about the relationship between failure and success and strongly suggest that failure can fuel greater success.

Digging beneath the relationship between failure and success, what are the pathways that connect the two? What are the benefits of failure that fuel success? Many were mentioned in the interviews. Some were specific to a particular situation and others were broad. For Lincoln, failure presented specific opportunities that opened doorways to greater success, like his defeat in 1854 feeding into his unanimous nomination for US Senate in 1858. Other opportunities emerged from subsequent failures that further spurred on his success. Consider other benefits of failure that emerged in the interviews in the words of interviewees.

Coach Mike Krzyzewski: "even more determined"; "learned from that"; "changed the way I coached"; "got stronger"; "opportunity"

Carl Hayden: "self-discipline"; "work even harder"; "failures create habits of mind and rules for self-governance that increase the likelihood that you will succeed"

US Senator Cory Booker: "facing up to my biggest fear"; "opportunity"

Mayor Pam Iorio: "growth"; "learned from it"; "motivating"; "better equipped to deal with future challenges"; "stronger"; "makes you a better person"

These benefits of failure connect failure to greater success. They carve the route. They are the pathways from failure to greater success. The visual below depicts pathways articulated in the interviews. The unlabeled pathways reflect that others exist.

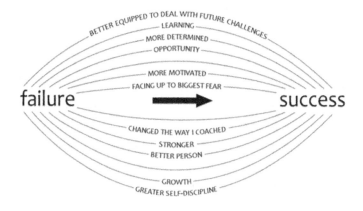

There are benefits of failure that have been established by research but get overlooked. For example, failures promote reflection and reevaluation more than successes do. One study found that managers in various business settings did not articulate a need for an intensive learning process when outcomes were positive, but the more negative the outcomes were, the more they called for this kind of evaluation. Managers also were more likely to recommend "doing nothing" after successful outcomes than after negative ones. Other research has shown that, more generally, failures motivate more of a response overall than positive events, eliciting more thinking, feeling, and action.

Failure is a better impetus for learning than success. Reverend Peter Gomes, longtime professor at Harvard University and minister at Harvard Memorial Church who passed away in 2011, spoke about this benefit in his baccalaureate address at Stanford University in 2008.

> This is where the unconventional wisdom comes in. I want to suggest to you that there's a great deal of virtue to be discovered in counting up your failures rather than your successes.... I want to suggest that failure may very well be your most important and useful teacher. When you succeed, as many of you have, leaping from mountaintop to mountaintop, you do not pause to say, "How did I get here?" Most of you are of the view, "I deserve to be here. I got here because I'm good. I'm clever. I know the answers. I not only bought the books, but I read a few of them from time to time." Failure, if it has any value, teaches us a great deal. And if an education is of any value, any good at all, it will help us to understand the constructive uses of failure.

Perhaps most importantly, research shows that failures are better catalysts for change and growth than success.

Imagine for a moment that failure's light side is a room in a house. What kind of room would it be? I picture it as a sunroom at the back of a house with big windows on three sides, or an enclosed porch with screens allowing in a lot of light. If you think of failure's light side as a room, we have been opening the door to the room and getting a sense of what is inside, but there is more to see. The door is not yet flung open. The next part of the quest is to expose one particular hidden pathway from failure to success that I stumbled upon and that is extremely meaningful and impactful in today's world. You can see it in *Walk the Line*, the 2005 biopic about singer-songwriter Johnny Cash.

3

A SECRET PATHWAY

There is a scene in *Walk the Line* in which the head of Sun Records recording studio offers Johnny Cash one shot to get a record deal. At the time, Cash sold appliances to support his family, but he wanted to make a living playing music. Desperate to get a record deal, he and his band played a well-known gospel song they thought the studio would approve of. The studio head cut the band off in less than a minute and yelled at them for playing such a hackneyed tune. Then he turned to Johnny Cash and asked him what he would play if he was dying in the road and had one last song. Cash played "Folsom Prison Blues," and he was offered a record deal on the spot.

Though the real story likely did not unfold in that exact way, the scene hints at a pathway between failure and success. First, desperate to succeed, Cash took a cautious approach. He played a song that he thought the studio would approve of even though it was not his style. Then he failed, and failing somehow pulled out all the stops. It freed him to play what he wanted to play. It extracted his originality. And his originality is what got him the record deal. Originality is the overlooked yet potent pathway between failure and success. Failure reveals greater originality, and, originality, in turn, drives success.

So what exactly *is* originality? It is what you do that feels most *you*—most aligned with who you are in your core. Originality is independent thinking and authentic action. It is your voice—fresh and novel because it is unique to you. Your originality springs from what you *really* think, feel, and want to do rather than what you believe you *should* think, feel, or want to do. Its source is your essence, your truth; it flows from what makes you feel alive, what lights you up, what nourishes you, what energizes you, and what makes you proud. And it draws on all your faculties, including your physical senses, analytical thinking, intuition, and passion.

Originality is similar to creativity, authenticity, and individuality. Individuality is an aspect of originality; in fact, the word *individual* is embedded in the dictionary definition of *originality*: "ability to think or express oneself in an independent and individual manner." But originality goes beyond individuality. Whereas individuality refers to a collection of qualities that distinguishes one person from another, originality is more active; it is what you express that comes from those essential qualities. Originality and authenticity are very similar because they both have to do with manifesting one's truth. But whereas authenticity describes how you act, originality is what you do. Authenticity is a way of being that reflects your truth, that is genuine, and originality is what you do that reflects that truth. And originality is a lot like creativity but with a twist. Two dictionary definitions of originality reflect the similarities between the two: "creative ability" and "freshness or novelty, as of an idea, method, or performance." Originality, like creativity, connotes freshness, novelty, and inventiveness. But originality is different. This definition of *original* sheds light on the twist: "firsthand, not imitative." Originality comes directly, firsthand, from a person. It is the unique manifestation of a person's independent thinking or action. Your originality is creativity with your fingerprint stamped on it. It is your unique brand of creativity. And since we are dynamic—we grow and change—originality is dynamic too. Uncovering it is an ongoing process rather than a one-time event.

It is worth noting that originality is not the opposite of convention. It is not equivalent to simply defying social norms or going against the grain. Those behaviors are still governed by the rules they defy; they predictably oppose the rule. And oftentimes, defying convention involves conforming to another set of social norms. Originality is about who you are rather than adhering to or opposing a set of rules or conventions.

Whereas Johnny Cash's story dropped clues about this secret pathway, the pathway leapt out at me while I was reading about three other individuals—a daring, imaginative writer, a revolutionary physicist, and a bold, innovative entrepreneur. These individuals have changed the way we imagine, think, and live. In referring to success in this pathway of failure originality success, I am not referring to any traditional definition of the word, like achieving short-term victories or favorable outcomes in everything you try to do, or attaining wealth, fame, position, or honors, which are two dictionary definitions of success. I am referring to a different kind of success—success marked by changing the world or maximizing your positive impact on the world. Originality is not necessarily the key to success in the traditional sense, but for this different definition of success, originality is your most powerful asset. To get a sense of how failure reveals originality and originality, in turn, fuels success, consider the stories of Albert Einstein, J. K. Rowling, and Steve Jobs.

Albert Einstein

Let's go back in time to 1901. Albert Einstein was twenty-two years old and trying unsuccessfully to find a job. When Einstein graduated from college at the Zurich Polytechnic in the spring of 1900, he set out to get an academic teaching position. As Walter Isaacson wrote in *Einstein*, "It was typical that each graduate would find, if he wanted, some such role, and Einstein was confident it would happen." Einstein applied to work with both physics professors in the department, but neither one wanted him. He applied to work with a math professor but didn't get that position either. Einstein became the only person in his graduating class not to get a job.

After he graduated, Einstein sent letters inquiring about job openings to professors all over Europe. He wrote in a letter to his girlfriend: "I will soon have graced every physicist from the North Sea to the southern tip of Italy with my offer." He rarely got a response. He started including a postage-paid card with a space for professors to reply so that he would get some type of answer. But, as Isaacson wrote, "Einstein did not even get the courtesy of a rejection." After months of failed efforts, Einstein became more desperate. In one letter to chemistry professor Wilhelm Ostwald, Einstein's desperation seeped out: "I am without money, and only a position of this kind would enable me to continue my studies." His father, pained by his son's predicament, wrote Professor Ostwald in April 1901 without telling his son. The following is an excerpt of that letter.

> Since then [graduating from the Zurich Polytechnic] he has been trying unsuccessfully to get a position as a teaching assistant, which would enable him to continue his education in physics. All those in a position to judge praise his talents; I can assure you that he is extraordinarily studious and diligent and clings with great love to

his science. He therefore feels profoundly unhappy about his current lack of a job, and he becomes more and more convinced that he has gone off the tracks with his career.... Since it is you whom my son seems to admire and esteem more than any other scholar in physics, it is you to whom I have taken the liberty of turning with the humble request to read his paper and to write to him, if possible, a few words of encouragement, so that he might recover his joy in living and working. If, in addition, you could secure him an assistant's position, my gratitude would know no bounds. I beg you to forgive me for my impudence in writing you, and my son does not know anything about my unusual step.

Ostwald still didn't respond.

Isaacson wrote in his book that it is hard to know what accounted for Einstein's trouble in finding an academic job. Einstein speculated that one of his physics professors at the Zurich Polytechnic who was a rival undermined his efforts by giving poor references. The fact that Einstein graduated near the bottom of his class at the Polytechnic might have contributed to the problem. Another possibility is that anti-Semitism was a factor. Whatever the case, Einstein remained jobless throughout 1901. He pieced together tutoring stints with temporary teaching assignments to make a basic living. Isaacson commented in *Einstein*: "Among the many surprising things about the life of Albert Einstein was the trouble he had getting an academic job."

In the spring of 1901, Marcel Grossman, a friend of Einstein, wrote to him that a position at the Swiss Patent Office in Bern was expected to become available in the upcoming months. Grossman said that his father knew the director and would put in a good word for Einstein. Einstein replied: "I was deeply moved by your devotion and compassion, which did not let you forget your luckless friend." After much waiting, the "luckless" Einstein got the job of examiner at the Swiss Patent Office in June 1902.

In *Einstein*, Isaacson described how Einstein's failure to get an academic job spurred his independent thinking, arguing that failing freed Einstein from common pressures in academic settings, unleashing his originality.

 Had he been consigned instead to the job of an assistant to a professor, he might have felt compelled to churn out safe publications and be overly cautious in challenging accepted notions. As he later noted, originality and creativity were not prime assets for climbing academic ladders, especially in the German-speaking world, and he would have felt pressure to conform to the prejudices or prevailing wisdom of his patrons....

As a result, the happenstance that landed him on a stool at the Swiss Patent Office, rather than as an acolyte in academia, likely reinforced some of the traits destined to make him successful: a merry skepticism about what appeared on the pages in front of him and an independence of judgment that allowed him to challenge basic assumptions.

Isaacson wrote that Einstein himself came to believe that being outside of academia benefited his science, saying that it was in "that worldly cloister where I hatched my most beautiful ideas." Isaacson described that period as "the most creative seven years of his life." Indeed, during that time, Einstein wrote his seminal papers that revolutionized physics, including the paper on his theory of relativity and one about the relationship between mass and energy that contained his famous formula $E = mc^2$.

J. K. Rowling

J. K. Rowling, author of the bestselling Harry Potter series, gave a commencement address at Harvard University in 2008 entitled "The Fringe Benefits of Failure, and the Importance of Imagination." Near the beginning of her speech, she told the graduating students how she decided on the topic of her talk.

 I have wracked my mind and heart for what I ought to say to you today. I have asked myself what I wish I had known at my own graduation, and what important lessons I have learned in the twenty-one years that have expired between that day and this.

I have come up with two answers. On this wonderful day when we are gathered together to celebrate your academic success, I have decided to talk to you about the benefits of failure.

She said that at the time of her own college graduation, she was "striking an uneasy balance" between her own dream of writing novels and others' expectations. Writing novels was the only thing she ever wanted to do, she said. But her parents, both from impoverished backgrounds, wanted her to pursue a career path that would ensure financial security; in her words, they "took the view that my overactive imagination was an amusing personal quirk that would never pay a mortgage, or secure a pension." During college, Rowling also felt caught between her parents' expectations and her own desires.

> So they hoped that I would take a vocational degree; I wanted to study English Literature. A compromise was reached that in retrospect satisfied nobody, and I went up to study Modern Languages. Hardly had my parents' car rounded the corner at the end of the road than I ditched German and scuttled off down the Classics corridor.
>
> I cannot remember telling my parents that I was studying Classics; they might well have found out for the first time on graduation day. Of all the subjects on this planet, I think they would have been hard put to name one less useful than Greek mythology when it came to securing the keys to an executive bathroom.

After graduation, she continued trying to balance her parents' expectations with her own, and seven years later, it was clear that the strategy had failed.

> So I think it fair to say that by any conventional measure, a mere seven years after my graduation day, I had failed on an epic scale. An exceptionally short-lived marriage had imploded, and I was jobless, a lone parent, and as poor as it is possible to be in modern Britain, without being homeless. The fears that my parents had had for me, and that I had had for myself, had both come to pass, and by every usual standard, I was the biggest failure I knew.

She spoke candidly about how painful failing was.

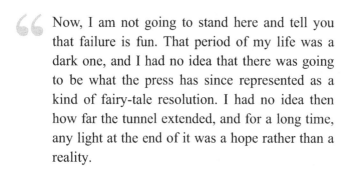 Now, I am not going to stand here and tell you that failure is fun. That period of my life was a dark one, and I had no idea that there was going to be what the press has since represented as a kind of fairy-tale resolution. I had no idea then how far the tunnel extended, and for a long time, any light at the end of it was a hope rather than a reality.

Then she asked rhetorically, "So why do I talk about the benefits of failure?" And answered: "Simply because failure meant a stripping away of the inessential." She went on to say:

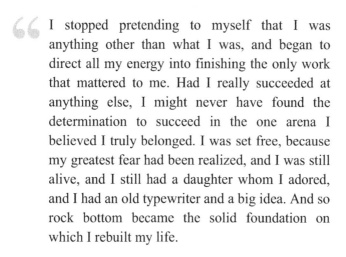 I stopped pretending to myself that I was anything other than what I was, and began to direct all my energy into finishing the only work that mattered to me. Had I really succeeded at anything else, I might never have found the determination to succeed in the one arena I believed I truly belonged. I was set free, because my greatest fear had been realized, and I was still alive, and I still had a daughter whom I adored, and I had an old typewriter and a big idea. And so rock bottom became the solid foundation on which I rebuilt my life.

J. K. Rowling went on to speak about other benefits of failure.

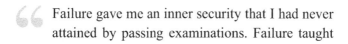 Failure gave me an inner security that I had never attained by passing examinations. Failure taught

me things about myself that I could have learned no other way. I discovered that I had a strong will, and more discipline than I had suspected; I also found out that I had friends whose value was truly above the price of rubies.

The knowledge that you have emerged wiser and stronger from setbacks means that you are, ever after, secure in your ability to survive. You will never truly know yourself, or the strength of your relationships, until both have been tested by adversity. Such knowledge is a true gift, for all that it is painfully won, and it has been worth more than any qualification I ever earned.

Of the multiple benefits she mentioned, the first benefit hit me the hardest: "failure meant a stripping away of the inessential." Or from another angle, failure revealed the essential.

Steve Jobs

Steve Jobs delivered a popular commencement address to Stanford graduates in 2005 that featured a story about "love and loss." The speech has circulated widely, so there is a good chance that you are familiar with it. If so, I would like to suggest that you take a fresh look at it here. Let me explain why by using a "Magic Eye" metaphor. If you were older than five in 1990, you may remember the 3-D "Magic Eye" pictures that were extremely popular in the mid-1990s. At first glance, the rectangular image was a two-dimensional, somewhat patterned design, but if you looked at the same image in a different way, which usually involved some special squinting situation, a 3-D image popped out. I think that looking at the familiar story of

Steve Jobs' failure in a different way may reveal a new dimension as well.

Jobs' story of "love and loss" was about starting Apple in 1975 and getting fired from Apple in 1985.

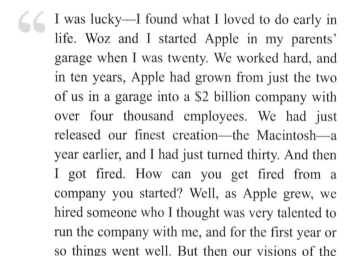

> I was lucky—I found what I loved to do early in life. Woz and I started Apple in my parents' garage when I was twenty. We worked hard, and in ten years, Apple had grown from just the two of us in a garage into a $2 billion company with over four thousand employees. We had just released our finest creation—the Macintosh—a year earlier, and I had just turned thirty. And then I got fired. How can you get fired from a company you started? Well, as Apple grew, we hired someone who I thought was very talented to run the company with me, and for the first year or so things went well. But then our visions of the future began to diverge and eventually we had a falling out. When we did, our board of directors sided with him. So at thirty I was out. And very publicly out.

Failing, Jobs said, was "devastating."

> I really didn't know what to do for a few months. I felt that I had let the previous generation of entrepreneurs down—that I had dropped the baton as it was being passed to me. I met with David Packard and Bob Noyce and tried to apologize for screwing up so badly. I was a very public failure, and I even thought about running away from the [Silicon] Valley.

But Jobs began to see possibility in the rubble. He said that failure made him feel lighter and freer. In his words, "The heaviness of being successful was replaced by the lightness of being a beginner again, less sure about everything. It freed me to enter one of the most creative periods of my life."

Jobs went on to describe how in the five years after he was fired, he started two companies: NeXT and Pixar. Pixar created the first computer-animated movie, *Toy Story*, and is regarded by many as the world's most successful animation studio. NeXT was a computer company that produced some computers but more relevantly an innovative operating system. Apple bought NeXT when Jobs returned to Apple as CEO in 1997, and the operating system that NeXT developed became the basis of the Macintosh operating system going forward. Jobs said that the technology developed at NeXT became "the heart of Apple's [then] current renaissance."

And Apple, it feels somewhat silly to note, experienced a new kind of success when Jobs returned as CEO in 1997. In other words, Jobs' big failure sparked creativity—"one of the most creative periods of my life"—which, in turn, fueled his subsequent success.

 I didn't see it then, but it turned out that getting fired from Apple was the best thing that could have ever happened to me.... It was awful-tasting medicine, but I guess the patient needed it. Sometimes life hits you in the head with a brick. Don't lose faith.

* * *

These three stories illuminate a single pattern. All three individuals felt a great commitment to meet others' expectations. Then failure hit, and it was extremely painful. And freeing. Failing peeled away what weighed them down and held them back. As J. K. Rowling said, "failure meant a stripping away of the inessential." It unmasked their originality. And their originality ignited our imaginations and changed the way we live and think. J. K. Rowling's original thinking created the Harry Potter series. Einstein's revolutionized physics. And Steve Jobs' personal brand of creativity led to Apple's renaissance. Their originality fueled their subsequent success.

The alchemy involved in the process—failure revealing originality, and originality fueling success—is mysterious. These stories are a start, but to unravel the mystery, we need to dig deeper. We will start by breaking the secret pathway into its two parts: (1) failure reveals originality, and (2) originality drives success.

First, consider how failure reveals originality, or as I prefer to say, how failure helps you fly your freak flag.

4
_____

FAILURE AND YOUR FREAK FLAG

It is clear from the beginning of the movie *The Family Stone* that Meredith Morton, the female protagonist in the film played by actress Sarah Jessica Parker, does not have many freak-like qualities. She is a business executive who is very uptight, seems like the consummate rule follower, and typically wears a slicked-back bun with pearl earrings and a business suit. When she visits her new boyfriend's family over the holidays, she is just as uptight about making a good impression with them as she is about every other aspect of her life. She desperately wants to fit in with the family, and perhaps because of this, she fumbles in her efforts to connect throughout the visit. At the family's Christmas Eve dinner, Meredith ends up saying something so hurtful that her boyfriend's dad yells, "That's enough!" several times. But she can't quite stop herself, even when it's painfully obvious that she has upset everyone at the table. She ends up leaving the dinner prematurely, in an awkward, abrupt, cringe-inducing exit, and goes to a local bar to escape. Her boyfriend's brother, Ben, played by actor Luke Wilson, follows her there to do some damage control. At the bar, Ben offers his analysis of her situation. He tells Meredith that she has been trying too hard to please the family. He suggests that she stop trying to play a part and just be herself: "Maybe you should stop. Just stop. Stop trying.... Here's the thing, Meredith. You have a freak flag. You just don't fly it."

Here's another thing: everyone has a freak flag, but as Meredith Morton's predicament illustrates, flying your freak flag is difficult to do.

The word *freak* and term *freak flag* have been used in various ways over time to both demean and empower. Here I use *freak flag* in a specific way—as a synonym for originality. I bring in the term *freak flag* for a handful of reasons. I think it hints at what makes it difficult for us to show originality; it taps into the fear of being judged for one's uniqueness. Also, I find the term empowering when used as an equivalent of originality because it takes the word *freak*, which has been used to denigrate people for showing uniqueness, and uses it in a way that elevates uniqueness. *Freak flag* reclaims a word that was used to provoke shame and gives it a new meaning that invokes pride. For all these reasons, I think *freak flag* captures the spirit of originality. And it's pretty fun to say.

Before getting into how failure helps us fly our freak flags, consider why help is welcome. It's needed. Flying your freak flag is hard to do.

Why It's Hard to Fly Your Freak Flag

So why is it hard to fly your freak flag? In a word, layers. You might have had an anxiety dream about showing up naked to work or school, but odds are, you arrive with clothes on every day. Just as we wear clothes on our bodies, we also tend to walk around with a layer or ten over the naked version of ourselves. These layers represent what we say and do that we don't really want to say or do but feel compelled to because of some outside reason—generally a version of a "should" or "supposed to." Imagine that beneath all the layers is a core. The core represents what we do because we really want to, for its own sake. The core is our essence, and the layers, to borrow J.K. Rowling's phrase, are "the inessential." Whereas the layers are fed by extrinsic motivation, our core is fueled by intrinsic motivation. Whereas the layers are dull, the core glows with vitality. The layers drape over the core, like wet towels thrown over a fire, and dampen, or snuff out, our originality.

Consider the following analogy of a gobstopper. Imagine a cherry red gobstopper. If you are not familiar with the candy, a gobstopper is a hard candy about the size and shape of a marble. It also can be called a jawbreaker. Gobstoppers with a solid color on the outside usually have solid-colored layers on the inside, so a red gobstopper might have a yellow layer underneath and then orange, etc. Each layer dissolves to reveal another layer until all the layers have dissolved and you reach the center of the gobstopper. It is the sweetest part, and the texture typically is different too. It is a softer candy as opposed to the hard, shell-like layers that cover it. If you think of yourself—what you do, say, and believe—as the gobstopper, the core represents doing what you most want to do, for its own sake—what you do out of intrinsic motivation. Moving outward from the center, the layers become more fueled by "should"— by extrinsic motivation—and less fueled by "want to." When you reach the outermost layer, it represents fully what you do out of extrinsic motivation—nothing that you want to do for its own sake.

(I tried to crack open a regular-size gobstopper with a lime squeezer so that I could show a picture of the cross-section. It didn't go well. I thought a picture would help you envision what I am talking about here, but as you can see, this picture is of no help.

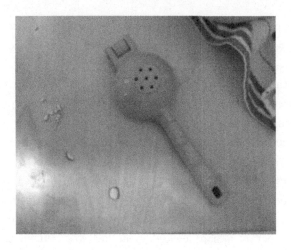

I later found a monster jawbreaker at a candy store, and a close friend's son volunteered to throw it on a stone patio. The results were marvelous and provided the kind of picture I was hoping for.)

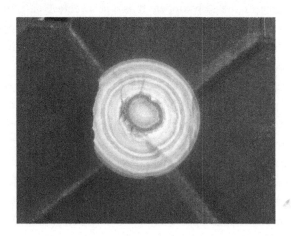

Back to the layers. The layers I am describing are not completely bad; they can serve a helpful purpose. Like clothes, they can make daily interactions more comfortable and shield the naked version of ourselves from outside elements and judgments. When that naked self is tucked away under multiple layers, it can feel cozy, safe, and invulnerable, untouchable. But it also can feel confining, suffocating, and isolating. Therein lies the big downside of layers.

Key to understanding what makes it hard to express originality is understanding how these layers come to be. In other words, what creates these layers? They can be created intentionally, like walls we put up or armor we put on to protect ourselves from potential hurt. They also can collect unintentionally, and often without much notice, by virtue of being human and interacting with other human beings. Layers tend to be created by expectations and pressures.

Expectations and Pressures

In October 2010, *New York Times* columnist David Brooks wrote an article entitled "The Soft Side" about Rahm Emanuel, then chief of staff for President Obama, now mayor of Chicago. Brooks offered his personal, insider's perspective on Emanuel, whom he had covered for a decade at that point. Brooks opened the article by summarizing the widespread perception of Emanuel as a fierce, no-holds-barred "political street-fighter" but then put forth another view. Brooks expressed admiration for how Emanuel has "somehow managed to remain true to his whole and florid self" in the midst of pressures to do otherwise. Brooks was not claiming that Emanuel is perfect, noting that he is "flawed like all of us," but pointed out that staying true to one's self is remarkable given formidable societal pressures.

 From the moment kids are asked to subdue their passions in order to get straight As to the time they arrive at a company and are asked to work seventy hours a week climbing the ladder, people have an incentive to suppress their passions and prune their souls.

That's especially true in Washington, a town with more than its fair share of former hall monitors, a place where politicians engage in these pantomime gestures of faux friendship and become promotable, hollowed-out caricatures of themselves.

Brooks' insight is penetrating: pressures permeate our lives and nudge people to "subdue their passions" to meet external demands.

Throughout life, other people, including parents, teachers, bosses, friends, and society in general, communicate expectations about what is good, right, important, desirable, appealing, and appropriate. As David Brooks points out, from the time we are kids, our success in the traditional sense, such as achieving in school, is contingent on meeting others' expectations. As adults, conventional success, whether it involves achieving a goal or attaining wealth, honors, or status, also is tied closely to meeting the expectations of others. So, there are powerful incentives to act according to what others think is good, worthy, or right. As a result, expectations exert a powerful influence over us and shape how we think, feel, and act.

And expectations are very helpful in ways. They can help us make sense of the world and provide useful information about other people's standards. Think of how confusing it would be if you never received instruction about what is right, appropriate, or good. But expectations have a major downside. Because they draw our focus to getting other people's approval, they can dim originality.

Pressures also can be originality dimmers. Consider some

common pressures: Make good grades. Get into college of choice. Get good job. Keep good job. Get promoted. Accrue wealth. Maintain wealth. Achieve status. Maintain status. Succeed. Like expectations, pressures abound, and they can provide information about commonly held beliefs and help us understand the world. But they have the same downside. They push us to act according to others' desires in a way that can drown out our own.

Viewing Four Established Social Influences from a New Perspective

Drilling down deeper, seminal research in psychology on four social influences—authority, conformity, conditioning, and modeling—helps to decode how expectations and pressures create the layers that dim our vibrant core. Looking at the impact of these social influences through a new prism—originality—reveals that they have a similar, dramatic effect. Applying the well-established research in this new way provides deeper insight into how expectations and pressures dim originality.

Authority

The classic "shock experiments" conducted by Stanley Milgram at Yale University in the 1960s sought to understand the influence of authority on behavior. The setup of the experiment involved three different roles: (1) a teacher, (2) a learner, and (3) an experimenter. The experimenter and learner were in on the experiment. The experimenter ran the experiment and was the authority figure in the scenario, dressed in a white lab coat to emphasize his position of authority. The role of learner was given to someone who posed as a participant but was actually working with the experimenter (a "confederate" in research jargon). The only actual participant in the experiment was always given the role of teacher. The experimenter instructed the teacher to give the learner a quiz involving various word pairs. The teacher and learner were put in different rooms and couldn't see each other but were able to communicate via intercom. The teacher was given a list of word pairs and instructed to read them to the learner and then administer tests relating to the words. The teacher was told that the learner would press a button to indicate a response; responses would light up on a panel in the teacher's room. If the answer was correct, the teacher should go to the next word pair, but if the answer was incorrect, the teacher should administer an electric shock to the learner. The first shock would be 15 volts and then shocks would increase by 15 volts with each wrong answer until the maximum voltage of 450 volts. The learner didn't actually receive shocks, but the teacher thought he did. Prerecorded tapes played fake responses of the learner indicating escalating distress with increased voltage—groaning, banging on the wall, yelling to be let out of the room—until the 315-volt level, after which point the learner made no more noise. When teachers expressed concern, as many did, the experimenter told them they were required to continue. Many teachers exhibited signs of distress, like trembling and stuttering, and expressed reservations about continuing, but about 65 percent of the teachers in the original experiment went all the way to the end, delivering a 450-volt shock to learners who had not responded since the 315-volt level. The remaining 35 percent of participants broke off the experiment but none before the 300-volt level. Milgram and others were in disbelief about the findings. When surveyed before the experiment, Yale seniors at the time predicted that about 1 percent of people would go all the way. Psychiatrists surveyed at the time predicted less than 1 percent. One of the most powerful aspects of Milgram's findings is that they have been replicated by him and other researchers many times.

The findings reveal that people in authority have a formidable influence on our behavior and that authority pushes us to obey instructions even when doing so involves overriding strong internal messages of what we think is right.

Expectations and pressures regularly are communicated by authority figures, like parents, teachers, bosses, doctors, professors, and religious leaders. The influence of authority permeates our lives. In best-case scenarios, capable, wise, and caring guides help us navigate different aspects of our lives in fruitful ways. But the profound impact of authority has a serious downside. In nudging us to act according to someone else's standards instead of our own, it can silence who we are.

Conformity

In 1955, Solomon Asch, another influential researcher in psychology, conducted a pioneering experiment investigating the influence of group standards on the individual. As is the case with Milgram's shock experiments, Asch's studies on conformity have been so influential that they are covered in nearly every Introduction to Psychology class. Asch's studies typically were conducted with a group of six or seven people, but only one participant was in each group. Everyone else was a confederate. Participants, typically college-aged men, were told that the study was about visual perception, and the experimenter started by asking everyone in the group to look at two cards, like the ones below, one with a single line and another with three lines. The group members sat in a row, all facing the cards, and the participant was the second to last in the group. Each person was asked to say which line on the second card matched the line on the first.

There were several rounds with different cards for each round.

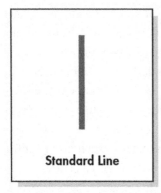

Standard Line

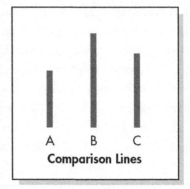

A   B   C
Comparison Lines

You can tell from the cards that this would seem like a boring experiment because the correct answer is so obvious. And in the first couple of rounds, it was. Everyone gave the correct response, but then confederates started giving incorrect answers. In many cases, the line they chose was dramatically different in length from the line on the first card. Participants often expressed confusion and frustration, but 75 percent of them went along with the incorrect majority at least once. Overall, participants conformed 37 percent of the time.

How could this happen? Asch's findings revealed that group standards exert enormous influence on us. They push us to adjust our opinions and behavior to be in line with the standards, even when doing so means going against what our own senses are telling us.

Expectations and pressures are frequently communicated through the rules, collective opinion, or norms of a group: group standards. Group standards involve what a particular group thinks is right, important, appealing, or valuable. They can relate to any group, ranging from family and friends to society as a whole, and group norms are ubiquitous. They can be explicit, but they also can be implicit, so they affect us in ways that are obvious and discreet. Both are powerful.

Let me tell you one way I unwittingly have conformed to group standards. From time to time, a thought like this will come into my mind: "I love the color mint green. It's just this personal, little thing I have. I guess I have never thought about it much but it's true. I love mint green, and I want to buy more clothes that are mint green." And that'll be the end of that random thought for the moment. Then, not much later, say within a month, I will walk by clothing stores and realize that there are *a lot* of items that are mint green. The trend, which I now realize had been building, has exploded. And as it was building, it had an impact on my tastes without my noticing. Here is what I think happens: at the beginning of the hypothetical mint-green clothing trend, I unconsciously register the message that the color is appealing, but the trend is incipient enough that I don't consciously notice it. I just absorb it subtly and find myself thinking about mint green, thinking it is my own personal taste. But I realize when the trend explodes that my "personal taste" was most likely created by group standards, in this case, what people in the fashion industry are telling me is appealing.

Group standards often influence us in ways that fly beneath our radars. They nudge us to conform in ways that are visible and invisible, and they squelch originality.

Conditioning

The kind of conditioning I am talking about here is operant conditioning, which is different from the kind that's talked about most—classical conditioning, which involves Pavlov's dogs, bells, salivation, etc. Operant conditioning is a scientific theory, based on many scientific studies, describing how we learn. It describes how consequences, like punishment and rewards, shape us by either encouraging or discouraging certain behaviors. Take punishment, for example, a well-known consequence. Punishment discourages a behavior by applying a negative consequence: a fine, suspension, probation, grounding, etc. Positive and negative reinforcement encourage a behavior in different ways. In positive reinforcement, a positive stimulus is added to strengthen a behavior. For instance, when you get a high five or a pat on the back for something you've done, it makes you feel good, and as a result, you want to do that thing again. One of my best friend's parents used to take her and her sisters out to dinner at Red Lobster when they got good grades. That is an example of positive reinforcement. In negative reinforcement, an annoying or aversive stimulus is removed to strengthen a behavior. A classic example of negative reinforcement is the beeping noise cars make if you don't put on your seatbelt. The beeping continues until you put your seatbelt on, so the behavior is encouraged because it eliminates the annoying stimulus.

Expectations and pressures often get communicated through consequences. Consequences are everywhere. They appear early in childhood and are present throughout our lives. They are a part of most of our relationships. Consequences have the same side effect as the other social influences: by prompting us to do what others want—what others reward or punish us for—they subdue originality.

Modeling

Modeling describes another way that we learn and, like operant conditioning, is an influential source of learning. We learn through modeling by observing the behavior of someone else and acting in that same way. If you are a teacher, you may find yourself imitating the behavior of your favorite teacher. If you are a singer, you likely started out imitating the music and style of bands you love. Many beginning lawyers probably have moments of recognizing that they were trying to imitate Perry Mason or Atticus Finch. Modeling can be a very positive influence, but it too can mask originality.

Authority, conformity, conditioning, and modeling are frequently used vehicles of expectations and pressures. Taken together, these four influences share a single downside. They nudge us to do, think, and say—to be—who others reward us for being rather than being ourselves.

The net effect of expectations and pressures, more generally, is that they make it hard to show and access originality—to fly our freak flags. The point is not to eliminate expectations and pressures altogether because, as I've mentioned, these influences can have a positive effect, and part of being human is allowing ourselves to be affected by other people. And to a degree, these influences are unavoidable; they often affect us in ways that we don't register consciously. But the effect of expectations and pressures does suggest this: that to see and show more of what is in our core, we have to slice through the layers. And we need help—a tool to cut through the layers. Surprisingly, this is where failure excels.

How Failure Helps Us Fly Our Freak Flags

In October 2005, *Newsweek* magazine ran a cover story entitled "How Women Lead" that featured eight influential women in leadership positions. The conductor Marin Alsop was one of them. Alsop is music director of the Baltimore Symphony Orchestra and chief conductor of the São Paulo Symphony Orchestra, and earlier that year, she had received a

MacArthur Fellowship, also called a "genius grant," awarded to individuals for exceptional creative work and potential for future creative work. At the time, Alsop was the only conductor in the fellowship's nearly twenty-five-year history to receive this grant. The article, a collection of firsthand accounts, focused on turning points in the women's lives. Alsop wrote about an interaction she had as a student at Tanglewood Music Center with her teacher, the acclaimed conductor and composer Leonard Bernstein.

 There was one rather cathartic rehearsal day where he came up to me and said, "The conducting's fine but it really isn't moving me." It was so devastating. Then he said, "Let's give the orchestra a break and then you'll come back and do this again." He said forget about conducting now. Just be yourself and be the music. But then I came back in and it was the weirdest experience. I felt like I'd had a massage. I thought I had nothing to lose. I'm just going to try it. I remember in the middle of the piece—this makes me cry—he came up to me and whispered, "That's it." It was so liberating.

Alsop punctuated the story with this insight: "Bernstein was more than a teacher; he coaxed the essence out of people." As Alsop's story implies, operating from your essence is difficult. We often need help. Failure provides that. It is a powerful tool for coaxing the essence out of us.

Oprah Winfrey, in a commencement address she gave at Stanford University in 2008, discussed how failing coaxed the essence out of her. Without using the word *modeling*, Oprah described how her efforts to model Barbara Walters' behavior squelched her originality, whereas failing unlocked it.

 A year after I left college, I was given the opportunity to co-anchor the six o'clock news in Baltimore.... It felt like the biggest deal in the world at the time. And I was so proud because I was finally going to have my chance to be like Barbara Walters, which is who I had been trying to emulate since the start of my TV career...

So, here I am, twenty-two, making $22,000 a year, and yet, it didn't feel right. It didn't feel right. The first sign, as President Hennessy [president of Stanford] was saying, was when they tried to change my name. The news director said to me at the time, "Nobody's going to remember Oprah. So, we want to change your name. We've come up with a name we think that people will remember and people will like. It's a friendly name: Suzie." Hi, Suzie. Very friendly. You can't be angry with Suzie. Remember Suzie? But my name wasn't Suzie. And, you know, I'd grown up not really loving my name because when you're looking for your little name on the lunch boxes and the license plate tags, you're never going to find Oprah. So, I grew up not loving the name, but once I was asked to change it, I thought, Well, it is my name and do I look like a Suzie to you? So, I thought, No, it doesn't feel right. I'm not going to change my name. And if people remember it or not, that's OK.

And then they said they didn't like the way I looked. This was in 1976 when your boss could call you in and say, "I don't like the way you look." Now that would be called a lawsuit, but back then they could just say, "I don't like the way you look." Which, in case some of you in the back, if you can't tell, is nothing like Barbara Walters. So, they sent me to a salon where they gave me a perm, and after a few days all my hair fell out and I had to shave my head. And then, they really didn't like the way I looked. Because now I am black and bald and sitting on TV. Not a pretty picture.

But even worse than being bald, I really hated, hated, hated being sent to report on other people's tragedies as part of my daily duty, knowing that I was just expected to observe, when everything in my instinct told me that I should be doing something. I should be lending a hand.... And meanwhile, I was trying to sit gracefully like Barbara and make myself talk like Barbara. And I thought, Well, I could make a pretty goofy Barbara. And if I could figure out how to be myself, I could be a pretty good Oprah....

And sometimes I wouldn't read the copy—because I wanted to be spontaneous—and I'd come across a list of words I didn't know and I'd mispronounce. And one day I was reading copy and I called Canada "Ca-nada" [Cuh-*na*-da]. And I decided, This Barbara thing's not going too well. I should try being myself.

But at the same time, my dad was saying, "Oprah Gail, this is an opportunity of a lifetime. You better keep that job." And my boss was saying, "This is the nightly news. You're an anchor, not a social worker. Just do your job." So, I was juggling these messages of expectation and obligation and feeling really miserable with myself.... I'd go home at night and fill up my journals about how miserable I was and frustrated. Then I'd eat my anxiety. That's where I learned that habit.

And after eight months, I lost that job. They said I was too emotional. I was too much. But since they didn't want to pay out the contract, they put me on a talk show in Baltimore. And the moment I sat down on that show, the moment I did, I felt like I'd come home... doing that talk show, it felt like breathing. It felt right. And that's where everything that followed for me began.

Libby Leffler Hoaglin

While working on this book, a friend told me about Libby Leffler (now Libby Leffler Hoaglin). My friend had seen a talk Leffler Hoaglin gave at the Digital-Life-Design (DLD) Women Conference in Munich about how to increase the presence of women in leadership positions in business. Leffler Hoaglin was the keynote speaker at the conference. My friend was impressed by the talk and suggested that I check it out. I did and I was impressed as well. Leffler Hoaglin was in her twenties at the time and already was very accomplished and forward-thinking. Leffler Hoaglin started her career at Google, where she worked in a group run by Sheryl Sandberg, current COO of Facebook. In 2008, she left to become a member of Facebook's inside sales team and soon became the business lead to the COO, Sheryl Sandberg, a position she held for almost three years before becoming senior manager of strategic partnerships, the position she held when I interviewed her. As senior manager of strategic partnerships at Facebook, Leffler Hoaglin led a division of Facebook partnerships that focused on helping nonprofit organizations and public figures engage others and create positive change through partnering with Facebook.

Leffler Hoaglin has received many honors and awards for her work in the field of business, technology, and social media. In 2013, she was named the "Most Important Woman Under 30 in Tech" by *Business Insider*. The next year she was on the "FORBES 30 Under 30" list as one of the "brightest stars" in media under thirty. In 2017, she was an invited speaker to the *Fortune* Most Powerful Women Next Gen conference, which brings together "preeminent rising women in business" and other fields, according to its website. I interviewed Libby Leffler Hoaglin in a conference room at Facebook Headquarters in Menlo Park, California, in August 2013.

I started our interview by asking which success had meant the most to her, and I was intrigued by her response; despite her concrete accolades, her answer was about an intangible achievement.

 When I was twenty-two, I was working at Google and I was recruited to come work at Facebook. And it was really hard at the time, because Google was like *Google*. Everyone wanted to work at Google. It was 2007/2008; I worked there. The company was really big. I think there were about 20,000 people. It was a huge company, super well known, everyone knew Google. Not that many people knew about Facebook.

Facebook was one of those things that, you

know, hit or miss, people who were on knew about, but it wasn't the global sort of phenomenon at the time that Google was. So, when I was interviewing at Facebook, I just—my instincts were very, very strong that this was the right place for me to be. Everything about it seemed correct, from the job I would be doing, to the team I would be joining, to the people that I met and talked to and the culture. Everything seemed right.

Even so, I was really afraid to kind of make the jump, you know. I mean, I've talked about this publicly before—like Facebook made me an offer and I didn't take it, because I was really scared, thinking to myself: I'm twenty-two and at this great company. Why am I like tossing aside this amazing experience and opportunity to go work somewhere that's really small that people don't know?

I asked: "It felt like too big of a risk?" And she continued.

 Yeah, it felt like it was a huge risk. So then I spent every night for a month sleepless thinking: oh my gosh, I've made the worst mistake ever. And that was a really important and very pivotal moment for me to always listen to my instinct. Because I ended up calling my recruiter back and coming to work at Facebook, which is the best decision I think I could have ever made. And the decision to come work at Facebook 100 percent changed my life. And changed the direction of my life.

Now, I joined a team at Facebook of five people. It was the beginnings of an inside sales team of, now we have, you know, a huge global inside sales team. But really it was a much less structured and defined role in a company that was relatively small—of several hundred people.

…And so when I think about my most personally meaningful success, my most meaningful success was listening to my instincts, and calling that recruiter, and basically having to call her and say: "I made a big mistake and I need to come work for you and here's why"—and having to suck up my pride and do that.

And I did and they made me the offer and I came to work at Facebook, and I love it at Facebook, right? That's why I'm here. I've done different things at Facebook, and this opportunity to be here has changed my life in incredibly meaningful ways, because of the things I've learned and the people I've been around and the projects I've had the opportunity to work on.

So that to me seems like the biggest personal success, because it was really hard for me as somebody who is very organized, loves to do things by the book, has everything, you know, the whole linear fashion of the way everything should be.

Ms. Leffler Hoaglin's biggest failure, she said, was an incident from her personal life. Interestingly, her biggest setback was similar to her biggest success in that it was, in her words, "another example of just really pushing myself to listen to my instinct and to do what I knew in my heart was the right thing to do." She called off her wedding two months before it was set to happen.

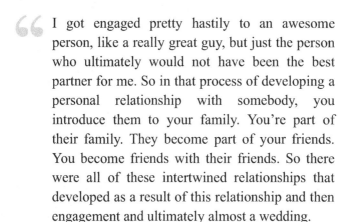 I got engaged pretty hastily to an awesome person, like a really great guy, but just the person who ultimately would not have been the best partner for me. So in that process of developing a personal relationship with somebody, you introduce them to your family. You're part of their family. They become part of your friends. You become friends with their friends. So there were all of these intertwined relationships that developed as a result of this relationship and then engagement and ultimately almost a wedding.

Leffler Hoaglin said that she started having serious doubts and ultimately realized that her fiancé at that time was not the right partner for her.

And so I ended up calling my wedding off two months before the wedding... It was incredibly stressful at the time, and I felt like it was *such* a failure. I really viewed it as *such* a failure and an immense disappointment. I felt like I had let down my parents. I felt like I had let down my partner's parents and family, my family, but most of all I felt like I let this person down who I promised to spend the rest of my life with, and it was a really hard moment for me.

It was a really tough moment of personal reflection. It was what felt like an immense setback personally because I just felt unsure of myself. You know, I was twenty-six at the time I ended up calling the wedding off. I got engaged when I was twenty-five, so it was a very fast engagement. And it felt like a major personal setback and disappointment. But from that I think I grew into the person that I'm ultimately supposed to become, an independent person who knows more about what she wants from life and... knows kind of the non-negotiables... it's about knowing what things you care about and what things you're willing to sort of compromise on, and feeling like... it's okay to be you and that authenticity is *really* important.

...And so in the last couple years, I've become more comfortable with trusting my instincts, and I think it's helped make me a more genuine and authentic person, and I'm really more confident. I'm not afraid to fail because I've developed that innate confidence. And that in turn makes me confident to put myself out into the world and put myself out there for more opportunities; to ask for more; to really set lofty goals for myself; to set almost audacious goals for myself because I'm just not afraid of what's on the other side.... I actually think that failure and setbacks can help make a person more confident.

When I asked Leffler Hoaglin to say more about the process of responding to the failure, she said:

At first, I felt really disappointed, like I disappointed everyone around me. And then instead of viewing it through that lens I started thinking about it more in the realm of, What do *I* really think about this? And how did this impact *my* life? How does this impact *me* and the things that I do? Am I a better sister, a better friend, a better daughter? Am I a better contributor at work, a better colleague, a better peer? Am I a better person overall? Do I understand what I'm looking for more? I think the answer to that is yes.

She then elaborated by saying that when you experience failures and setbacks, "you often think: 'I'm never going to get through this. There's like no light on the other side of the tunnel. This is impossible,' and you do. You know you can do anything. And it gives you that confidence to know like, I've been through this one thing, I can do anything." I nodded and said "yes" as she continued.

 I am fearless. And my twenty-one-, twenty-two-year-old self was like by the book, checking every box, making sure everything's perfect. And that's just not reality.... Life is messy. Life is complicated.

And I really believe that every setback has something to teach you about yourself and about being more authentic. And if you can learn something about yourself, you can become therefore more innately in tune with your instincts and hopefully more confident with those instincts too.

And... I think that's what made me more confident, that I was confident in my instincts and that I knew that if I pursued the things that I was passionate about or pursued the things I was deeply interested in, that I could get to a point where I felt comfortable putting myself out there and that I wasn't kind of having to do everything by the book exactly the way someone else said it needed to be done.

By the time I asked her whether she thinks failure is related to success, she already had shared thoughts on the topic through her responses to other questions, but she offered more. After saying that she thinks they are related, she spoke specifically about her situation: "I think that personal failure gave me the confidence to listen more closely to my instincts, and since then I've listened very, very closely to the things that I think—just my gut reactions to things. I process things in a very analytical way, but I also pay very close attention to what instinctually... I know to be important to me." I said: "And you were doing less of that before?" And she said:

Yeah, I think before it was more box-checking, thinking: "I've got to go to this school. I've got to do this. I've got to spend this number of years. I need to work in consulting. I need to go to work here. I need to do this." And at some point, I think I just became more comfortable with who I was as a person. And I think when you become more comfortable with who you are, you can be more successful. You've opened yourself up to the opportunity to further develop skills you maybe never knew you had. You open yourself up to the chance to... take on new opportunities and really challenge yourself to dream big and to do cooler, more interesting things that kind of

spark your interest. So I think failure, if it leads
you to a place where you can become more
confident and therefore take bigger risks, I think
that's a success... that can only fully develop you
in more interesting and valuable ways.

Leffler Hoaglin's failure put her in touch with what she
really wanted. It got her to listen to messages she had been
ignoring about what she really wanted. It gave her more confidence not only to listen to her instincts, but also to trust them,
and it gave her more courage to act on them.

So how does failure reveal originality? The alchemy is
indeed mysterious; to my knowledge, there currently is no
empirical evidence that speaks directly to this point, but here is
how I see it. The problem—that it's hard to fly our freak flags
—actually has two parts: (1) it's hard to access originality, and
(2) it's hard to express originality. Failure helps with both.

Accessing Originality

Over time, expectations and pressures put us out of touch
with messages of what we really think, feel, and want to do.
When we repeatedly act according to external demands and
reject internal ones, the internal messages become fainter or
harder to interpret, or they stop coming altogether. In this way,
expectations and pressures make it hard to get in touch with
what is on the inside; originality becomes hard to access.

We receive information constantly from the outside, and
every day we make innumerable decisions, automatically and
intentionally, to accept (i.e., listen to) or decline (i.e., ignore)
incoming information. Like a switchboard operator, expectations and pressures exert control on which "calls" get through
and which are denied. And they order our priorities to focus on

external rather than internal messages. Preoccupied with meeting others' desires, we dismiss our own, and over time, valuable information from ourselves gets hidden out of reach. Like a physician straining to hear a patient's heartbeat under layers of clothing, we struggle to hear what we really desire and believe at the deepest level. Like listening to a foreign language you once spoke but haven't heard in years, the messages are hard to interpret. Expectations and pressures end up compromising or cutting off vital lines of communication with our core selves. They muffle the messages, making it hard for us to tune into our own desires.

Failure cracks us open, allowing hidden contents to spill out. Like a wooden bat smacking a piñata, failure sends what was hidden inside flying out. It releases what was dammed up, or held in, as we focused on avoiding failure. And failure digs up what was buried out of judgment, burping up hidden information, forcing it to surface. The pain of failure turns us inward. This is reflected in language we use when we are in pain. Research shows that people who are in emotional pain use more first-person singular pronouns like "me," "my," and "I," reflecting that attention is focused inward. The pain of failure grabs our attention and pushes us to reflect. It also gets us to listen. Pain, with its loud megaphone, brings clear messages. It helps us to hear what we couldn't hear before, or what we were ignoring, about what we really think, feel, and want. It restores lines of communication with our core selves that had been compromised or cut. If expectations and pressures serve as a switchboard operator, controlling which "calls" get through, failure fires the switchboard operator. Messages that were previously denied come flooding in. Not meeting others' standards can give us permission to listen to our own. In other words, failure removes the censor, and that which was pushed down springs up. It puts our eyes on what we overlooked.

Failure elicits truth like a truth serum—it extracts truth out of us. Failure decloaks our core self, exposing it.

Failure clarifies what is essential. Like an abrasive cutting through layers of buildup to uncover a gem, failure scrapes away layers that cloud originality. Failure strips us bare—helping us see the naked, unvarnished version of ourselves more clearly—putting us in touch with our core. It reveals us in a more authentic form to ourselves. Failure brings into relief what we really care about and what we don't. It separates the layers from the core, the wheat from the chaff. It teases apart what we truly think, feel, and want from what we believe we're supposed to think, feel, and want. By burning off the clutter, failure puts us in touch with what is most vital. Near the end of my interview with Senator Booker, he made comments that speak directly to this phenomenon I am describing here.

 There's a soulfulness I find from people who have had spectacular failures or have hit the rock bottom of drug abuse or who have had public humiliation. There's a soulfulness, I think, that comes from that where you do get better in line with what really matters. And there's a liberation too, also, when you go through hell. When you say, "Oh my God, I'm still here. All those horrible things have happened and I'm still here. There's still breath in my bones. And I can still move forward." And I think there's a wonderful alignment in that, and what is important becomes more crystal clear and what's not important gets pulled away.

Failure also makes us dig deeper. It introduces us to deeper reserves than we had previously known, exposing us to unplumbed resources. As an analogy, consider this story about how the Frog's Leap Winery in Napa Valley, California, grows its grapes. Several years ago, when I was on a tour of its vineyard, the guide told the group about the vineyard's approach to growing grapes. She said something like this: "We don't put our grapes on a Coke and candy diet." She explained that they don't indulge their grapes with a lot of water. They water the grapes less than most other vineyards. Why? Less water forces the roots to go deeper into the soil. The roots then are exposed to richer, deeper resources in the soil, and drawing on these resources enhances the quality of the grapes. Similarly, failure forces us to go deeper into ourselves—acquainting us with richer resources we had not been able to reach before, unearthing more of our originality.

And failure nudges us to trust our truth, the inner authority, that we have found. It helps us trust our own experience. In stripping away what we wish we felt, saw, and believed, failure gets us to own what we actually see and believe, what we actually love, yearn for, think, dream, feel. Consider this quotation about self-trust and originality from Emerson's essay "Self-Reliance": "We but half express ourselves, and are ashamed of that divine idea which each of us represents.... Trust thyself: every heart vibrates to that iron string." Whereas expectations and pressures lead us to "half express ourselves," failure helps us to trust ourselves.

Failure is a portal to originality, and it can provide a nudge —a shot of courage—to express what we have found.

Expressing Originality

Expectations and pressures are like gatekeepers. They control what comes out and what stays in. They nudge us to screen parts of ourselves. Like a baseball pitcher acting on certain suggested pitches and waving off others, expectations and pressures prompt us to act according to others' desires while waving off our own. When others' standards are in line with our own, there is no problem. But when others' standards are not in line with our own, we may say yes when we really want to say no. We may twist, bend, or shrink to fit someone else's standard.

Failure can provide freedom to be more ourselves. Why? Failing to meet others' expectations can unbridle us from trying. It can liberate us from focusing on trying to meet others' standards, freeing us to act according to our own. Failing often is the realization of one of our biggest fears, so when that fear is realized, it can feel like we have nothing to lose. When we feel we have nothing to lose, we feel freer—to release the holds and let things flow from deeper sources: to voice what we have been reluctant to say and do what we really want to do. So failure not only reveals originality, it provides a dose of courage to express it—to bring to the outside more of what is inside. Failure can free us to think, act, create, imagine, lead, and produce in bolder ways that feel even more authentically like ourselves.

* * *

In 2007, the writer Joan Acocella published a compilation of essays entitled *Twenty-Eight Artists and Two Saints*. The essays, as the title implies, are about artists and saints, including the writer and Holocaust survivor Primo Levi, ballet dancer Mikhail Baryshnikov, dancer and choreographer Martha Graham, and Joan of Arc. Though the essays had been published individually, she realized that a theme tied them together, as she pointed out in the introduction of the book: "As I read through them," she said, "a single theme kept coming up:

difficulty, hardship." She clarified that she was not talking about hard childhoods, though some of the people featured in her essays did have hard childhoods. The hardship had to do with the work itself: "…the pain that came *with* the art-making, interfering with it, and how the artists dealt with this." She concluded that difficulty was a common theme in the art-making process of these acclaimed individuals. When the writer Kathryn Harrison reviewed the book in the *New York Times Book Review*, she distilled Acocella's discoveries about how great art is made like this: "Corrosive disappointment can strip away the veneer of culture and refinement that an immature artist typically acquires, revealing the more genuine sensitivity, the art, beneath." This comment about how exceptional art is made summarizes what I put forth here: the "corrosive disappointment" of failure, the pain of it, strips away "the veneer of culture and refinement," the influence of expectations and pressures, revealing the true beauty—originality—that lies beneath. The stories of these artists divulge a very similar pattern to the one we saw in the stories of J. K. Rowling, Albert Einstein, Steve Jobs, Johnny Cash, Oprah Winfrey, and Libby Leffler Hoaglin. The pattern begins with a universal tendency: to focus energy on meeting others' expectations and adapting to outside pressures. Then failure. Failing peels away the influence of expectations and pressures that weigh us down and hold us back. It reveals the essential—our essence, our originality.

That is the first part of the secret pathway from failure to success: failure reveals originality. Now we put a magnifying glass on the second part of the pathway: originality fuels success. In other words, flying your freak flag fuels success. How exactly does that happen?

YOUR FREAK FLAG AND SUCCESS

When Steve Jobs returned to Apple as CEO in 1997, Apple launched a major advertising campaign that encouraged people to "think different." Full-page print advertisements featured historic figures, big thinkers, and doers, like Einstein, Cesar Chavez, Muppets' creator Jim Henson, Miles Davis, and Richard Feynman, with just the two words "Think different" in a corner. Similar ads covered entire sides of buildings. And in a one-minute television advertisement, brief clips of black-and-white film footage rolled of some of the most influential people of the twentieth century, like Martin Luther King Jr., Mahatma Gandhi, Amelia Earhart, Thomas Edison, Einstein, and John Lennon, while actor Richard Dreyfuss read the poem "Here's to the Crazy Ones" in a voice-over narration.

 Here's to the crazy ones. The misfits. The rebels. The troublemakers. The round pegs in the square holes. The ones who see things differently. They're not fond of rules. And they have no respect for the status quo. You can quote them, disagree with them, glorify or vilify them. About the only thing you can't do is ignore them. Because they change things. They push the human race forward. And while some may see them as the crazy ones, we see genius. Because the people who are crazy enough to think they can change the world, are the ones who do.

The word *originality* is not used in the ads, but the idea is at the center of them. The phrase "Think different" is itself encouragement to think in an original way, and the grammatically incorrect phrasing offers another nudge to pause and think more deeply. Originality is what unifies the featured group of people: the "crazy," status-quo-scoffing, genius individuals. The poem in the television ad makes the case explicitly: "the crazy ones... who see things differently... and have no respect for the status quo... change the world." Apple's "Think different" advertising campaign captures the second part of the secret pathway: originality fuels success.

Your originality is your genius. Not kidding. Let me explain my thinking. Consider how the MacArthur Foundation, the organization that awards "genius grants" like the one the conductor Marin Alsop received, describes who receives genius grants: "talented individuals who have shown extraordinary originality." And there's more. The Foundation explains that the aim of genius grants is not simply to pat people on the back for past accomplishment but to invest in future work of the recognized individual: "The fellowship is not a reward for past accomplishment, but rather an investment in a person's originality, insight, and potential." Just as originality is essential for receiving a genius grant, more generally, originality is essential to genius. A current definition of *genius* is an individual of exceptional natural ability, but an antiquated definition is "a guardian spirit." Genius was considered something that everyone had—each person having a unique version rather than a quality reserved for a small group. It seems like there is wisdom in the old definition. It is possible that we all have genius within us—in as many forms as we are individuals. Your unique genius is your originality, and your originality is your greatest power—your greatness. When originality gets covered by layers that build up over it, those layers smother the greatness. Whereas acting from the layers saps power, operating from the core provides power; it empowers, which is why originality fuels success.

Thomas Friedman, columnist for the *New York Times* and Pulitzer Prize–winning author, advised graduates in his 2005 commencement address at Williams College to "do what you love" and quickly added that this advice is no longer "warm and gooey career advice"; it is a survival strategy. Why? Because, as he put it, "the world is getting flat"; there now exists a much greater capacity to automate work with computers and software and a new level of global interconnectedness, which allows for work to be sent to other parts of the world to be done more efficiently or cheaply. And in this flat world, he said, different qualities are valued.

 The flatter the world gets, the more essential it is that you do what you love, because... all the boring, repetitive jobs are going to be automated or outsourced in a flat world. The good jobs that will remain will be those that cannot be automated or outsourced; they will be the jobs that demand or encourage some uniquely human creative flair, passion, and imagination. In other words, jobs that can only be done by people who love what they do.

Friedman does not use the word *originality*, but what he says characterizes originality: "uniquely human creative flair, passion and imagination." Similarly, the type of workers he identifies as being the most valuable—"people who love what they do"—characterizes people operating from their core. Years later, in an op-ed in the *New York Times*, Friedman echoed what he said in his address at Williams: "We live in an age when the most valuable asset any economy can have is the ability to be creative—to spark and imagine new ideas, be they Broadway tunes, great books, iPads, or new cancer drugs."

Other writers, as well as economists, have made similar arguments indicating that originality is especially valuable in today's world. Economist Alan Blinder, professor at Princeton University, argued that creativity and inventiveness are among the most important skills for success in the twenty-first century. Walter Isaacson wrote: "For this new century of globalization... our success will depend on our creativity." And the writer Daniel Pink argued in his book *A Whole New Mind: Why Right-Brainers Will Rule the Future* that we are transitioning from a society of knowledge workers to a society of creators and that professional success increasingly will depend on the ability "to invent something new by combining elements nobody else thought to pair." The notion that originality fuels success may be more true in the twenty-first-century economy than ever.

Consider a more concrete way of describing how originality fuels success. Originality is the seed of innovation, and innovation drives progress. A 2011 article in the *New York Times* described innovation as "the crucial ingredient in all economic progress." Innovation could mean coming up with a new idea or creating a new product. It also could mean taking a new approach to an existing issue or devising a new solution to an old problem. New ideas drive innovation, and originality is what generates new ideas. As Einstein said, "It is important to foster individuality for only the individual can produce the new ideas." And new ideas change the world.

Thomas Friedman spoke about his belief that innovation is actually essential for all workers in the twenty-first-century economy in an interview at the Aspen Ideas Festival in 2011. Walter Isaacson, who is not only an author but also the president and CEO of The Aspen Institute that puts on the Aspen Ideas Festival, was interviewing Friedman about his book *That Used to Be Us: How America Fell Behind in the World It Invented and How We Can Come Back.* Friedman said that his belief that innovation is now essential for all workers came from his experience interviewing a group of employers from a range of sectors: "one high-end white collar, the head of a Washington law firm; one low-end white collar, the guy who ran—actually, the outsourcing firm where I wrote *The World Is Flat*; third, a blue collar, Ellen Kullman, the chairman of DuPont; and fourth, the head of the biggest green-collar employer in America, Major Martin Dempsey, the head of the US Army education team, now promoted to chairman of the Joint Chiefs of Staff." These employers, when asked what kind of employees they were looking for, responded in a strikingly similar way. They said that just to get an interview, workers need to be able to do critical thinking and problem-solving. Friedman's takeaway was that "average is officially over. So whatever you do, you better find your extra." He told a story about his interview with the head of a Washington law firm, Jeff Lesk, to illustrate his point:

 I said, "Jeff," subprime crisis hits, I said, "What's happened to your law firm?" He said, "Oh we're laying people off." And I said, "That's interesting. Who gets laid off first?" Just kind of curious. He says, "It's not who you think. It's not last in, first out. The people who are being laid off are when the credit bubble was at its height and we had all that work, we handed it to those lawyers, they did that work in a very nice way and they handed it back. Those are the ones who are gone. The ones who are staying are those who can say, 'You know, Jeff, we could do this old work in a new way, or actually there's a whole new set of work we can do.' So his section actually in the book starts with him explaining, "My law firm just hired a Chief Innovation Officer." Okay. So basically what's happening now is people don't want just critical thinking and problem solving, they want people who can invent, reinvent any job they're doing. And that is going to be the new thing I think in the labor market.... You and I, Walter, we had the privilege, I'll just end here, when we got out of college we got to *find* a job. I think our kids are going to have to *invent* a job.

The idea that originality drives success has roots in history. Consider the words of poet and philosopher Ralph Waldo Emerson in a journal entry from September 1830.

Every man has his own voice, manner, eloquence, and, just as much, his own sort of love and grief and imagination and action. Let him scorn to imitate any being, let him scorn to be a secondary man, let him fully trust his own share of God's goodness, that, correctly used, it will lead him on to perfection which has no type yet in the universe.

For success marked by changing the world or maximizing the positive impact you have on the world, originality is your most powerful asset. Offering up your unique perspective—your vision, voice, and thinking—is your best tool for adding value. Each of us has something that no one else can offer. You have cornered the market on your unique brand. Whether you are an entrepreneur, a scientist, an educator, a student, a stay-at-home dad, a stay-at-home mom, a singer, an actor, a bus driver, a political leader, a middle manager—whoever—your voice is your best shot at adding value. Whether you make an impact in ways that are small or large, private or public, originality is your greatest power.

Flying your freak flag also fosters another kind of success: psychological success, or happiness. Evidence that originality fosters happiness is rich and varied, and it spans centuries. This idea is supported by empirical research and has been articulated by philosophers and poets.

Originality and Happiness

In the mid-twentieth century, influential psychologists Abraham Maslow and Carl Rogers argued that expressing one's inner self and strengths was essential to well-being. Since then, many scientific studies have demonstrated that doing what feels aligned with who we are at a core level contributes to our happiness. Emerging research in psychology on the "true self," defined by "the essence of who a person really is," indicates that one's true self plays a vital role in creating a fulfilling, meaningful life. Other research has shown that pursuing intrinsically rewarding goals as opposed to focusing on extrinsic rewards or demands is deeply satisfying. Psychologists Ed Deci and Richard Ryan have written extensively about the benefits of living one's life according to internal values as opposed to focusing on extrinsic rewards or demands. They have found that when people's goals are aligned with their deeper needs and values, psychological well-being is enhanced. Relatedly, psychologist Martin Seligman and colleagues have found that drawing on one's signature strengths—strengths that reflect a person's most essential values—fosters happiness. And, in the job context, workers who pursued goals that employed their greatest strengths reported not only higher job satisfaction but also higher life satisfaction.

There is a chapter in *On Liberty*, an essay by the philosopher John Stuart Mill published in 1859, entitled "On Individuality, As One of the Elements of Well-Being." Mill uses *individuality* and *originality* interchangeably in the essay, and as the title of the chapter implies, he argues that originality is an important part of well-being, but he goes further in the essay and calls it "one of the principal ingredients of human happiness." Emerson conveys a similar sentiment in this untitled poem from 1832.

> I will not live out of me.
> I will not see with others' eyes...
> I would be free; I cannot be
> While I take things as others please to
>   rate them.
> I dare attempt to lay out my own road.
> That which myself delights in shall
>   be Good,
> That which I do not want, indifferent;
> That which I hate is Bad. That's flat.
> Henceforth, please God, forever I forego
> The yoke of men's opinions. I will be
> Light-hearted as a bird...

Expressing originality makes him "light-hearted as a bird."

Manifesting originality not only helps us change the world, it brings us joy. That is the effect that expressing originality has on you and me, as individuals. Consider what it means for us as a society.

You, Me, and Us

Since manifesting originality helps you as an individual change the world, at a collective level, many individuals manifesting originality would change the world dramatically. It would propel progress at a societal level, a point that John Stuart Mill made in *On Liberty*. Mill argued that originality is "quite the chief ingredient of individual and social progress." Here he elaborates on why that is.

> It will not be denied by anybody, that originality is a valuable element in human affairs. There is always need of persons not only to discover new truths, and point out when what were once truths are true no longer, but also to commence new practices, and set the example of more enlightened conduct, and better taste and sense in human life.... There is only too great a tendency in the best beliefs and practices to degenerate into the mechanical; and unless there were a succession of persons whose ever-recurring originality prevents the grounds of those beliefs and practices from becoming merely traditional, such dead matter would not resist the smallest shock from anything really alive, and there would be no reason why civilization should not die out...

On a societal scale, expressing more of our originality is vital to progress.

Einstein alluded to the idea that originality drives progress in a conversation he had near the end of his life. Isaacson wrote of it, "Einstein was asked by the New York State Education Department what schools should emphasize. 'In teaching history,' he replied, 'there should be extensive discussion of personalities who benefited mankind through independence of character and judgment.'" Isaacson noted: "Einstein fits into that category."

And since manifesting originality brings joy to you as an individual, at a collective level, it would elevate our happiness as a society, which is also a point that John Stuart Mill made in *On Liberty*. He describes how expressing originality—"cultivating it and calling it forth"—enriches not only the individual but also society. You will notice that Mill uses the word *individuality* in the following quotation, whereas he used *originality* in the previous one, reflecting how he uses the two words interchangeably in this essay.

 It is not by wearing down into uniformity all that is individual in themselves, but by cultivating it and calling it forth, within the limits imposed by the rights and interests of others, that human beings become a noble and beautiful object of contemplation; and as the works partake the character of those who do them, by the same process human life also becomes rich, diversified, and animating, furnishing more abundant aliment to high thoughts and elevating feelings, and strengthening the tie which binds every individual to the race, by making the race infinitely better worth belonging to. In proportion to the development of his individuality, each person becomes more valuable to himself, and is therefore capable of being more valuable to others. There is a greater fulness [sic] of life about his own existence... it is only the cultivation of individuality which produces, or can produce, well-developed human beings, I might here close the argument: for what more or better can be said of any condition of human affairs, than that it brings human beings themselves nearer to the best thing they can be?

What value does originality have for society? In short, greater success as defined by progress and happiness.

* * *

Part 1: The Light could be summarized with this graphic, slightly modified from the one you saw previously.

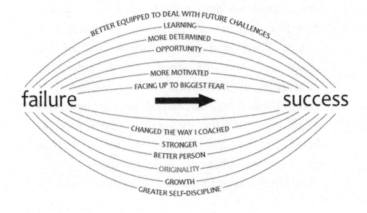

Science and stories reveal that failure can fuel greater success, and it can do so in many different ways. Originality is a particularly powerful one. Failure reveals greater originality, and originality fuels success. This may be true in the twenty-first century more than ever. And failure can foster happiness by the same route: failure originality happiness. Exposing new dimensions of failure's formidable, multidimensional light side illuminates more of the whole truth of failure, and as the light pierces the dark, we see failure in a fuller, truer way.

For most of us, however, the prevailing belief that failure is completely bad is deeply rooted, so uprooting it is not easy. To have a shot at uprooting it, we have to understand what feeds it. So what feeds the belief that failure is bad? Failure's downside, or what I will call failure's dark side: pain and humiliation. A deep, enduring shift in how we view failure can only occur by acknowledging the true pieces of how we see it now.

PART II

THE DARK

"FAILURE SUCKS"

I n late October 2009, Max Levchin, cofounder of the online payment service PayPal, was a guest on the NPR show *Morning Edition*. Levchin is considered one of the best innovators in the world. The magazine *MIT Technology Review* named him Innovator of the Year in 2002 and that same year named him one of the top 100 innovators under thirty-five in the world. When Levchin appeared on *Morning Edition*, he had recently spoken at the first FailCon, a conference about failure that brings together technology entrepreneurs, investors, and other businesspeople to talk about their failures in an effort to build greater success. FailCon started in 2009 in San Francisco and since then, conferences have been hosted in many countries around the world. Levchin's achievements can make you wonder if he has ever failed. He shared on *Morning Edition* that he has—many times. "The very first company I started failed with a great bang. The second one failed a little bit less but still failed. The third one, you know, proper failed, but it was kind of okay. I recovered quickly. Number four almost didn't fail. It still didn't really feel great, but it did okay. Number five was PayPal."

Around the same time, Levchin talked with *Wired* about what it feels like to fail. He put it bluntly: "Failure sucks."

The comedian Conan O'Brien had a similar message in a commencement address he gave at Dartmouth College in 2011. His speech came about a year after he was fired as host of *The Tonight Show* after just a seven-month stint, and he spoke about the pain of failing: "Nietzsche famously said, 'Whatever doesn't kill you makes you stronger.' But what he failed to stress is that *it almost kills you*. Disappointment stings, and for driven, successful people like yourselves, it is disorienting. What Nietzsche should have said is, 'Whatever doesn't kill you makes you watch a lot of Cartoon Network and drink mid-price Chardonnay at eleven in the morning.'"

Just as we tend to assume that people who have achieved extraordinary success don't fail, we tend to assume that they would be emotionally immune to failure if it did happen. This assumption is perpetuated because most people don't feel comfortable talking about failures. Even fewer talk about how failure *feels*. Because acknowledging the pain of failure is rare, we assume that experiencing pain after failure is rare. But it's not. Max Levchin and Conan O'Brien bravely offered a peek behind the curtain.

People I interviewed also spoke frankly about what failure felt like. You might recall that "hurt" is the word Dr. McPherson used most to describe how Lincoln felt after his most painful failure. Lincoln reportedly used that word too. Take a look at the language others used.

Coach Mike Krzyzewski: "like a leper"; "angry"; "dark moment"; "emotioned out" to the point of "no feeling"

Mayor Pam Iorio: "lots of self-doubt"

US Senator Cory Booker: "humiliating"; "devastating"

Carl Hayden: "broke my heart"; "no matter how hard you try, you take it personally"; "just this awful feeling, this sting-y sort of feeling"

Libby Leffler Hoaglin: "immense disappointment"; "like I disappointed everyone"

The stories of J. K. Rowling, Einstein, and Steve Jobs reveal similar feelings.

Albert Einstein: "profoundly unhappy" is how Einstein's father described him when he couldn't find a job.

J. K. Rowling: "Now, I am not going to stand here and tell you that failure is fun. That period of my life was a dark one…"

Steve Jobs: "devastating"; "awful tasting medicine"

Science offers evidence that experiencing negative emotions after failure is universal. In one experiment, William Swann, a psychology professor at the University of Texas, and his colleagues investigated the emotional impact of failure in a social setting: getting rejected. They considered the possibility that some people don't feel pain after rejection, investigating whether people with high self-esteem experience negative emotions after being rejected.

When participants came into the laboratory, they completed a questionnaire assessing their self-esteem in social situations. The questionnaire consisted of items like, "I have no doubts about my social competence." Then participants gave a short speech that involved reading excerpts from a novel, and afterward they received feedback on their performance from an evaluator. Unbeknownst to participants, however, the feedback had nothing to do with how well they delivered the speech. Participants had been randomly assigned to receive either positive feedback or negative feedback, the negative of which is shown here in this example.

> From the way he (or she) looked reading this speech, this person doesn't seem real socially self-confident. I'd say he probably feels somewhat uncomfortable and anxious around other people he doesn't know too well. He seems to have some doubts about his social competence. That's about all I could tell about him.

After receiving feedback on their performance, participants completed questionnaires about their level of negative emotions. Findings showed that receiving negative feedback increased negative emotions irrespective of one's level of self-esteem. People with low and high self-esteem experienced negative emotions after being rejected.

If having high self-esteem doesn't inoculate a person from the pain of failure, what about another likely characteristic—not caring what other people think of you? Mark Leary, professor of psychology at Duke University, and his colleagues asked that question. They conducted two studies investigating whether people who report not caring what others think of them are affected by social rejection.

In the first study, when participants, who were college undergraduates, came into the laboratory, experimenters asked if they believed that their self-esteem was affected by approval or rejection of others. Participants then completed a questionnaire about themselves, including questions about hobbies, favorite movies, personality traits, and lifestyle habits. Afterward, participants received either approving or disapproving feedback and were told that the feedback was based on the personal information they shared on the questionnaire, but actually they had been randomly assigned to receive either approving or disapproving feedback. The approving feedback indicated that evaluators liked them—thought that they were well adjusted and would like to have them as a friend or as a member in a group they belonged to. The disapproving feedback was the opposite. After receiving feedback, participants completed a short assessment about how they felt about themselves at that time—called "state self-esteem"—and a questionnaire measuring their level of positive and negative emotions. Researchers found that people who were rejected felt worse about themselves afterward—had lower "state self-esteem"— and experienced more negative emotions and fewer positive emotions. This finding held true for people who reported before the experiment that they did not care what others thought of them.

Diving deeper, Leary and his colleagues conducted a second study. It was similar to the first with a few small changes to the design. Instead of completing a questionnaire at the beginning of the experiment, participants were presented with questions through prompts on a computer that they responded to through a microphone. At first, the prompts were general: "What is your first name?" Then they became increasingly personal: "Describe the last time you felt lonely." Participants were told that someone was listening to them in another room, and they received ongoing feedback through the computer monitor about how approving the listener was. Feedback was in the form of a numbered scale ranging from 1 to 7 indicating how much the listener wanted to "get to know" the participant; "1" was "I do not wish to get to know the speaker at all" and "7" was "I wish very much to further get to know the speaker." Disapproving feedback caused people to feel worse about themselves and to experience more negative emotions, including anger, hurt feelings, and sadness, than approving feedback did. And again, findings held true even for people who reported before the experiment that they were not affected by what others think of them.

Emerging research shows that emotional pain in response to failure can even be "seen" at a physiological level—in our hearts, hormones, and brains. The pain of failure is actually manifested in our bodies. For example, people experiencing social rejection had a cardiovascular response that mirrored the response of a person under threat or severe stress. And at a hormonal level, rejection produces more cortisol, a hormone associated with stress. Research using functional magnetic resonance imaging (fMRI), which measures functional processes in the brain by tracking blood flow and oxygen, demonstrated that when individuals who recently had experienced an unwanted romantic breakup viewed a photograph of their former romantic partner while thinking about the rejection, their brain was activated in essentially the same places as when a device was placed on their arm that produced enough heat to cause pain. In other words, the regions of the brain that light up when people experience social rejection overlap substantially with those that light up when people experience physical pain.

There is some truth in our view that failure is bad. It *is* painful. Just as failure is not all dark, it also is not all light. Science and stories provide converging support for what Max Levchin said: "Failure sucks." And the sentiment is universal. The idea that "failure sucks" for virtually everyone is mundane in ways but also radical. It's mundane because to our conscious minds it is not surprising; there is a certain *duh* factor in hearing that failure is painful. But it is radical because of the universality, which contradicts unconscious assumptions we have at an "in-the-bones" level: assumptions like, people who have achieved extraordinary success are not affected emotionally by failure; or people with high self-esteem are not hurt by failure; and people who say they don't care what others think of them are emotionally immune to failure. The evidence that feeling pain after failure is universal flies right in the face of those assumptions. Take a moment to let this simple, somewhat mundane and also radical idea penetrate your thinking and settle into your bones.

Humiliation is another aspect of failure's dark side. Although humiliation can fall under the umbrella of pain, it merits a separate conversation because it creates a specific, significant problem for us. It governs how we react to failure, and this way of reacting robs us of the opportunity to reap failure's rewards.

"THE GREAT AMERICAN TABOO"

When I was applying to doctoral programs in psychology, I decided to take the GRE, the standardized test for entrance into graduate school, a second time. I was in a master's program for public policy at the time. I had taken the GRE to get into that program and did well, but I was applying now to PhD programs in psychology with little background in psychology, so I needed every bit of help I could get. My professor in a math-intensive course in the policy program said that he thought bumping up my score would be very doable, and so I decided to go for it. And people—I bombed. I don't mean a stumble or a near miss or a run-of-the-mill "off day." I mean a fall-off-the-bike-on-your-face day. My math score plummeted. I don't really know what happened. Anxiety from pressure I put on myself probably was a big factor. Incidentally, my score went up on the other two sections I wasn't trying to improve, but that was little consolation for my nose-dive of a math score. Afterward, I didn't want to tell anyone. I didn't want to think about it or even know it. I wished that it hadn't happened, and I wanted to act like it hadn't. I told close friends and family, but my overriding urge was to hide it.

Failure is embarrassing, often humiliating. And the humiliation makes us want to do one thing: hide the failure.

Hiding failure has real allure, and the desire to hide it is very understandable. We hide it in hopes that we will be protected from humiliation. And in the short term, we might be right. But in the long term, hiding failure has a major cost: it also protects us from failure's benefits.

Philip Schultz, author of a Pulitzer Prize–winning collection of poems entitled *Failure*, called failure "the great American taboo." That label feels so fitting. Few topics evoke silence like failure. We don't like to talk about it. When I read that Shakespeare was private about his failures, it made me realize that I felt self-conscious about my failures. At the time, I thought this insight was about a personal idiosyncrasy, but I realized over time that the tendency to hide failure is common.

There are many ways to hide it, too. In a July 2006 *Bloomberg Businessweek* article entitled "How Failure Breeds Success," Thomas Kuczmarski, a new-product development consultant, described a typical response that companies have to failure: "What most companies do," he said, "is put a wall around a failure as if it's radioactive." We may try to excise it from our lives, to surgically remove it. Try to sweep it under the rug, cover it up with blankets, or bury it in the yard. Often, we not only hide failure from others, we try to hide it from ourselves—to bury it in our own minds. We may try to ignore it, deny it, or twist the truth of it to convince ourselves or others that it didn't actually happen. Whatever the form, hiding failure has the same effect: it shuts us off from the possibility of absorbing failure's benefits. It wastes the potential benefits.

* * *

One reason that failure is scary is that it doesn't always lead to something better. Failure creates raw material that can be converted into something better, but the process doesn't happen automatically. If we don't convert the raw material, it is wasted. And there is effort involved in the conversion process, as a quotation from the beginning of the book implies: "Last night, as I was sleeping, I dreamt... that I had a beehive here inside my heart. And the golden bees were making white combs and sweet honey from my old failures." If we are to be buoyed by failure, we have to respond to it in a way that allows us to extract its benefits. But what is that way?

In his baccalaureate address at Stanford in 2008, Reverend Peter Gomes highlighted the importance of understanding how to respond well to failure.

 I want you to first think about the virtue of failure. Think of the things that haven't gone right, the things that don't go well, because there will be many more of them in your lives, and how will you sort out those failures? What will you learn from them? What will you make of them? Become acquainted with failure, for failure will become acquainted with you. It will know your name. It will know your vanity. It will know your weak spots. So, you'd better be prepared to deal with it.

Emerging research sheds light on how people can respond to negative experiences, like failure, in a way that fosters growth. Whereas traditionally research on responding well to failure has focused on how to rebound quickly from it—return to previous levels of functioning—recent research has investigated how to grow from failure.

Drawing on research, as well as stories from a range of

sources, including literature, television shows, film, and a centuries-old spiritual, we now consider how to respond to failure in a way that allows us to extract its growth benefits. Ralph Waldo Emerson wrote that if a person "harvests his losses," then he "turns the dust of his shoes to gems." How can we turn the dust of our shoes to gems?

PART III

TURNING THE DUST OF
OUR SHOES TO GEMS

HOW TO GROW FROM FAILURE

A PRIMER

R eflect for a moment about a goal you have right now in any part of your life—personal, work, relationships, anything. Now imagine that you fail, falling flat on your face. What would be the worst outcome of your failure—your nightmare scenario of the fallout? By the way, this is not building up to a "see, it's not that bad" resolution. I actually would like you to indulge your biggest fear for a moment. The details of our scenarios will be different, but for many of us, the main theme will be the same: some spiraling downward situation possibly ending in an incapacitated state. In a word: helplessness. Helplessness typically is considered the worst outcome of failure in research too. Now think about what the best possible outcome of your failure would be. In this case, I have no idea what you imagined, but you might have envisioned bouncing back quickly and fully to life as it was before your failure. That is resilience. And resilience traditionally has been considered the best outcome of failure in research too. Resilience entails bouncing back readily to a prior state after a setback, as is reflected in the dictionary definition of *resilient*: "springing back to its original form after being bent or stretched." For example, let's say you run track, and you usually run the mile in six minutes. (This example, by the way, bears no resemblance to my own life. I have only run that fast once, and it was in a dream.) Then you have a horrible race for whatever reason, and you run a seven-minute mile. Resilience, in terms of your performance, would mean getting back to a six-minute mile within the next race or two. Traditionally, research on responding to negative events, like failure, has focused on these two outcomes: one bad—helplessness—and one good— resilience. Conventional wisdom of how to respond well to failure is informed by this research, so let's examine the research a bit more closely.

One of the many strengths of this line of research is that findings are strikingly similar across studies conducted by many researchers over the course of decades. Studies on helplessness and resilience largely have been laboratory experiments, and they typically unfold in a similar way. Participants come into the laboratory and are asked to perform some cognitive task, like solving a set of math problems. Then they encounter a failure. For example, they are asked to solve math problems that are unsolvable. Right after, they perform another cognitive task, like a new set of math problems. Researchers use performance on that subsequent task to measure helplessness versus resilience. If performance deteriorated after failure, that indicates helplessness. If it was maintained or dipped briefly but bounced back readily to the prefailure level, that is resilience. These studies also commonly assess participants' emotional state after failure as compared to before failure, as well as persistence on the subsequent task. The studies show overall that participants who show greater resilience in performance also report less negative emotion and more positive emotion, and they demonstrate greater persistence. Conventional wisdom about responding well to failure, which can be characterized as "be positive and persist," is consistent with this research.

Although this research has contributed in a massive, meaningful way to the understanding of how to respond well to failure, it is predicated on a particular "good" outcome of failure, resilience. Emerging research considers a new "good" outcome —one that goes beyond bouncing back to prior levels.

A New Possibility

Traditionally, research on how to respond well to negative events, like failure, has distinguished between helplessness and resilience as possible outcomes.

Emerging research, however, investigates a new possibility: growth.

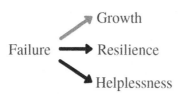

Growth entails ultimately improving after a setback— getting to a higher level than you were before. More recently, researchers have been tilting their perspectives upward from resilience to growth, investigating the possibility that negative events can lead to something better than before. This research, building on the remarkable foundation of previous work, entertains the possibility that surviving failure relatively unscathed may not be the ultimate positive outcome. This new angle elicits the question: Does the new "good" outcome—growth—entail a new "good" response?

Diverse research from many areas cutting across a wide range of negative experiences—including failure, relationship problems, trauma, and disease—provides converging evidence for how to respond to negative experiences in a way that fosters growth. Stories from many sources, including television shows, literature, movies, and an old spiritual, provide further support. The kind of response to failure that is associated with growth differs dramatically from the "be positive and persist" approach associated with fostering resilience. Extracting failure's benefits requires a new, different kind of "good" response than the one we traditionally have espoused. The response I put forth here is what I gathered from sifting through a lot of evidence from a wide range of sources, the science and stories that I mentioned. It is compelling to me because of how many different sources pointed in the same direction, including stories from centuries ago that mapped onto current scientific findings. But it is worth keeping in mind that it is *a* response to failure that can foster growth. It is not *the* response. Although I am not aware of other responses supported by research at this time, there most likely are myriad responses to failure that could foster growth. Point being: this is not *the* way. It is *a* way. It's not a recipe to follow precisely. It's more like a roadmap to consider.

So, what exactly is this new "good" response to failure? It has two parts. The first relates to how we think and feel—the cognitive/emotional part. The second part relates to how we act, or what we do—the behavioral part. Let's consider the cognitive/emotional part of the response first. It is counterintuitive and goes against conventional wisdom, and it has been shown to foster positive change in the context of confronting negative experiences. It is called *acceptance of negative emotions*, or as I once saw on a T-shirt: "embrace the suck."

"EMBRACE THE SUCK"

In the 2005 film *Batman Begins*, Bruce Wayne, who later becomes Batman, has a nightmare about a traumatic childhood experience: he fell down a well near his family's house in Gotham City and landed in a cave full of swarming bats. Bats were his biggest fear at the time. The experience was terrifying and cemented his fear of bats, a fear that followed him stubbornly into adulthood. Many years after Bruce Wayne fell into the well, and soon before he became Batman, he traveled to the country of Bhutan to learn how to master fear. His mentor, Ducard, told him that mastering fear requires a journey inward. As part of the training, Ducard instructed Bruce to breathe in a toxin from an exotic flower found in Bhutan that causes people to see their worst fear: "Breathe. Breathe. Breathe in your fears. Face them." As Bruce inhaled the toxin, he began having flashbacks of bats swarming. Ducard continued to instruct: "Feel terror cloud your senses. Feel its power to distort—to control. And know that this power can be yours. Embrace your worst fear." Through Ducard's training, Bruce Wayne learned to master fear. Later, when he returned to Gotham City, he went back to the well that he fell in as a kid. He climbed down into the cave where he knew the bats would be, and, in what seemed like a test of his training, he shined a light to attract bats to him. Then, he stood up tall and breathed calmly and steadily as the bats swarmed all around him. Embracing his biggest fear had changed him. Soon thereafter, Bruce Wayne became Batman and set out to drive crime and corruption from his hometown of Gotham. Transformed into a superhero through learning to master his biggest fear, his new name, Batman, reflected his journey.

This fictional story suggests something about real life: embracing negative emotions may transform you. It may foster positive change, elevating you to a new level of your potential.

What exactly does embracing negative emotions mean? It involves allowing yourself to experience negative emotions without trying to control or suppress them. It entails a willingness to experience negative emotions. *Acceptance of negative emotions* is a term that has been used in research to describe this phenomenon; in line with the dictionary definition of *accept*—"to treat as welcome"—accepting negative emotions involves welcoming them in—embracing them—rather than pushing them away. It is worth noting that allowing negative emotions to surface is different from dwelling on them. Dwelling on negative emotions, or thinking about them repetitively, is rumination, and rumination is not beneficial. It is associated with negative psychological outcomes and inhibits action required to effect positive change. Whereas rumination results in negative emotions staying inside—getting stuck—accepting negative emotions allows us to metabolize them. To digest them.

Before exploring the science, consider what a centuries-old spiritual, the novelist John Steinbeck, and a television doctor, in addition to the life of Batman, suggest about the value of accepting negative emotions.

A Spiritual: "Wade in the Water"

Consider some lyrics from a centuries-old spiritual: "Wade in the water, children; God's gonna trouble the water." The lyrics allude to a pool of water in Jerusalem that people would gather around in Biblical times, the Pool of Bethesda. According to the Bible, when an angel touched the water, the touch created ripples, and people who jumped into the water when it was turbulent were healed of any illness or disability: "For an angel went down at a certain season into the pool, and troubled the water: whosoever then first after the troubling of the water stepped in was made whole of whatsoever disease he had." Dr. Cornel West, author, philosopher, and professor emeritus in the Center for African American Studies at Princeton University, distilled the meaning of "wade in the water" like this: "You've got to be in trouble to be transformed. If you do not have the courage to be where the crisis is, where the catastrophe is, you will never be changed." The idea here is similar to that in the Batman story: allowing oneself to experience the negative can be transformative. Being willing to wade into uncomfortable emotions fosters positive change. This idea is at the heart of the novelist John Steinbeck's philosophy on life—a philosophy he called "is thinking."

John Steinbeck: "Is Thinking"

John Steinbeck wrote that this kind of thinking "concerns itself primarily not with what should be, or could be, or might be, but rather with what actually 'is.'" This philosophy encourages an acceptance of things as they are without judgment. The working title of his novel *Of Mice and Men*, "Something That Happened," reflects his approach of taking things as they are. Steinbeck believed that "is thinking" fosters understanding and, counterintuitively, change. He juxtaposed "is thinking," which he also called "non-teleological thinking," with "teleological thinking" and argued that whereas the former is based on *what is*, the latter is based on what *could be* or *should be*. He believed that seeing life as it is actually provides a foundation for change whereas seeing things only as they could be or should be impedes change: "In their sometimes intolerant refusal to face facts as they are, teleological notions may substitute a fierce but ineffectual attempt to change conditions which are assumed to be undesirable, in place of the understanding-acceptance which would pave the way for a more sensible attempt at any change." In other words, denying *what is* by choosing only to see what you wish were true ironically thwarts change. In contrast, accepting the reality of how things are —*what is*—provides a foundation for change.

Applying Steinbeck's philosophy to a failure scenario, the best way to foster positive change after failure would be to start by accepting painful emotions. Why? Consider *what is* after failure. In a word: pain. As the science and stories indicated, experiencing pain after failure is universal. It occurs for people with high self-esteem and low self-esteem. It occurs for people who say they don't care what others think of them. It can be observed in the way we report on our own emotional experiences and can be seen in the physiological processes of the body—in the heart, in the brain, and in the hormones.

There is no easy way to transition from a literary giant to a modern-day television show, but a character on *Grey's Anatomy* offers relevant commentary about how we heal from the pain of failure.

Grey's Anatomy: "Expose the Unhealthy"

Grey's Anatomy is a show about the personal and professional lives of a group of surgeons and surgical residents at the fictional Seattle Grace Hospital. The show typically begins and ends with the main character, Dr. Meredith Grey, delivering a voice-over narration. Almost as if she is talking from a journal, Meredith offers her perspective on issues that characters are grappling with at the time. Usually what she says isn't just about being a surgeon, it's about being a human, as is true in the following excerpt. In this narration, she reflects on the counter-intuitive process of healing.

 In surgery, the healing process begins with a cut, an incision, the tearing of flesh. We have to damage the healthy flesh in order to expose the unhealthy. It feels cruel and against common sense, but it works. You risk exposure for the sake of healing.

This television character suggests that in order to be trans-formed in the face of something bad, you first have to expose the problem. Although it hurts, it is necessary for real healing. What does her idea suggest about responding to failure? Expose the pain. The first step in transforming after failure is to expose the pain. Accepting negative emotions is more painful in the short term than ignoring them, but in the long term, it may be essential for growth.

Near mile eight of a half marathon that I ran in Austin a few years ago, I saw a runner in front of me whose T-shirt grabbed my attention.

I had never heard the phrase "embrace the suck," but I felt immediately that it captured perfectly, if not delicately, what accepting negative emotions means. Negative emotions are the suck, and accepting them is embracing them. Later, I learned that "embrace the suck" is a military term. It has been translated into everyday language like this: "The situation is bad but deal with it." In other words, embracing negative aspects of a hard situation leads to better results rather than resisting or denying them. Research provides empirical evidence for what the life of Batman, a centuries-old spiritual, John Steinbeck, and Meredith Grey have suggested. Accepting negative emotions cultivates positive psychological change, or growth.

The Science: Benefits of Embracing the Suck

Much of the research on accepting negative emotions comes from the area of clinical psychology, where studies have examined how accepting the negative fosters positive psychological change in therapy situations. One study from research on couples' therapy pitted two styles of therapy against each other to see which led to better results for distressed couples. One style, called integrative behavioral couple therapy (IBCT), encourages accepting a romantic partner's challenging aspects with little emphasis on change. The other style, called traditional behavioral couple therapy (TBCT), is a more traditional approach that focuses only on change. The study found that both husbands and wives participating in IBCT showed greater increases in marital satisfaction than couples participating in TBCT. The therapy style that emphasized acceptance did a better job of fostering change than the style that emphasized making change. The researchers, in reflecting on what could explain the results, wrote: "Paradoxically, acceptance interventions are also predicted to produce change in addition to acceptance, often more efficiently than the direct change-inducing strategies that constitute TBCT, because at times the pressure to change may be the very factor that prevents it from occurring." In addition, two established therapies for treating people with post-traumatic stress disorder (PTSD), prolonged exposure therapy and cognitive processing therapy, involve exposing individuals to their anxiety through a guided process of revisiting the traumatic experience. In other words, psychological improvement happens by allowing anxiety to surface rather than batting it away. More generally, acceptance-based strategies have been associated with positive change in a range of psychological conditions, including depression, social phobia, and work stress. Research on mindfulness—a highly related idea—offers further support that accepting the negative fosters positive change. Mindfulness involves a "cultivation of an attitude of 'acceptance' and 'allowing' toward difficult and unpleasant experiences," and it has led to improved psychological well-being in several therapies and studies.

Research outside of the therapy setting also shows that openly expressing emotions about negative experiences leads to positive change. James Pennebaker, a psychology professor at the University of Texas, has demonstrated in many studies over the course of decades that writing in an open, emotional way about a traumatic experience increases health and well-being. Similarly, Annette Stanton, a psychology professor at UCLA, has found that when patients coping with breast cancer engaged in emotional disclosure, their distress decreased and vigor increased.

Carl Rogers, an influential psychologist in the twentieth century, argued that "unconditional positive regard" is essential for healthy psychological development. When someone listens to you with unconditional positive regard, according to Rogers, that person offers you nonjudgmental, compassionate support or acceptance no matter what you share. You are free to confide your most shameful thoughts, feelings, or actions without being judged. It is worth noting that unconditional positive regard does not entail condoning your actions; it simply means that the person values you unconditionally no matter what you say. Rogers argued that therapists best foster growth in clients by offering this unconditional acceptance and, more generally, that everyone needs unconditional positive regard to reach their full potential. "So I find that when I can accept another person," he said, "which means specifically accepting the feelings and attitudes and beliefs that he has as a real and vital part of him, then I am assisting him to become a person." Rogers contended that when people offer this kind of unconditional acceptance to themselves, even with negative parts, they help themselves grow: "...the curious paradox is that when I accept myself as I am, then I change."

To get a better sense of the benefits of embracing the suck after negative experiences, consider the costs of not embracing the suck.

Costs of Not Embracing the Suck

Consider the story of Kristina Braverman, a character on the television show *Parenthood*, which follows the lives of three generations of the Braverman family who all live near each other in Berkeley, California. *Parenthood*, which is no longer airing, mixes drama and comedy and has an uncanny knack for making you care about the characters. The show reels you in at an emotional level. The characters are both good-hearted and flawed and eminently loveable because of the combination. At one point in the show, Kristina, in her forties, receives a breast cancer diagnosis. To provide some context, she is in a support-ive, vibrant relationship with her husband, Adam. Of all the romantic relationships in the Braverman family, Adam and Kristina's might be my favorite. But the way Adam tries to help Kristina cope with her cancer diagnosis, though well inten-tioned, has a negative effect. In a scene that takes place in a coffee shop, Kristina talks about how she is feeling with another cancer patient she recently met, Gwen, who is further along in the treatment process.

> Kristina: And I, uh, I also feel like I'm kind of scared, you know?
> Gwen: Of course.
> Kristina: I feel like I can talk to you. I don't even know you, it's like, you're a perfect stranger, but I can't really, I can't really talk to my husband.

Gwen: Why do you feel like you can't talk to him?
Kristina: Because he is so positive. He is like this relentlessly positive person who can fix everything and make everything better.
Gwen: That's, that is a good man. He wants to protect you from anything bad happening, and here's the thing: the bad thing is already happening.
Kristina: Right.

Adam is trying to help by being "relentlessly" positive, but his approach is hurting. He is making Kristina feel like it is not okay to have negative feelings. Later in the same episode, Kristina and Adam are talking in bed, and Kristina tells Adam how his efforts make her feel.

Kristina: Adam, I know that you're trying to make everything okay for me. You always have our whole lives. And I love you so much for that. But you have to let me be scared. I want to be able to come to you and just say, "Adam, I'm, I'm really scared today," and I just want you to hear, and I don't want you to tell me to think positive or that everything's going to be great. Because right now I'm not sure that it's going to be, and I just want to be able to feel scared. That's just what I need from you right now.
Adam: Okay, I can do that.
Kristina: I love you.
Adam: I love you too so much.

Here's the thing: Kristina is not alone in feeling this way, and Adam is not alone in acting this way. Most of us have been in both positions. We absorb messages that "thinking positively" is the best response to setbacks, and, in turn, we communicate them. But, as Kristina implies, forcing positivity in a painful situation has negative effects. Research actually offers evidence for what Kristina suggests.

Research on how people show support for a loved one who is a victim of trauma, for example, indicates that significant others often respond by forcing cheerfulness and displaying an optimistic façade—for example, saying that the victim "should look on the bright side." Although these efforts are often well intentioned, they have negative effects on the person's psychological health. Forced cheerfulness minimizes the victim's situation and can make the person feel abandoned or rejected. It is associated with more depressive symptoms and greater overall psychological distress. Forcing optimism in the context of a traumatic event is described by victims to be one of the most common and least supportive responses. Similarly, research on cancer victims' perceptions of social support found that one of the most frequent complaints of cancer victims was feeling that social support providers, such as family, physicians, and nurses, minimized their trauma. Ironically, responding to another person's negative situation by telling them to be positive, or to look on the bright side, can have a negative effect on physical and psychological health. The same is true for relating to ourselves in the midst of a painful situation.

Why does pushing positivity in a painful situation have a negative effect? The answer undoubtedly is multidimensional, but here is one dimension: it disconnects us from truth. And truth telling is needed for growth. Forcing positivity ignores the truth of what we feel if we are the person in the painful situation. Accepting negative emotions involves offering air time to what we actually feel, allowing truth to surface. Short-circuiting the pain may protect us in the short term, but in the long term, it short-circuits growth.

A yoga teacher in a class I once took illustrated a similar

phenomenon by using a road-trip analogy. In speaking about how to make a positive change in your life, she said something like: "If you are going on a road trip to California, and you act like you are in Florida when you actually are in Texas, it's going to be hard to reach your destination. You have to acknowledge where you actually are starting to reach your destination." To get where you want to go, you have to be honest about where you are. This sounds obvious when you are talking about a road trip, but in practice with life challenges, it can be hard. After failure, it is often hard to tell the truth about our starting point. It involves telling truths that are difficult to acknowledge even to ourselves, like "I screwed up," "I am embarrassed," "I am doubting myself," or "I feel badly." Telling the truth after failing entails acknowledging a reality that we might not want to admit or at least would like to twist a bit to be more appealing or acceptable. But just like going on a road trip to California and pretending you are starting in Florida when you are actually in Texas will prevent you from getting to your destination, not being honest about where you are after failure impedes you from getting to where you want to go. Exposing the truth of what we feel after failure can transform us. It may mean experiencing more pain in the short term, but in the long term, it means reaping more of failure's rewards. This idea is reflected in the motto of FailCon, the conference on failure: "Embrace your mistakes. Build your success." Counterintuitively, embracing *what is* provides a foundation for change, in getting to *what could be*.

But there's a catch: embracing the suck is difficult to do. What exactly are the hurdles that make it challenging?

Barriers to Embracing the Suck

Pain is one hurdle. Embracing the suck is painful, which makes it hard to do.

Facing hard truths is another hurdle. Acknowledging that we feel badly to others and even to ourselves is difficult. It's particularly difficult because of a third obstacle: pressure to be positive.

Psychologists have observed that there is societal pressure to be positive most of the time, especially in Western culture. Relatedly, we feel pressured to respond with positivity to negative events. The pressure to be positive makes it hard to allow oneself to experience the negative. It can make us feel that allowing ourselves to experience negative emotions is not advisable or acceptable. As a result, we tend to resist negative emotions as soon as they appear. Psychologist Tal Ben-Shahar, an author and lecturer, has written and spoken insightfully about this topic. Ben-Shahar taught a course on positive psychology, the science of happiness and well-being, at Harvard University for several years. His course had the largest enrollment of any course at Harvard—more than one thousand students were in the class. In his book *Happier: Learn the Secrets to Daily Joy and Lasting Fulfillment*, Ben-Shahar articulates how pressure to be positive makes it hard for people to allow negative feelings to surface. He argues that giving yourself permission to experience negative emotions—what he calls "permission to be human"—cultivates happiness.

Relatedly, a fourth obstacle to embracing the suck is conventional wisdom. If the idea that "failure sucks" is radical in some ways, the idea of embracing the suck is even more radical; it is counterintuitive and goes against conventional wisdom. Conventional wisdom about how to respond well to failure suggests that responding well means not being affected emotionally. Praise for people who have responded "well" to a setback often begins: "Rather than getting upset, he or she did

_____." The underlying idea is that experiencing negative emotions after failure is not desirable. This makes it difficult to allow negative emotions to surface. Likewise, conventional wisdom suggests that people who benefit from failure do so *because* they don't experience negative emotions—making the hurdle higher.

These barriers make it hard to accept negative emotions. But new science and old stories challenge this common wisdom. They disabuse us of the idea that experiencing negative emotions after failure and growing from failure are mutually exclusive. They actually suggest the opposite: that accepting negative emotions fosters growth. The individuals I interviewed said that they experienced pain after failure *and* they grew. It is possible that allowing oneself to experience negative emotions might reflect a natural dip that people who will ultimately grow after failure must experience. In the short term, allowing negative emotions to surface after failure may be more painful, but in the long term, it is vital for growth. Acknowledging our true starting point after failure is a necessary first step for change; what we *do* after failure matters too.

* * *

The question of what to *do* after failure usually comes down to this: persist or quit? In other words, keep going or give up? Conventional wisdom is clear on this front: always persist, never quit. And research has shown that persistence in the face of negative experiences, like failure, is associated with resilience. But is it associated with growth?

10

"DOES THIS PATH HAVE A HEART?"

Harvey Merrick is the main character in Willa Cather's short story "The Sculptor's Funeral," though the story begins after his death. He grew up in a tiny town in western Kansas but lived his adult life in Boston, where he became a world-renowned sculptor. He was known there as a genius: "Surely, if ever a man had the magic word in his finger tips, it was Merrick. Whatever he touched, he revealed its holiest secret." Right before he died, after his lungs had shut down to the extent that he knew he wouldn't survive, he asked one of his students to return his body to his home in Kansas. The arrival of Merrick's body in his hometown sparks conversation about him among local residents, and the reminiscences, largely negative, are the pith of the short story. The theme of their talk is that Harvey Merrick was a fool and an embarrassment to his family because he was not good at farming, which was his family's business and that of many others in the rural Kansas town. One man recalled how Merrick was absentminded and would let cows get loose when he was bringing them back from pasture, once killing a cow that way: "Harve, he was watchin' the sun set acrost the marshes when the anamile [sic] got way." Another person commenting on Merrick's ineptitude said: "Harve never was much account for anything practical, and he shore was never fond of work." So Harvey Merrick, a world-renowned artist as a man, was a bad farmer as a boy. Consider for a moment if he had responded to failing in his farming duties by persisting. What if he had ignored his desire to become an artist and had stayed on the family farm to improve his farming skills, refusing to give up? He would have neglected what mattered most to him, probably would have been unhappy for it, and definitely would have robbed the world of his genius.

The story suggests that persistence may not always be the best strategy. Recently, research has punctured the conventional assumption that persistence is always optimal and indicates that it actually can be detrimental. In one study, psychology professors Gregory Miller and Carsten Wrosch found that people who had more difficulty disengaging from unattainable goals (i.e., quitting) showed greater concentration of the inflammatory molecule C-reactive protein (CRP), a marker of inflammation in the body. Inflammation is thought to underlie many diseases, including heart disease, cancer, stroke, diabetes, Alzheimer's, and depression. Other studies have shown that individuals who disengage from unattainable goals—who quit—have better well-being compared to people who have trouble disengaging from unattainable goals. Sometimes people persist with a strategy that has failed many times just to convince themselves or others that their resources have not been spent in vain; they persist with a failed strategy even when viable, possibly more fruitful, alternatives exist. So persistence is not always the optimal strategy. Sometimes quitting is best. And sometimes persistence is actually harmful and results in deleterious effects on health and well-being. Furthermore, recent research indicates that focusing on just these two responses—persistence versus quitting—is too narrow a focus. Missing in this dichotomy is a vital question: Do I care? Or said another way: How much do I care?

Some researchers have explored another behavioral response altogether: engaging with new, more meaningful goals. *Goal reengagement* is a term that has been used in scientific literature to describe pursuing new, meaningful goals. *New* may entail a dramatic change in goals—for example, switching fields from biology to acting, or art to finance—but also could mean pursuing a new angle in the same field. Steve Jobs described responding to getting fired from Apple by pursuing new goals that excited him more deeply, but they were still in the same field of business and technology. *Meaningful* connotes goals that are intrinsically exciting, aligned with your core self. The opposite of going after a meaningful goal would be going after a goal based on extrinsic motivators—like status, wealth, or trying to impress or please others. Emerging research suggests that in the context of negative experiences, like failure, engaging with new goals that are more intrinsically meaningful may foster positive psychological change. Importantly, this is true irrespective of whether people quit or persist with the old goals. Both persisting and quitting are associated with improved outcomes; sometimes one is better and sometimes the other, but goal reengagement is consistently associated with improved outcomes. Research shows that when people confront unattainable goals, reengaging with new, intrinsically meaningful goals is consistently a strong predictor of greater well-being. Relatedly, research on responding well to crises in early adulthood demonstrates the benefit of exploring new possibilities and then rebuilding one's life with more intrinsically satisfying commitments. Research on goal reengagement challenges accepted notions of how to respond well to negative events, and at the same time, it coheres with well-established research in related areas of psychology. Previous research indicates, for example, that when people's goals are in step with their deeper needs and values, psychological well-being is enhanced; some of the research also demonstrates that engaging with new, meaningful goals gives purpose to life and that a sense of purpose fosters long-term personal development.

What research on goal reengagement suggests is that, irrespective of whether you keep going or give up on old goals after failure, this question is important to consider: What is a new, more intrinsically meaningful goal I can pursue? In other words: Will I go after a path that has more heart? The author Carlos Castaneda wrote: "Look at every path closely and deliberately. Try it as many times as you think necessary. Then ask yourself, and yourself alone... Does this path have a heart? If it does, the path is good. If it doesn't, it's of no use." Goal reengagement is about pursuing a path that has more heart—going after what you care about even more deeply. Though failure provides a window of opportunity to shift what you are doing and reveals information about what you really want and a shot of courage to act on that new information, taking a path with more heart is a decision. It doesn't happen automatically. Goal reengagement is that decision. It involves taking the new information coupled with the window of opportunity to act and the nudge to act, and then taking action. If the goal is to extract growth from failure, the most important question after failing may not be "Should I persist or quit?" but rather "How can I take action toward a goal that is more meaningful to me?" The answer to the question of "What can I *do* after failure to foster growth?" may be: pursue goals that excite and energize you even more. Doing what matters most to you is vital for fostering growth after failure.

You may wonder: If going after new, more meaningful goals enhances well-being, why don't we do it without the failure part? An answer is that it is hard to do. An outside impetus helps. We are less likely to do it without an impetus. And, it's always possible to get closer to the center. Going back to the gobstopper analogy, the core is hard to access because of the multiple layers covering it. To reveal the core, we have to shed the layers. And to shed the layers, there often has to be some outside force that dissolves the layers or cracks the gobstopper open. Failure is that outside force. It hacks past the layers and exposes the core. Since failure reveals more of what you really want to do and don't want to do, it sheds light on the question: Do I care about this path? Or put in other ways: Does this path matter to me? Does this path have heart? The simple story of a gobstopper becomes more complex with human beings. Although failure reveals our core, we can choose to ignore what has been revealed. If we do, we stay where we are, foregoing the opportunity to get closer to the core. Or we might choose to run the other way, further from the core, traveling to more of an outside layer, adding stripped layers back on. Failure opens us to messages that we couldn't hear, but we can choose to close down to them. We can choose to harden or turn away. We have to decide to take advantage of the opportunity. That is the goal reengagement part. Goal reengagement is taking that action. It is deciding to take the opportunity and go after goals that are more intrinsically meaningful and satisfying. And taking action toward what matters most to you is vital for fostering growth after failure.

* * *

Although there is a significant and fast-growing body of scientific literature on the benefits of goal reengagement and accepting negative emotions in responding to myriad negative experiences, these two bodies of literature are largely separate. To my knowledge, when I started my dissertation studies, no one had tested these two aspects of responding to negative experiences together. In addition, there is little research in either area that focuses specifically on failure. My research brought together these two bodies of literature to propose a new model for responding adaptively to failure. I proposed and then tested a model of how people could respond to their biggest job-related failures in a way that was associated with greater subsequent flourishing. The model consisted of two parts: acceptance of negative emotions and goal reengagement. My hypothesis was that responding to failure by accepting one's negative emotions and reengaging with new, intrinsically meaningful goals would be associated with greater subsequent flourishing.

Through these studies, I hoped to build on previous research on responding well to failure in a few ways. The first, as I've established, was by shifting the outcome of interest from resilience to growth. The second was focusing on real-world failures. Most previous research on responding to failure consists of controlled experiments in a laboratory setting. This is a major strength in certain ways because experiments allow you to infer causality. But it can be a limitation because it is hard to generalize findings of tightly controlled experiments to real-world situations. Failure on an anagram task in a labora-tory, for example, is quite different from getting fired or losing a business. As such, the best way to respond to one situation may not be the best way to respond to the other. Third, I wanted to account for the role of time in people's process of responding to failure. I felt that doing so also would make findings more applicable to real-life situations. In most previous research, participants engaged in a task immediately after failing, and performance on that task was a measure of the participant's response. This approach doesn't take into account the possibility that growth after failure may be evident only after some time and that ultimately growing from failure may actually involve a dip in performance and mood in the immediate aftermath.

11

TENDER AND TOUGH

When I was planning these studies in the fall of 2007, I decided to choose a domain of real-world failures—either professional or personal. Somewhat arbitrarily, I chose job-related failures. I didn't know how painfully relevant the topic was about to become in 2008, when the economy crashed.

I conducted two studies using different methods and different participant samples to investigate one question: How can people respond to their biggest job-related failures in a way that relates to greater subsequent flourishing? *Flourishing* is an umbrella term I used to describe the cluster of specific outcomes I measured across both studies. The first study consisted of interviews about people's biggest job-related failures. The second, an online study, further tested the proposed model by using questionnaires to assess each participant's response to the biggest job-related failure ever experienced and current level of flourishing. Because I suspected growth after a major failure would take time, I had one criterion for people as they chose their failure: it had to have occurred more than a year prior. This would allow me to learn about the process of responding to failure over a stretch of time. Consider the interview study first—what we (my research team and I) did and what we found.

Fifty people from the Austin area, representing a wide age range—thirty-two to ninety years—participated. Participants' jobs at the time of their biggest failures also varied greatly: entrepreneurs and business owners, manual laborers, educators, accountants, and government workers; one was a member of the armed forces. The failures they discussed included getting fired, getting demoted, poor job performance, being passed up for a promotion, having personal problems that caused trouble at work, a failed project or business deal, and problems with interpersonal relationships, such as difficulty getting along with coworkers or supervisors. For the interview, participants came to the University of Texas laboratory that I was a member of as a graduate student, and their interviews consisted of the same set of questions. Following an introductory statement, the interviewer, either myself or a research assistant, asked the participants to identify the biggest job-related failure they had ever experienced. Next, the participants were asked to describe their failure experiences in detail. Then the participants were asked about the trajectory of their responses to failure, starting with how they "reacted right after the failure" and ending with how they "feel about it now." Transcriptions of the interviews were coded to assess participants' responses to failure, on the dimensions of accepting negative emotions and goal reengagement, as well as current level of happiness. Happiness was the specific outcome for this study and was defined as the level of meaning, fulfillment, and satisfaction in a person's life. Each variable was rated on a scale from 1 to 7, where 1 was "not true at all" and 7 was "extremely true," indicating to what extent that variable was reflected in the writing. We used statistical analyses to determine what kind of response was associated with greater happiness.

We found that at a cognitive/emotional level, responding to failure by accepting negative emotions was associated with greater subsequent happiness. The following quotations from participant interviews illustrate how accepting negative emotions after failure was tied to happiness later on.

(Age 52) I didn't really react with anger I guess it was more... disappointment, but yes I definitely felt it and I went through a period of time where I think you question yourself and question, um, whether, you know, why you weren't good enough and really kind of feeling not good enough and so I did have to work through that.... I do not know that there was a point [when I felt better], I think it was more gradual turning. I just don't turn on a dime... I do the big circle [*laughing*] and so it was working around it and accepting it.... I think that in reflecting on disappointments you really do learn much more from going through the disappointments than just from the successes... life is really a series of disappointments and successes.... So it's just recognizing that all those things are chances for you as an individual to reflect on what is truly important in your life.

(Age 64) I was let go and it was very hurtful.... I was more frightened than anything.... I'm an eternal optimist; I believe for every door that is closed another one opens and that things happen for a reason. It was real hard when I was scared to death because it didn't seem that that would ever be true. So, I'm not saying I'm happy I lost my job at that time, but it has been a great benefit, and I've had a lot of life experiences that I would have never had.... It made me a better person or made me realize that maybe I was better than I thought I was. I certainly realized that I can conquer and be forgiving, and caring, and grateful.

At a behavioral level, responding to failure by engaging with goals that are new and intrinsically meaningful was associated with greater subsequent happiness. Two other quotations from participant interviews reflect how engaging with new, intrinsically meaningful goals after failure was related to subsequent happiness.

(Age 37) I did look for new purposes.... Experiment with different things and look for something that you like.... Do not stop. If you failed, do not stop. Look for other purposes and other alternatives.... Look for something you like.... I became stronger. So, I said, if you do not value me, I am valuable to many people. I have my own value.

(Age 57) It outlined for me that that wasn't the kind of work that I wanted to be doing with my life.... I would much rather be designing things than running an organization... what I do now is much more my pride.... It's much more of what I wanted as a kid.... You know, it took a long time before I realized, but... I feel very much happier with what I'm doing now. It satisfies the urge to design, create, modify, build... it's a need that fulfills me. I wish I had done it a long time ago.... I'm a whole lot happier than I had been...

so for me it [the failure] was an affirmation of things that I clarified in my heart.

The second study built on the first by using a different method and different participant sample to test the proposed model of adaptive response to failure further.

There were 101 participants in this online study, recruited from thirty cities in the United States, and ranging in age from eighteen to seventy-three years. Study 2 used online questionnaires to investigate how people can respond to the biggest job-related failure in their lives in a way that relates to greater happiness and fewer depressive symptoms. The types of jobs they held at the time of their biggest failures included work in sales, government organizations, childcare, exotic entertainers, janitorial staff, managers of companies or organizations, and waitresses. The types of failures participants described included being fired, conflicts with coworkers, quitting a job, serious emotional issues or health problems, and being denied a job, an advancement, or another opportunity.

Participants first were asked to identify the biggest job-related failure they had ever experienced, and then they completed questionnaires relating to their response to the failure. Those questionnaires measured acceptance of negative emotions and goal reengagement. Then, participants completed questionnaires assessing happiness and depressive symptoms at the present time.

We found that responding to failure with greater acceptance of negative emotions and greater goal reengagement was associated with greater subsequent happiness and fewer depressive symptoms. In other words, the same pattern of results emerged across these two studies with different participant samples and different methods, providing converging evidence for the proposed model of adaptive response to failure.

Before expanding on the findings, it is important to note limitations of the studies. Neither study is an experiment, so findings cannot address causality. That is to say, we can't conclude from these findings that responding to failure by accepting negative emotions and reengaging with new, intrinsically meaningful goals caused greater subsequent flourishing. We only can say that the response was associated with greater subsequent flourishing. In addition, the studies were based on retrospective accounts of people's responses to failure, which can be influenced by recall. Future work is needed to address these limitations and understand the topic more deeply.

Overall, our findings highlight the value of accepting negative emotions and engaging with new, intrinsically meaningful goals when confronted by failure. Taken together, the two studies involving individuals from diverse stages of adulthood (overall age range was eighteen to ninety years) suggest that accepting negative emotions and reengaging in new, intrinsically meaningful goals is an adaptive response across the lifespan. Furthermore, our findings on the value of accepting negative emotions suggest that experiencing negative emotions immediately after failure may reflect a natural dip that people who will ultimately grow after failure, not just hold their own, must experience.

Also of note: the two aspects of responding to failure—acceptance of negative emotions and goal reengagement—were not correlated in either study. People who accepted negative emotions were not more likely to engage with new, intrinsically meaningful goals, and conversely, people who were high in goal reengagement were not more likely to accept negative emotions more. Why is this finding noteworthy? It suggests that these two aspects of responding to failure do not commonly coexist in us. It is very possible that we have a strength in one of these areas but likely that we don't have strengths in both.

More broadly, knowing our proclivities along the two dimensions of response—allowing and action—can help us navigate our way forward better. This is significant because cultivating one's natural strength while trying to strengthen the complementary aspect may help us respond more effectively to failure.

Personally, I have a clear weakness in one area that would behoove me to develop and a natural strength in the other. Consider this story about a childhood swim meet—my tendencies along these two dimensions soon will become painfully clear. When my two sisters and I were younger, we participated in swim team in the summers. Meets were usually on Saturday evenings at our neighborhood pool or the pool of one of the rival teams. The meets were fun, and we got to eat powdered Jell-O to refuel between races, which made them even more exciting. My sisters and I also were pretty serious about competing and wanted to do well. During one particular meet, probably the summer between second and third grade for me, I was lined up on the edge of the pool with five or so other swimmers for a 25-meter freestyle race. The announcer at these meets started races in the familiar way: "Swimmers, take your mark. Get set. Go." When she said "go," she would fire the starting gun in the air. If there was a false start, she would fire the gun twice to signal to the swimmers to stop. The person who false-started would be given a warning, and the race would start again. For this race, I was in one of the middle lanes, maybe three lanes in from the announcer's chair, which was on my left side. With our toes at the edge of the cement, fingers gripping the side, the announcer made the call: "Swimmers, take your mark. Get set. Go!" and the gun fired. Then the gun fired again, unbeknownst to me. I don't know if I was focusing so intently on swimming hard that I didn't hear the gun fire a second time, or if I heard it but wasn't 100 percent sure that there was a false start and wasn't going to risk stopping. Either way, I kept swimming. Apparently, people were shouting at me to stop, but I didn't register that either. I kept going. This is where the story gets embarrassing. Race officials lowered the line of racing flags that hang several feet above the pool to get me to stop. I swam into the line of racing flags, picked it up with one hand, keeping my head down, put it behind my head, and kept swimming. Finally, a lifeguard jumped in and plucked me out of the water. I am kind of surprised that I didn't try to bat him away and keep on swimming, wondering how many obstacles a girl has to put up with in one race.

So, I tend to be an effort person. Putting forth effort—trying, taking action—generally comes naturally to me, but I struggle with allowing things to happen. It is hard for me to accept realities I don't like and to accept that exerting more effort sometimes is not productive. Knowing that these two aspects of responding to failure—broadly, acceptance and action—typically are not related and knowing my proclivities can help me respond more effectively to failures.

These two studies are a small part of a large, growing body of research suggesting that accepting the negative and taking action toward the positive in response to painful events may foster positive change. Cutting-edge research investigating how to grow in the face of a range of other negative experiences, including marital problems, psychological disorders, trauma, and disease, provides converging evidence for the growth-promoting effect of this two-part response.

* * *

Research on posttraumatic growth—growth after trauma—indicates that being open to experiencing trauma-related cues and emotions while taking action toward valued life goals is associated with growth. Two major, empirically supported therapies center on the combination of accepting the negative while taking positive action. Acceptance and commitment therapy (ACT), which has been effective in treating people with depression and anxiety, encourages clients to be willing to experience negative emotions while also taking positive action toward valued life goals. Dialectical behavior therapy (DBT), which has been effective in treating people with borderline personality disorder, teaches clients to accept their feelings while working to make positive changes to improve their lives. In a writing experiment, colleagues and I tested a similar strategy in a non-therapy situation. This strategy used the context of coping with the biggest problem in one's life and found similar results. Participants who responded to the biggest problem in their lives by accepting the negative and then seeking out the positive increased their emotional well-being more than participants who used other strategies, like only seeking out the positive. In a subsequent study, researchers and I analyzed the language participants used in the experiment's writings because research has shown that linguistic analysis can be like an x-ray illuminating people's cognitive processes. Our findings revealed that over the course of writing about their problem, participants who used the strategy of accepting the negative and then seeking out the positive increased more in their use of words that researchers have established as associated with insights (e.g., *think, know, consider*). This increase in insight words demonstrated increased insight by the participants. The findings also revealed that using this strategy led people at first to look inward, engage with the past, ventilate negative emotions, and then, over the course of writing, to shift their attention outward—psychologically distancing themselves from the problem and focusing more on social connections—and engage less with the past and more with the future. Together, these two seemingly conflicting ideas—accepting negative emotions and attempting to seek out the positive—create an engine of change.

Essentially this same theme came up in the lecture series that then mayor Booker gave at Princeton University, The Unfinished Journey of America's Spirit. Mayor Booker spoke about how we as a country can progress in the context of the pain of our past. You may remember that the titles of the three lectures in order were "The Past: A Testimony to the Impossible," "The Present: Through Cynicism, Negativity, and Self-Doubt," and "The Future: Humble Hopes and Insane Idealism." Mayor Booker said, "What is so urgently necessary: for people to see the world unapologetically as it is, but still within that, still within that, have a vision for what we must be, what we can be, what we should be." His vision for how the nation can respond to past painful events in a way that fosters progress maps onto how we as individuals can confront painful events in a way that fosters progress, or growth: accepting *what is*, including the negative, while taking positive action toward what could be. Mayor Booker underscored his point by drawing on a quotation about how optimists, pessimists, and idealists approach the world: "'An optimist is a person who sees only the lights in the picture, whereas a pessimist sees only the shadows. An idealist, however, is the one who sees the light and the shadows, but in addition sees something else: the possibility of changing the picture, of making the lights prevail over the shadows.' That's what we need. That's the idealism that I believe is inherent in America." His comments capture the essence of what I am saying here. It is in a sense a distilled answer to the question of how to turn the dust of our shoes to gems. To make progress in the context of painful events, to grow, to be transformed, requires a counterintuitive, paradoxical combination: accepting the negative—allowing it to surface, acknowledging it, exposing it—while taking action toward the positive, toward what is best, what is highest, and what matters most. If we want to grow from failure, we may need to allow ourselves permission to feel the pain that is inherent in failure while also nudging ourselves to take positive action.

Bear with me for a minute because what I am going to say next will sound strange at first. There was a cleaning spray in a friend's house where I stayed while I wrote this book, and I think the name of the spray speaks to the dialectic of acceptance and action: Tough & Tender. Here is a picture of the Tough & Tender on my friend's kitchen floor.

For the purpose of this analogy, the reverse is most apt: Tender & Tough. This spray, which saved me from having to explain many tea spots, spaghetti sauce splashes, wine stains, and rust marks, is an environmentally friendly cleaner, and I am guessing that it is called Tough & Tender because it is hard on stains but gentle on the environment. But the name of the spray also speaks to another pairing: allowing and action, or ease and effort. If we respond to failure by allowing negative emotions to surface and then taking positive action, failure can foster growth. Allowing and action are needed.

In a more general way, an experience I had whitewater rafting on a family trip when I was younger, maybe in seventh grade, speaks to how vital both allowing and action are. As my family and I rafted down the last stretch of water before stopping for lunch on this daylong whitewater rafting trip, the water was calm, so the guides said we could jump into the river and swim to shore. To help you imagine the surroundings, this particular stretch of water was like an "L." Our rafts were heading down the long part of the "L" toward the elbow. The place where we would stop to eat lunch was near the bend of the "L" where the river turned to the left, and the rapids picked up. After a little consideration, I decided to get out and swim— more like float since the current was carrying us along. I was apprehensive and a little scared because I was aware of the current, but I also was excited. As I floated along with the current and approached the bend, I was feeling pretty cool and brave that I took the guide up on his offer. I remember looking up at some point and seeing my parents on the shore already at the lunch area, up ahead and a bit to the right; it was about time to swim over. When I started to swim in that direction, though, I felt resistance. I couldn't go forward. I tried to swim harder, pulling with more strength and kicking harder. That didn't work. I looked up, and although I was facing my parents and trying to go in their direction, I could feel myself being pulled in the opposite direction, down the river. I remember feeling panicky, and then I went all out and tried as hard as I could to swim toward the shore. Even by giving every ounce of my effort, I made no progress. At that point, I waved to my parents to signal for help. They quickly understood what was going on —not only that I was in a current that would be useless to swim against but also that I was scared—and they ran in my direction. They told me through motioning and shouting to go with the current, put my feet up, and aim for the shore ahead. I am not sure exactly how far away I was from the lunch spot. I remember looking at my parents as I was starting to freak out and thinking that they looked so far away. But I also remember that when the current swept me to the left at the river bend, they were running beside me telling me what to do, so I'm guessing the shore was not the half mile away that it felt. As the current swept me to the left and my parents coached from the shore, I went feet first into the rapids on my back. The rapids seemed big but were probably small. Fairly quickly, I was able to make my way to the bank on the right side of the river. When I got on land, I was rattled but okay. I didn't have any injuries. I don't remember even being scraped up, but the incident scared me. Looking back, I can see that stopping all of my trying sooner in the process would have saved me energy and probably would have gotten me to a solution more quickly. I was working extremely hard to solve a problem but to no avail. My efforts were having no positive impact on the problem. They were actually delaying a solution and tiring me. I say this sweetly to my younger self because I was young and scared, and I know that I handled it the best I knew how at the time. But I was trying too hard. This story speaks to how allowing and action are both needed. I was exerting too much effort, specifically, too much effort in the wrong area as I tried to swim against the current. I needed to relinquish some of that effort and literally go with the flow of the river. I also had to exert some effort though to get to the shore. If I had not exerted any effort, I would have continued to be taken down the river. The combination of allowing what is to occur while exerting effort to work toward what we want to happen is valuable.

Our current understanding about how to respond well to

failure is informed primarily by research on resilience, and research indicates that being positive and persisting are associated with resilience. Conventional wisdom—"be positive and persist"—squares with research on resilience. But shifting our perspective upward to growth changes the story. It brings a new way of responding and a new way of understanding what it means to respond well to failure.

Science and stories suggest that in the face of negative events, like failure, an answer to the question of how to respond in a way that fosters growth looks like this: (1) accept negative emotions and (2) take positive action—toward more intrinsically meaningful goals. In other words, accept "what is" while taking action toward "what could be." Embrace the suck and go for yourself. These two do not coexist frequently. But the two together—a rich, rare combination—foster growth.

Imagine that we now see more of the whole truth of failure: failure's powerful light side in addition to its dark. We understand that failure can foster greater success and see myriad pathways that can take us from one to the other. We also now see a single pathway quite clearly, one that often gets overlooked but is exceptionally powerful, especially in today's world. And we have a roadmap for how to respond to failure in a way that allows us to extract its growth benefits. Why does all that really matter? What impact do these insights have on our lives? My answer: seeing a fuller view of failure changes the way we think about it. And shifting the way we think about failure—changing our relationship with it—could change the way we lead our lives. But how exactly?

PART IV

HIDDEN MAGIC

12

THE WAY WE THINK ABOUT SUCCESS

J ust like we tend to view failure as strictly bad, we tend to have a one-sided view of success too. Here I am talking about straight-up, standard, short-term success: achieving a favorable outcome in what you attempted to do. You landed the job, got the promotion, won a game, won an election, pulled off a delicious meal, got into the school of your choice, made partner, got a new client, got a raise. That kind of success. We see it as completely good. And this way of thinking makes sense. Success has a shimmering light side that attracts our attention. Not that it would take research to convince you of success's upside, but research does show that success has meaningful benefits. It increases our sense of confidence and competence, and it strengthens our belief in our ability to reach goals —what psychologists call self-efficacy. After Coach K told me that his first championship was among his most gratifying successes, I followed up later in the interview to ask if he would say more about what made it so special for him. His answer was about confidence. He said that the first championship makes you believe "that you could do it."

199

I mean you talk about, I wonder what it would be like and whatever, but there was no wonderment —you did it. And you accomplished—we did that. I was able to coach a team that did this. And so there's a certain confidence level that's built.

Boosting confidence is among success's many strengths, but thinking of success as purely good hides part of its truth. Success's obvious beauty monopolizes our attention and governs the way we think about it. Success's sparkly light side blinds us to its dark. And success has a dark side. Research reveals it.

The Whole Truth of Success

Successes do not promote much reflection or reevaluation, like failures do. Successes encourage stability and provide momentum to stay on course. If you are achieving success in your job, for instance, you might feel inclined to stay, even if it does not fulfill you. If you started a certain career when you were younger and had success, odds are you kept going even if it didn't excite you. Successes tend to impede change and growth.

Successes make us more risk averse and foster complacency. The comedian Conan O'Brien used an analogy of a white tuxedo to convey how success makes us less likely to take risks: "Success is a lot like a bright white tuxedo. You feel terrific when you get it, but then you're desperately afraid of getting it dirty, of spoiling it in any way." When I interviewed James McPherson about Abraham Lincoln, he told a story that spoke to this aspect of success's dark side. The story was about two generals in chief of the Union army during the Civil War: General George McClellan, who led from November 1861 until he was fired in March 1862, and General Ulysses S. Grant, who led from late 1863 until the end of the Civil War in April 1865.

 I'm often asked about General McClellan and General Grant. Why McClellan, who seemed to have it all, turned out to be such a failure and Grant, who had been a failure for many years in the 1850s in civilian life and was a very obscure colonel and then brigadier general in the early months of the war, turned out to be the best Union commander. I have answered that by saying... that McClellan was born with a silver spoon in his mouth to a wealthy, prominent family in Philadelphia, educated at the best schools, admitted to West Point by special permission at the age of sixteen—a year early—graduates at twenty, rises fast in the peacetime army.... When the war comes, he is appointed very early at the age of thirty-four, as first commander of the Army of the Potomac, the principal army in the Union, and then general in chief of all the armies in the United States. So he has never known failure. Yet he turns out to be the most risk-averse commander, always making excuses for inaction. And my pop psychology is that he was afraid of failure because he had never experienced it, and that's why he wouldn't take risks. You can't be a successful commanding general if you are not willing to take risks because risk is inherent in the very process of commanding an army in combat.

...Grant [in contrast] had dealt with failure, so he was not afraid of it because he had already been through it, and he becomes a very risk-taking general, and that is one of the secrets to his success.... in McClellan's case... there is so much evidence that he really is afraid of failure and therefore he is not going to take, as he said himself, he is not going to undertake a particular military operation... unless assured of success. Well, you cannot be assured of success in those circumstances.

I believe that all these downsides of success lead to another shortcoming: success can cloak originality. If we succeed in meeting other people's standards, we tend to stay on course. We keep going in that direction. When we are rewarded by positive feedback, we find a way to keep getting rewarded. If that direction is also where we want to be headed, there is no problem. But if not, success's dark side implies there will be momentum to keep going, little impetus to change course, and difficulty getting in touch with what feeds us. When we are succeeding, it can be particularly easy to ignore whether the path we are on feels genuinely fulfilling. Let's say you start out in law, for example, and you do well, but you realize at some point that it does not fulfill you. Success will propel you to stay the course and will not help you move closer to what drives you.

And there's another potential downside of success.

Redefining Success

Standard dictionary definitions of success can be divided into two categories: short term and long term. The short-term definition is what I just described, achieving a favorable outcome in what you attempted to do. The more long-term definition is this: attainment of wealth, fame, position, or honors.

Taking the long view of our lives reveals fault lines in the traditional definitions of success; it makes clear that these definitions are lacking, misguided, and inadequate. For example, we pursue this conventional kind of success with an implicit understanding that achieving it will feel highly satisfying, yet research shows that often this is not true. Much research on the connection between money and happiness has shown that there is a small, positive relationship between money and happiness but that after one's basic needs are met, there is virtually no relationship between the two. Furthermore, longitudinal studies exploring the connection between income and happiness over time, including my own, have shown that an increase in income, even over a ten-year period, is not associated with any increase in happiness. As it turns out, the notion that getting a big raise in the future will make us happier is misguided.

Conventional definitions of success fall short in other ways too. For example, they do not consider the quality of one's work or impact of one's work on others. They are not democratic in important ways. Take the "wealth" definition of success. According to this definition, large swaths of people are categorically disqualified from success irrespective of the quality or impact of their contributions. Such groups include those who are poor, who are middle income, and whose primary work is unpaid, like a full-time parent, as well as those who are systematically underpaid. A similar situation exists for the "status" definition of success: people whose positions are deemed low status are categorically barred from success. They may add significant value to the lives of other people and feel fulfilled and joyful because of it, but they are not considered successful. Conventional definitions of success are not only misguided, they are inadequate; they fail to tap into the deepest desires we have for our lives, and they fail to reflect our highest ideals. They don't capture what matters most. During my interview with Libby Leffler Hoaglin, she spoke about how conventional definitions of success fall short: "And frankly, awards and things like that and these lists [referring to the honorary lists she has been named to], to me those are not according to my personal definition of success. Success to me is, How did I learn as much as I possibly could and develop myself into just a better person, contributor, manager, peer, colleague, friend? Those are my personal successes to me."

This book puts forth a new, unabashedly idealistic definition of success—one that is marked by changing the world or maximizing the positive impact you have on the world. Steve Jobs articulated a similar idea back in 1994 when he was interviewed by John McClaughlin of the Santa Clara Valley Historical Association. Near the beginning of the interview, Mr. McClaughlin asked Jobs: "If this was going to be viewed forever by young high school kids and college kids, young entrepreneurs who want to go out and do something... what advice would you give them?" And Jobs responded:

 So, the thing I would say is, when you grow up, you tend to get told that the world is the way it is and your life is just to live your life inside the world. Try not to bash into the walls too much. Try to have a nice family life. Have fun. Save a little money.

But life, that's a very limited life. Life can be much broader once you discover one simple fact. And that is—everything around you that you call life was made up by people that were no smarter than you. And you can change it. You can influence it. You can build your own things that other people can use.

And the minute that you understand that you

can poke life and actually something will—you know, if you push in—something will pop out the other side. That you can change it. You can mold it. That's maybe the most important thing—is to shake off this erroneous notion that life is there, and you're just gonna live in it, versus embrace it, change it, improve it, make your mark upon it.

I think that's very important. And however you learn that, once you learn it, you'll want to change life and make it better because it's kind of messed up in a lot of ways. Once you learn that, you'll never be the same again.

There is a flaw in the way we think of success as well as failure. Both views are one-sided: success = good and failure = bad. These prevailing views shape our relationships with success and failure, and more generally, they govern the way we act, leading us to lust after success and revile failure. Pursue the first, avoid the other. And they obscure the whole truth of success and failure. Failure and success both have a light and dark side. And here's the thing: failure shines in the very ways success falls short. Whereas success encourages stability, providing momentum to stay on course, failure knocks us off a path, providing a window of opportunity for change. We benefit from failure and success—in different, complementary ways. This realization implies that the way we tend to lead our lives—with "avoid failure" as top priority—is not optimal.

13

A SIMPLE, REVOLUTIONARY SHIFT IN
THE WAY WE LEAD OUR LIVES

In May 2013, through the courage of an aunt and the kindness of a stranger, a letter I had written to Dr. Maya Angelou asking to interview her for this book arrived in her hands. Dr. Angelou inspired, enlightened, comforted, and delighted so many people with her poetry and books, including me. One afternoon, a couple of weeks after I sent the request, I received a phone call that she had said yes to an interview. I still remember where I was when I got the call—standing in the kitchen of a close friend I was visiting in Chicago. I fell to my knees. I was elated and in a state of semi-disbelief. My excitement escalated further when I was told that Dr. Angelou said she had been thinking about the relationship between failure and success for a long time, would enjoy talking about it, and would be happy to help in any way she could. Soon thereafter, the interview was scheduled for a month or so later at Dr. Angelou's home in Winston-Salem, North Carolina, where we ended up having a wide-ranging conversation over the course of nearly three hours. As it turned out, our conversation was in the last year of Dr. Angelou's life; she passed away in May of 2014.

Dr. Maya Angelou was a poet, memoirist, novelist, teacher, actress, filmmaker, and civil rights activist, among other talents and roles. Her list of published poetry, nonfiction, and fiction consists of more than thirty bestselling titles and spans decades. Her first autobiography, *I Know Why the Caged Bird Sings,* was published in 1969, and her most recent book, *Mom & Me & Mom,* was published in 2013. In 1993, Dr. Angelou read her poem "On the Pulse of the Morning" at the inauguration of President Bill Clinton, who requested that Dr. Angelou write a poem for the occasion. In 1995, she delivered her poem "A Brave and Startling Truth" at the fiftieth anniversary celebration of the United Nations. Dr. Angelou's poetry includes other well-known titles, such as "Phenomenal Woman," "Still I Rise," and "Life Doesn't Frighten Me." Dr. Angelou was the Reynolds Professor of American Studies at Wake Forest University and received numerous awards for her work. In her memoir *Wouldn't Take Nothing for My Journey Now*, she described women in her family stepping away from the expected path to find success on their own terms. They succeeded, in her words, by "cutting a brand-new path." Dr. Angelou clearly cut a brand-new path for herself, as well. She blazed trails with her words, guided by her own instinct, voice, and style.

When I met Dr. Angelou, she was seated at the head of a long dining table in the sunroom of her house. The room, with windows on three sides, looked out over a lush, large backyard where Dr. Angelou liked to entertain; a gazebo was at one end and a statue garden at the other. She greeted me with a vibrant, warm smile, and I was struck immediately by how comfortable and welcome I felt. I was little more than a random stranger to her. I went to her house with a colleague and dear friend of hers from Wake Forest University, the kind stranger I mentioned at the start. He knows two of my aunts from church, but I had just met him outside her home a few minutes before. With my level of excitement about this opportunity, Dr. Angelou could have been merely cordial, and I would have been thrilled. But she not only made me feel comfortable and welcome, she also made me feel valued. Somehow, in her larger-than-life presence, she made me feel bigger rather than smaller. That phenomenon mystified me and struck me as rare and remarkable. I think this ability was due in part to how present she was. At the beginning of the interview, I thought to myself how present she was, and shortly afterward, she said something that supported what I sensed: "I bring everything I own, everything I've been through, everything I've survived here to this table this minute to make myself available to you." I felt her full presence throughout our conversation.

Soon after I sat down, to the right of Dr. Angelou at the dining table where we would do the interview, I asked to use the restroom before we started. In the bathroom, on a small hutch to the left of the toilet was a cup full of writing utensils, the kind that most people would have next to their home phone or on a desk. I thought: This must be the sign of being in the house of a such a remarkable writer—writing utensils in the bathroom; insights could strike at any time. On the same hutch sat a stack of *O, The Oprah Magazine*s. This delighted me for some reason. I wasn't surprised to see the magazine itself; I love *O Magazine* and also knew that Dr. Angelou and Oprah were very close friends, but there was something that felt way too mundane and at the same time surreal about seeing "Maya Angelou" and her street address on a magazine label. I don't know how else the magazine would have gotten to Dr. Angelou, though; hand-delivered by Oprah? That would seem to make sense, or maybe delivered by some official-looking messenger in uniform on a horse. I stared at the label and ran my fingers across it, trying to put my hands on concrete evidence that I was in fact where I thought I was. When I got back to the table, I told Dr. Angelou that I had seen the writing utensils in the bathroom and supposed that it was a sign of being in the home of a truly amazing writer. Right as I said it, I thought, *What* are you saying? Seriously! That is probably a completely inappropriate thought to share! But she didn't miss a beat and responded by saying something like: Oh, yes, and there are notepads in the drawers too.

As we started the interview, I confided that I'd brought two audio-recording devices. I said something like, "Because you are Maya Angelou, you don't know what it's like to interview Maya Angelou, but I have to tell you I am very excited to be here and very nervous that I will somehow botch the recording of our conversation, so please indulge me in allowing me to use two recording devices." She graciously said that was fine and replied by telling me how she used to feel talking to her friend, the acclaimed author James Baldwin. I pressed *record* a little after the start of her story: "And we would sit up sometimes— I'd visit him in his place in France or he'd come here, and we'd sit up drinking scotch and talking into the night and all of a sudden, I'd look and think, *'That's James Baldwin!'*" She started laughing and continued: "For just a minute, I'd be stalled, but then I knew I was right, whatever I was saying, so…"

I asked Dr. Angelou about the moment she knew she wanted to be a writer, and she replied: "Well, I seem to always have written. At Wake Forest in the rare books room—I've given papers to Wake Forest—and there's a tablet which I wrote in when I was nine. And in there, there's some of the worst poetry west of the Rockies." We both laughed and I said: "I have a hard time believing that." And she said, "But it's there," and continued: "I know I loved Paul Laurence Dunbar and I loved Edgar Allan Poe. *I just loved them.* And Dunbar and Poe,

I memorized everything I could read of theirs. And I love Shakespeare. I loved it, and I memorized sixty sonnets or something." I muttered, "Oh my goodness," and she went on:

 I know—amazing, but there was nothing else to do. You know, I didn't have radio.... Radio was only on Sunday.... We didn't listen to music, worldly music. I know that when the gandy dancers who'd work over on the railroads putting down railroad tracks, they would sing, there'd be always a singer, and she [her grandmother, whom she called "Mama"] would let the door stay kind of cracked open. But we never had anything else to do but go to church. And, uh, we couldn't say "hotdog." Mama said that was just a way to get around cursing. We said "by the way," and it was just terrible because Mama said Jesus was the way, the truth, and the light, and we were just cursing in her house, and she wouldn't have it.

So, all of that. I mean, I just, I remember what the poetry meant to me and the *rhythm* of the poetry. So I thought if they wrote it, I'd write it. [*Starts laughing and continues talking.*] It's pretty bad, but anyway. I'm going to go over there one day and look at that tablet.

When she finished talking, I commented: "So it was kind of always in you." And she said: "Yes, it was," and added a bit more: "I loved the human voice. I've never heard a human voice that I didn't like. I've heard what they've said that—some of the intent, but the voice itself, I love to hear people talk. Those years when I didn't speak, I could think of my own body as an ear, and I could just go into a room and absorb the sound."

Dr. Angelou brought up the topic of failure before I asked about it and indicated that she was well acquainted with failure. "The rejections, which came automatically, and threats of failure came automatically, and they come, I guess, just staying alive. But to be black, and female, and six foot tall and all that, and not cute…" I asked about her most challenging setbacks, and she talked about personal disappointments and professional struggles in her adult life and rejection she experienced as a child. She said her most painful personal disappointments as an adult were "usually romantic."

 I married or nearly married a number of men, and I brought everything I knew to the relationship. My fidelity, and not forced fidelity, but really, that was the only person in the world. My appetites—all of them. I love a pretty house. I keep it pretty. And good food and all that. So when a marriage has broken up or a relationship, the disappointment, that I know. I know that. I've been secured because of that statement, "This too shall pass away." If I can just stay alive, keep myself in some order, and get my work done, I won't hurt so bad next week. If I can just—and then I won't question myself so much. I will have questioned, "What did I not do?" or "What did I leave undone?" or "What did I overdo?" When I'm satisfied that I did everything I know to do, then I have to say, "Well, this is life."

In the professional realm, Dr. Angelou spoke about a time when she lived in Europe and was a first dancer, *premier danseur*, with *Porgy and Bess*. She had a singing role, the role of Ruby, Sporting Life's girlfriend, even though she had no training as a singer. Other singers, she said, were extremely well trained: "Among some thirty-five people, there were one hundred degrees in music. There were so few places for black singers trained in European classics to work. The company could afford to get a person who had one degree from Curtis and another from Juilliard just to be in the chorus." After each performance, other singers criticized her: "Every night or two, after we closed, the curtain went down, one or another of the singers would say, 'Maya, I'm sorry to tell you, but you flatted that F, or you sharped that G.' I didn't even know I was singing in the alphabet." More generally, she said she experienced a lot of headwind in her professional life. "Professionally, yes, I've been told, 'You can't,' and 'You won't,' and 'You never will,' and all that." She talked about how she responded to those messages: "I don't even know—I just don't believe any of that. I don't believe that. If I don't know a thing, I study it. I bring all my energy to it. If there are ten books on the subject, I read them and make notes and quibble with the author though the author may be long dead. I would still say, 'I don't believe that. I believe that. I don't believe that.' Then read more and more until I could get a hold of it." She paused briefly and added: "I feel if it was a matter of climbing Everest, I have to admit where I am. I have to admit that I'm now assailed by this COPD, so the altitude would be against me. But then, I wouldn't even attempt it."

Curious about this last comment, I later asked her to elaborate on what she meant about the need "to admit where I am" when facing disappointment. She said it was about telling the truth. "And tell the truth to yourself first," she said. "I know I can't run the ten-yard dash or one-hundred-yard dash. I know that, so I wouldn't attempt it, I don't think. But if I just wanted to see, How far could I run?—ah, that's another matter. But if I can only run two yards, then I'd find out. That's okay. I know that now. But I also know that what is true today may not be true tomorrow. That too shall pass away."

Dr. Angelou also spoke about rejections from her childhood. After experiencing sexual violence as a seven-year-old, she didn't speak for many years. Because of her silence, people at school called her names, like "idiot," "dummy," and "moron." She said that the unconditional love of her brother, Bailey, and her grandmother, who raised her for much of her childhood, were pivotal in helping her handle the rejection and overcoming self-doubt. In talking about her brother, she said, "My family came closest to making genius when they made my brother. Because people called me 'dummy' and all of that because I didn't speak for years, he told me often: 'Don't worry about those people. They're stupid. In fact, you're the smartest person here, except me of course.' I never argued with him because I knew he was right." Before describing how her grandmother helped her deal with painful rejections, she reflected on her grandmother as a person.

 My grandmother, I can't imagine what kind of woman she was. At one time until I was about ten, I thought she was God. She was *so tall*. When she died, she was over six foot. She was about my size, never large, you know, just—but in the teens of the twentieth century, she opened a store in this little village in Arkansas [Stamps]. All the jobbers were white men. How did this woman, the daughter of a former slave, how did she convince these white men that she was reliable enough for them to buy goods in Texarkana, or in Little Rock, or Pine Bluff, and bring it to Stamps, and that they would be repaid? …When she'd braid my hair, she'd say,

"Sister, Mama don't care what these people say about 'you must be an idiot or a moron because you can't talk.' Sister, Mama don't care. Mama know when you and the good Lord get ready, Sister, you're going to be a teacher. You're going to teach all over this world." And, of course, I thought, "This poor, ignorant woman—I'll never speak, let alone teach." But I have taught all over the world now.

So, I had my brother, my grandmother, and my mother. So somehow that was my bulwark, you see. I don't know if anybody survives the outrageous fortune of being bullied or looked down upon or rejected without having *something* given to you, something you may have earned as well, but something that you can fall back on in the sleepless nights.

Dr. Angelou told another story of a time from her childhood when her brother and her grandmother showed her love and then added: "So those kinds of things. They get in the spleen and in the ribcage."

When I asked Dr. Angelou whether she thought there is a connection between failure and success, she immediately said yes. Then she took the conversation to a whole other level. She talked about death and spoke of how confronting her fear of death in her twenties shaped the way she lived her life. Overcoming this fear was not a moment, it was a long process—about a year—set in motion by the passing of her grandmother. And it was a struggle; she called that period a "terrifying, yawning chasm." As she spoke, I started to realize that her comments about death contained a metaphor about failure. I don't know for certain whether she intended the metaphor, though by answering my question about the connection between failure and success by discussing the impact of confronting the fear of death, I imagine she did.

 In my early twenties, I came face-to-face, mind-to-mind to the fact that I was mortal and that I would die. My grandmother had died, and it just worried me because I thought nowhere on Earth, if I had billions of dollars, there's nowhere on Earth I could find her. And that meant that if she could, I will someday. And, it really bothered me for about a year. My mother talked to me about it, my brother, because I would lock the doors in my own house and put a chair under the door. Whenever my mother or my brother came over and they found this out, that I had put broomsticks in the windows.... they asked and asked and finally I said, "I'm afraid to die." [And their response was:] "Well then... there you are. Well, who isn't? Or, so what?" Something like that. And I realized that that's just silly. That will happen.

When I got over that, when I came through that terrifying, yawning chasm, I thought I could probably do anything. I will do that, ready or not. So in that case, I can do anything good.

When she completed her thought, I said: "The word that just came into my mind is *liberated*." She replied: "Absolutely. Free to—" And she added: "Yes, ma'am—if it's a good thing. If it's not hurting anybody. If it's a good thing, I can do anything."

When I asked Dr. Angelou about her most personally mean-ingful success, she didn't point to a particular achievement. She started telling stories. I realized at a certain point that the stories were about the way she approached life, specifically about times that she took risks, times that she dared. She said that "to risk having a failure is exciting" and shortly thereafter continued to reflect on my question: "What is the most satisfying? Every day that I awaken and have some clarity of mind and some control over my body is a success. I am eighty-five years old, and I'm still kicking it, you know, with all the— maybe not all—but with some of the ambition I've had all my life to be as good as I could be at anything and to dare many things." Right after she finished that sentence, I said, "That word is really central in your life, isn't it?" Take a look at what followed.

Dr. Angelou: *Dare*?
Me: Yes.
Dr. Angelou: I suppose so.
Me: Yeah, from an outsider's perspective, you have
dared a lot....
Dr. Angelou: It seems so. I just don't like the feeling of
being thought of as unable to or unequal to or not on par
with anybody. I don't want to think I'm better than
anybody, but I certainly will not think I'm less, under no
circumstances.

Dr. Angelou's approach to life, forged by overcoming her fear of death, was characterized by daring.

Later in the conversation, I asked Dr. Angelou how people can go about "cutting a brand-new path"—the phrase she used in her writing to describe stepping away from the expected path to find success on one's own terms. Her answer again: overcome the fear of death. She said, "I think that each person, whether she or he admits it or not, is afraid to die. And you have to get over *that*. Once you can get over *that*, you're liberated." Looking for a step-by-step manual, I probed, "So how do you do that?" She replied:

 Well, you can't help it. It's like wishing water wasn't wet, but it is. It is. So once you admit, *Well, you know, ready or not, I'm going to do it—* Look at all the people who've already done it. People with talent and people without, and people with good intent and people without, fat people, and short and thin, and pretty and plain, and gay and straight. People have already done it. I think that that's the best... the surest way of being—of liberation. If you can just admit that what will happen, will happen. All you have to do is look at people in your family; they've already done it, who didn't want to. There it is. There's no other assurance that's more assured than that—nothing. You can't say, *Well, I'll finish this tomorrow.* You're not sure about that. *I'll see you next week.* You're not sure about that.... So there's no assurance other than that; you can be sure of that.

Then she added: "And if you can deal with that assurance, then until it comes—you don't have to help it to come by being sour and dure and all that and putting the bad mouth on yourself. That's not smart. I think it's wise to know that you're probably a lot smarter than you admit, because if you were as smart as you admit, you'd take on more things. You'd do more. [*Starts laughing and continues talking.*] So I think you may as well admit, I'm pretty smart. [*Laughter continues.*]" Overcoming the fear of death, she said, frees us to live more courageously and to cut a brand-new path for ourselves. And that, from my vantage point, is exactly how she lived. I am not an expert in the art of learning to deal with the certainty of death. In fact, I would guess that I am worse at this skill than the average person. But I am trying. Hearing how overcoming the fear of death shaped the way Dr. Angelou lived her life—her trail-blazing, awe-inspiring, courageous, full life—is compelling evidence for its value.

The metaphor that emerged as Dr. Angelou spoke is based on the parallel between the fears of death and failure. The two fears seem very similar in nature, though maybe different in magnitude. Confronting the fear of death seems like an advanced version of confronting our fear of failure, having a similar impact but in an even bigger way. Both fears heavily influence how we lead our lives and do so in a similar way. Just as fear of death confines our lives and holds us back, as Dr. Angelou shared, fear of failure does too. Changing the way we think about death—overcoming the fear of death—would free us, inject us with courage, and help us cut a brand-new path for ourselves, as Dr. Angelou described. Changing how we think about failure—and overcoming the fear of failure—also would make us feel freer and more courageous. It would embolden us to take more risks and seek out more challenges because we would be more willing to approach situations in which failure is possible. It would allow us to dare to do what we would do if we weren't afraid, or if we were less afraid, to fail. It would help us carve our own path.

Seeing the whole truth of failure enables us to overcome the fear of failure. It starves the fear, which is fed by the single story we have about failure. And it shifts the way we view failure. When we think of failure as bad and lead lives in which avoiding failure is a top priority, our focus is on getting away from what we don't want rather than going toward what we yearn for most deeply. Seeing the whole truth of failure switches that focus and invites us to live in a new way. Whereas the first approach to life can be characterized by the mantra "avoid failure" (i.e., "don't eff this up"), the second can be characterized by the governing principle: "Let your freak flag fly." Changing our view of failure frees us to pursue what matters most to us.

Cory Booker described how confronting his fear of failure helped him pursue a big dream. At the beginning of our interview, before asking about his biggest failure, I asked if there was a moment when he realized he wanted to serve Newark for his career. He said that there was a pivotal moment; it happened when he was in law school, at a time when he was uncertain about what he wanted to do with his future.

I have this wonderful mother who challenged me to answer the question: If you couldn't fail in life —you were guaranteed success—what would you do? And in a sense, that's what you should do. You know, there are a lot of little vignettes and moments in time when I was struggling trying to figure out what I was going to do in law school that I really couldn't see out of my mind. Those moments where my mom's sort of prodding me really helped give me the courage to say, You know what? I'm going to just do it: my dream would be to go to stay in New Jersey where I grew up but also go to one of the more difficult parts of Newark, New Jersey—the city that I felt most aligned to—and start a nonprofit as a street lawyer.

And that is what Senator Booker did. He worked as a lawyer in Newark, started a nonprofit there, was later elected to the city council, and then became mayor, and now as US senator of New Jersey, he still serves Newark and lives in Newark today. After he spoke about that defining moment, I asked: "So you feel it was like your mom's kind of challenging you, but also her unconditional love?" And he replied: "Yeah, I think fear is the biggest block to success. I think that it's a really corrupting emotion and many of us don't live lives: If I could dream the greatest day possible, what would make this day incredible? And try to figure out how to make that—how to imagine and create your reality. And so, fear of failure is stifling, and that's why I think that many people have their biggest successes early in their careers because they've got nothing to lose, and then they start to play conservative. Or in politics, I think there's reverence breeds conformity. The more people revere you, the more you want to conform to their reverence." He brought up Martin Luther King Jr. and observed: "He was in a wonderful, safe space around the civil rights movement and earned a lot of reverence. Nobel Peace Prize, but then he picked up the antiwar movement and showed a lot of courage because he didn't yield to popularity or convenience, and that's a really wonderful thing." Near the end of our interview, Senator Booker added: "I do know that for me when I'm talking to young people... risk-taking, having the courage to step out, to be different, to take a courageous stand are things that I like to celebrate. Because I think they're values that correlate to great success. And innovation and help for human evolution."

Mayor Iorio also mentioned a recurring theme in many of her speeches and conversations, and it was quite similar to Senator Booker's. "I do encourage all young people and all audiences of any age that it's kind of like the Teddy Roosevelt quote about the man in the arena. The important thing is that you're in the arena. The important thing is that you went back to school. Not that you maybe didn't make an A in every course, but you went back to school. The important thing is that you put your name out to run for office. Most people never do. The vast majority of people never put their name on a ballot. The important thing is that you took a risk and had a child. That's a huge risk in life to say, "I'm going to raise a child in today's world," but you went ahead and did it. The important thing is that you started a business. Maybe it didn't last. Okay, most small businesses fail, most do. Statistically, most fail. That doesn't mean you're a failure. It means you tried something. You ought to be given credit for trying."

When Mark Zuckerberg, CEO and founder of Facebook, was a guest on *The Oprah Winfrey Show* in 2010, a short video was shown about daily life at Facebook headquarters. The hallway walls were covered with posters of encouraging messages, and one caught my eye: FAIL HARDER. (When I visited Facebook headquarters to interview Libby Leffler Hoaglin, I saw many FAIL HARDER posters.) Although the advice to fail harder might seem out of place at one of the most successful companies, it is apparently a key part of Zuckerberg's business philosophy. You may remember from earlier in the book that Zuckerberg told Oprah that he celebrates failures at Facebook. To explain why, he said: "We want people to keep on taking risks and trying to do crazy stuff—right?—because that's what pushes the world forward."

In that same video about Facebook that aired on *Oprah*, I saw another poster that caught my eye: WHAT WOULD YOU DO IF YOU WEREN'T AFRAID? The question is essentially the same as the one Senator Booker's mother posed to him: What would you do if you weren't afraid to fail? Put another way, the question could be: What would you do if you knew that failure could benefit you in profound ways? Although the wording of the questions is different, the gist is the same because if we knew how much failure could benefit us, we would be much less afraid to fail. I saw this poster again when I visited Facebook, among other posters on a vibrant wall behind a receptionist's desk. I was struck by how the combination of this poster with the one directly below it—DREAM BIG—spoke to the impact that overcoming the fear of failure would have on the way we live. WHAT WOULD YOU DO IF YOU WEREN'T AFRAID? would be a guiding question in our lives, and DREAM BIG would be a significant part of the answer.

So, what would this shift in the way we lead our lives actually look like?

A "Freedom to" Kind of Life

The twentieth-century philosopher and psychologist Erich Fromm, in his book *Escape from Freedom*, offers language that provides a useful framework for describing a "let your freak flag fly" approach to life. He distinguishes between two types of freedom, negative and positive, and characterizes negative freedom as "freedom from" something undesirable and positive freedom as "freedom to" something desirable. "Freedom from" involves getting away from something we don't want, whereas "freedom to" involves going toward something we do want. Drawing on Fromm's language, seeing the whole truth of failure would shift us from a way of living characterized by "freedom from," where the focus is on getting away from failure, to one characterized by "freedom to," where the focus is on going toward our greatest aspirations. Seeing the whole truth of failure enables us to overcome the controlling fear of failure, and overcoming the fear of failure frees us to go after what we most want, what matters in our own estimation, rather than trying to elude what we don't. It shifts us to a *freedom to* kind of life.

A key distinction between a *freedom to* and *freedom from* way of living entails being driven by intrinsic motivation—doing something for its own sake, because you really want to—versus extrinsic motivation—doing something for any other reason. In a *freedom to* approach to living, motivation is sourced from deep internal reserves, so it is fierce and abundant and transcends victories and defeats. The *freedom to* approach to life entails investment that is not contingent on a particular outcome. It involves placing top priority on bringing to the outside what is inside rather than subduing what is inside to meet outside demands. In other words, it prioritizes manifesting your originality. It is defined by less fear and more freedom and courage, and specifically more courage to go toward what you care most about, including your purpose, passion, and ideals.

The problem with the *freedom from* approach is that, to use Conan O'Brien's metaphor, it is like going through life wearing a bright white tuxedo. Who wants to get to the end of life and realize that their tuxedo is in pristine shape, but that they didn't live as fully as they could have? A *freedom from* approach may lead to more successes in terms of short-term victories but possibly on a path that you don't even care about. A *freedom to* approach may involve more defeats and rejections but far fewer regrets. In the short term, piling up only victories might feel more comfortable and better, but in the long term, staying so fully within our limits leads to a more shrunken life. It is a life that will not reveal the full extent of your human capacity and unique potential.

This shift in the way we lead our lives would look like this: taking more risks and seeking more challenges in areas that are deeply important to us. In other words, not just taking more risks and seeking more challenges for the sake of taking on *more* risks and challenges—but taking on more *meaningful* risks and challenges. This way of living, characterized by the mantra "let your freak flag fly," involves feeling freer and more courageous and taking more risks and seeking more challenges on paths that have heart.

Steve Jobs, in his Stanford commencement address in 2005, talked about the value of this kind of approach to life.

 Your time is limited, so don't waste it living someone else's life. Don't be trapped by dogma —which is living with the results of other people's thinking. Don't let the noise of others' opinions drown out your own inner voice. And most important, have the courage to follow your heart and intuition. They somehow already know what you truly want to become. Everything else is secondary.

And this way of living is what people who were dying regretted not doing, according to palliative care nurse and author Bronnie Ware, whose work "Top 5 Regrets of the Dying" was discussed earlier. As you may recall, the number one regret was, "I wish I'd had the courage to live a life true to myself, not the life others expected of me." Because the desire to live a life that is true to ourselves is among the deepest yearnings we have and is extremely hard to do, one of the big questions posed at the beginning of the book was: How can I find the courage to live a life that is true to myself rather than one that others expect of me? We now have an answer: seeing the whole truth of failure changes the way we see failure, enabling us to overcome the controlling fear of failure, and changing our view of failure endows us with courage to live the life we want to live. It frees us to go after what we most want, what matters in our own estimation, rather than trying to elude what we don't. It shifts us to a *freedom to* kind of life.

BECCA NORTH

This way of living sounds pretty good in and of itself, but what else might it yield?

A New Kind of Success:
"Cutting a Brand-New Path," Happiness, and
Changing the World

Consider another big question posed at the beginning of the book: How can I reach my full potential? This question also reflects one of our deepest yearnings in life, and because of this, realizing one's full potential would be a valuable part of a new definition of success. It is equivalent to finding success on one's own terms, or what Dr. Angelou called "cutting a brand-new path." "Cutting a brand-new path" is contingent upon manifesting your originality. It is based on the belief that self-trust is valuable, a point that was made clear in a comment Dr. Angelou made (when she says "you" here, she was speaking in a general way, not directly to me): "I think what's best for you, you will know. You have yourself. You keep yourself open and courageous, and what's best for you will be offered to you. Life will offer it whether you're ready or not." Since living in a *freedom to* way prioritizes manifesting originality, it allows you to fulfill your unique potential. Fulfilling your unique potential is not only what maximizes your ability to change the world; it is gratifying at the deepest level. As such, this kind of success dissolves the tension between acting selfishly and selflessly and reflects the idea that what is best for the world is best for us as individuals as well.

Think back to this big question posed at the beginning of the book: How can I cultivate greater happiness? Science and stories discussed in this book reveal that expressing your originality fosters happiness. So living your life with manifesting originality as your guiding principle—"let your freak flag fly"—will enhance happiness greatly.

And this *freedom to* approach to life is freeing and emboldening in and of itself. Like the opposite of a vicious cycle, this way of living, born out of reduced fear, greater freedom, and greater courage, further reduces fear and enhances freedom and courage. Being more deeply invested in the input and less worried about the outcome is liberating. This idea came through in the interviews.

Dr. Angelou spoke of how a *freedom to* way of living liberates us and endows us with courage. Her words were different, but the spirit of her message was strikingly similar. Instead of talking about intrinsic goals, she talked about the value of doing right for its own sake. When she first spoke about doing right for right's sake, we were finishing lunch. I had stopped recording while we ate. She seemed to care so much about this point that she said I might want to get this part of her comments on the recording: "I think when you love right for its own sake, not because it's going to bring you an increase in salary or a raise in your title, [but] because it is the right thing to do right, in a marvelous way that also liberates a person from fear. You can really know that when I do the right thing because it's the right thing to do, whatever happens as a result of it, I'm satisfied that I've done the right thing for its own sake." When she finished her answer, I said that it seemed like that liberation she referred to is key to the art of living a good life. She said, "I think so." Similarly, she said that being of use to somebody helps to overcome fear. As she put it, "I think that's one way you get over being afraid. You say, *I will be of use to somebody.*" The next story illustrates the impact of her philosophy of doing right for its own sake and of being useful. And it reveals another effect of a *freedom to* way of living life. It helps you change the world.

Dr. Angelou, at the time she shared this story, was remembering her close friend Dolly McPherson. In the midst of talking about how the two of them often traveled together, this story surfaced of a speech Dr. Angelou gave at Brigham Young University in November 1972. To provide some context, after Dr. Angelou told the story of her speech at BYU, she commented that she hadn't thought of the story in a long time, "a month of Sundays." She said she had never written about it either. So in the middle of our interview, she called an assistant in one of her offices, a media expert, to ask if she could remember when the speech took place. Dr. Angelou was deeply surprised and humored to learn that the speech had been recorded and that her office had received a DVD of the speech that morning.

 I was invited to speak at Brigham Young University. I was living in San Francisco, and she [Ms. McPherson] was in New York at Hunter. So I called her. I said, "Sister, meet me in Salt Lake City. I'm sending the ticket, because I'm really scared. These Mormons have asked me to speak, and they hate me." You know, according to their belief at that time, black people not only didn't go to heaven, they couldn't become members of the church. And I talked to my mother. She said, "You must be going there for some reason, so go there."

So Dolly met me in Salt Lake City and we went to a hotel. And I called my mother again. I was already forty years old, and I called my mother and she said, "You must be—is your sister there yet?" I said yes. She asked me, "Do you have your little portable bar?" I said yes. She said, "Make a drink."… The next morning two young men came to the hotel to pick us up and drive us to Provo, where Brigham Young is. And in the car, they showed me their brochure. Brigham Young had a speaker for every month. The other eleven speakers were white men. The speaker before me had been Spiro T. Agnew, the then vice president. They told me there were 11,000 students, and people, in the stadium.

I went to the—oh my God, I haven't thought about this—I went—they sat me down on the platform. There were forty old white men sitting on it. And they put Dolly over there somewhere.

She said the audience seating went up high, and the incline was steep.

It looked like all those white people were going to fall on top of me. And way up there at the corner was another black face. And so somebody gave a perfunctory prayer. Somebody said something else, then somebody said, "And here's Maya Angelou." They didn't say, "I tried to," "I attempted," "I succeeded," "I failed" at anything. "And here's Maya Angelou."

So I went up, I had my speech [in my hands], and I put it back on my chair. This is all so—I just said, "Lord, if you want it said, put it in my mouth; otherwise, I have nothing to say." So I walked up to the platform and I said, "I thank you for inviting me. I thank you for coming out to back up your invitation. I'm told that you are some 11,000. I'm amazed that you have the nerve to come here because I know that you have some religious aspirations." There was a little titter. I said, "But as I understand it, one person with God constitutes a majority. I commend you for coming in your minority to face me this morning. *How dare you try to deny me God?* You can't put one eyelash in my eyelid and bid it grow, and you've decided I'll be a hewer of wood and a drawer of water, world without end. Amen. *Who made the rules? How dare you?*"

I went on. I talked for about an hour. And when I finished, these children came down these steep stairs trying to touch my feet. And these old men were crying, and we embraced. I was crying.

And the two young men took me and Dolly back to Salt Lake City. And, I called my mom. I said, "It's all right." She said, "I know it's all right. I prayed all night." [*Laughs.*] The phone rang, and a person said, "Miss Angelou, I'm the international elder of the Mormon church. I was on the platform this morning." I said, "Yes?" "We are going to ask you to do something we've never asked a non-Mormon or woman to do. We invite you to speak this evening in the temple. We'll pay you the same money."

…So I said, "I'll have to say the same thing." He said, "That's what we want."… I asked him, "What time?" He said, "Around seven." I said, "Well, can you get people in in that amount of time?" He said, "Young lady, that's not your lookout."

So when I got there, I said pretty much the same thing. And in the morning—Dolly came out to California to spend the weekend with me, and then I sent her back to New York. I said, "McPherson, these people—I haven't done anything, these people know it's time to make a change, and somebody's been hearing me speak. And someone has said, 'Get Maya Angelou in here. She'll lay a foundation for a change. Watch and see.'"

Within a few weeks, the elder died. But the next elder came in, and he spoke directly to God, to Jesus, and he said black people had worked out their salvation and so that we could become members of the church.

Later, Dr. Angelou's close friend and colleague who accompanied me to her house, Dr. Wilson, said, "There must have been somebody at Brigham Young who invited you who wanted the church to change." Dr. Angelou said, "Exactly. Oh, absolutely. I think more than that, Brigham Young, maybe at the church itself. That's what I told Dolly, that somehow the people had—somebody had heard me speak, and I'd spoken about [the fact that] human beings are more alike than we are unalike, which is my—the melody of my song, the burden of my song."

In June 1978, the Mormon church declared that black men could become priests, and, as Dr. Angelou recalled, she later met the first black Mormon minister. When they met, he told her that he was in the audience when she spoke at Brigham Young and at the Mormon temple. This chance meeting happened at a Baptist church in West Oakland during a trip Dr. Angelou took to see her friend Ruth Love, who had been superintendent of schools in Chicago and at the time of the visit was a superintendent in California.

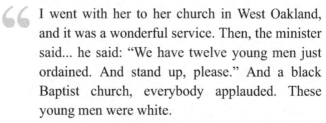 I went with her to her church in West Oakland, and it was a wonderful service. Then, the minister said... he said: "We have twelve young men just ordained. And stand up, please." And a black Baptist church, everybody applauded. These young men were white.

And so when church was over, Ruth and I were going to her car in the parking lot, and one young black man came, and he said, "Miss Angelou, Miss Angelou, wait a minute." I said, "Yes?" He said, "Miss Angelou, I was at Brigham Young. I was way up in the corner when you spoke and I was there that night when you spoke, and I want to introduce myself to you and tell you I'm the first black minister in the Mormon church." Isn't that something? I had forgotten about that.

So now, on the street where Lydia had lived in Harlem—my assistant—the Mormons are building a temple in Harlem.

But this is to be of use, you see? Anybody who can't be of use is useless. I will not be abused. I will not be misused. But I will be of use. I think that's one way you get over of being afraid. You say, "I will be of use to somebody."

To emphasize her point that being of use to somebody also helps to overcome fear, she brought up a song—one she has written about admiringly.

There's an incredible song that was inspired by a statement in Genesis. Genesis said rain had persisted so unrelentingly that people thought it would never cease, so God put a rainbow in the sky. But in the nineteenth century, an African American lyricist wrote, "God didn't just put the rainbow in the sky; God put the rainbow in the clouds." Which meant that at the worst of times, there's a possibility of seeing hope. That's what you want to be, is a rainbow in the clouds. And so if you make that decision, you have all the help. You have no idea where you get the help, but you have all the help you need to be a rainbow in somebody's cloud.

The *freedom to* way of leading our lives is characterized by two of Dr. Angelou's lessons—doing what we feel is right for its own sake and being of use to somebody. By leading our lives in this way, we may find that this approach is a priceless tool in helping us change the world. We may also find our lives blooming more fully and more beautifully than we could have imagined. "Yes," Dr. Angelou told me, "I'm sure that life loves the liver of it." I am deeply grateful for hers.

Consider what the Pulitzer Prize–winning historian Dr. James McPherson said about the impact of Abraham Lincoln assuming a *freedom to* approach to life. In 1849, Lincoln said he was done with politics forever after experiencing some painful defeats. He said that he was going to concentrate on his legal career and on making a living for his family. He stayed out of politics for the better part of five years until he returned to run for US Senate. What brought him back in 1854? His passion for a single issue: the Kansas-Nebraska Act. McPherson told me that Lincoln himself "said later that it was the Kansas-Nebraska Act that hit him like a thunderclap and propelled him back into politics. It was the issue, and there is no reason to disbelieve him." Lincoln stayed in politics even though he lost in 1854 because of his conviction: "This time he doesn't foreswear politics. He stays in politics and helps to found the Republican Party and moves on from there." Given that the 1854 defeat was so painful and that Lincoln had just gotten back in politics after a five-year break during which he said he swore off politics forever, I would think that Lincoln would have felt an even deeper conviction to abandon politics. "But," Dr. McPherson said, "that isn't what happened. He stayed right in after that, and it may well have been the issue because from then on, he made dozens and dozens of political speeches in campaigns in Illinois and other midwestern states between 1854 and 1859, and they were all issue-oriented, on this issue of restricting the further expansion of slavery, which became the central theme of American politics in the mid- to late 1850s, and the issue which eventually prompted Secession and war, and he hammered away at that. So, clearly, it was the issue that drove him after this." Lincoln's conviction for the issue of eliminating slavery not only sustained him through many personal defeats but also shaped our country and world.

Changing our view of failure would change the way we lead our lives, and this notion answers and connects the diverse set of big questions underlying the book. Changing our view of failure would help us feel freer and less afraid. It would ignite our courage to lead lives that feel true to our deepest selves. It would enable us to realize our full potential and cultivate greater happiness. It would help us to change the world. Changing our relationship with failure would have profound benefits for us as individuals and as a society. It would expose hidden resources within us—unleashing innovations, break-throughs, joy, meaning, and magic yet to be discovered.

The Bottom Line

The bottom line is not that we should go out and try to fail as much as possible or reject successes. Success, in the sense of achieving what we set out to do, can be extremely valuable. The bottom line is that knowing we can benefit from failure and feeling equipped to respond well to it will embolden us to take more chances, seek more opportunities, and approach more challenges, however shaky-kneed we feel. As Reverend Gomes said in his baccalaureate address at Stanford, "If we are to profit from failure, to learn from it, then we are free to imagine, take on impossible things that we would otherwise avoid for fear of failure."

Successes, for all of their sparkle and glory, can fall short—and leave us wanting more. Failures enrich us in precisely the ways successes do not. Successes fortify us. Failures can transform us. Failures can help and even be needed in moving us toward what we most yearn for—to tap our full potential, to change the world, to be happy, to be our best possible selves—to succeed, to fly as high as we are capable of flying. It is possible that that is what Dr. Angelou's Facebook post from May 15, 2014, one of her last posts, suggests; it is also the quotation you saw at the very beginning of the book: "We delight in the beauty of the butterfly, but rarely admit the changes it has to go through to achieve that beauty." Ultimately, failure may become a helpful, organic, even welcome factor in our lives, allowing us to unfold our full potential and achieve fulfillment of the deepest kind. And together, failures and successes may collaborate in a powerful, symbiotic, and complementary way to behoove us in a larger cycle of growth in our lives.

HIDDEN MAGIC

 O my friends, there are resources in us on which we have not drawn.

— RALPH WALDO EMERSON, "THE DIVINITY
SCHOOL ADDRESS," 1838

A s the top regret of the dying implies, the desire to live a life that is true to ourselves is one of the deepest desires we have. But discovering what that looks like and then finding the courage to do it is difficult. Failure—a dread-inducing, shame-creating thing that we try to avoid—is part of the answer. Failure strips us bare and cracks us open, unearthing originality, and originality is a hallmark of a life that is true to yourself. Living a life that manifests your originality is not just deeply fulfilling to you personally, it is perhaps your greatest tool in trying to have a positive impact on the world, your greatest gift to the world. To unfold our full potential, failure not only helps enormously, it may actually be needed. In a strange way, failure—what we want the least—can be a catalyst for bringing about what we yearn for the most—to live a life that is true to ourselves. Rewriting the story we tell ourselves about failure will ignite our courage to lead lives that feel true to our deepest selves and help us realize our full potential. It will help us foster happiness and change the world.

Seeing more of the whole truth of failure—the light and dark—may shift the way we think about it—and a shift in the way we think about failure may shift the way we lead our lives.

It is possible that we will not know the boundaries of our fullest selves unless we are willing to venture into areas of greater challenge and risk. Doing so would result in more failures and successes, with each benefiting us in its own way. Realizing our full potential is not something we are endowed with or something that is inevitable. It is a practice, a process, that requires active participation. When I asked Dr. Angelou at one point if she thought that she was born with all the courage that she had, her reply underscored the vital importance of active participation: "I don't think anybody is born with courage. I don't think so. I think circumstances give you chances to learn. To see what you dare to see. Chance what you dare." When I followed up by asking, "So you think that staying open to those opportunities where you can build and practice courage is the key?" She replied, "It is *a* key."

We sit on unseen sources of power and unrealized potential. Unpacked gifts. Hidden magic. Failure, far from disqualifying us from manifesting our full capacity, may qualify us for reaching our highest potential. Failure, like Bruce Wayne's bats, trips us up and scares us, but it has the potential to reveal our own superpowers.

So, that is the impact that a shift in the way you think about failure might have on the way you lead your life and the way I lead my life. Think of the impact that a shift in the way *we* think about failure—a real cultural shift—could have. Think of what that might elicit for society. Ultimately, it could expose unseen resources, hidden magic, for us as a society too.

You, Me, and Us

Discovering your hidden magic is best for you, but it's also what's best for the world. We are all pioneers of the human experience, equipped to explore new frontiers within ourselves and report back with the findings. We, as a society, need individuals to explore their own part of the frontier of human experience. To manifest their unique truth, their personal brand of creativity. These individual pieces together create an even more vibrant, more truthful, richer mosaic. Just as a shift in the way we think about failure may elicit undiscovered resources in each of us, it might do the same for us as a society—unleashing innovations, breakthroughs, and magic yet to be discovered.

EPILOGUE

HOW FAILURE HELPED ME WRITE THIS BOOK

You may remember this popular saying from the movie *Field of Dreams* about the building of a baseball stadium: "If you build it, they will come." That saying has rattled around in my mind for the past several years because I feel like something similar has happened since I started researching failure: "If you study it, it will come." I feel like the number of failures I have experienced—trying to get interviews for this book, searching for an agent and publisher, applying for jobs and research fellowships, etc.—has skyrocketed since I started researching the benefits of failure. Maybe it is the universe's way of helping me understand the topic more fully—with my heart and mind—and making me live what I believe. The failures have been painful, and they paved the way to let me write this book.

One failure in particular opened up the way for this book. It happened in March 2010 just a couple of months before I graduated with my PhD in psychology. I found out that I did not get a postdoctoral fellowship that I applied for and that seemed likely I would get—for reasons that are boring and tedious to explain. The night I found out though, the idea to write this book came flying into my head. And it didn't let go. In the summer of 2010, I secured a position as a postdoctoral researcher and lecturer at UT and started contacting people for interviews.

I was so excited by the topic of the benefits of failure and bubbling with enthusiasm to dive deeper, so in some ways, I felt strong conviction and a deep sense of purpose, but there was also a lot of bashfulness about my plan at first. I was reluctant to share my idea and tended to talk about it in hushed tones. Oddly, two magazine covers provided comfort during this fragile, early time and encouraged me to keep going, convincing me that I was on the right path.

The first, the *Princeton Alumni Weekly* magazine, I found in my mailbox in the beginning of April, the day that I delivered my dissertation to the committee of professors who would evaluate it. Literally, I came right home after dropping off my dissertation to the last professor, checked my mail, and found the magazine in my mailbox with this headline on the cover: "The fruits of failure." Above the headline and next to the drawing of a beaten-up, bruised, and embattled person with stitches on his chin, a lens broken on his glasses, right arm in a cast, and left hand holding a paper that says "Nobel Prize" are the following words: "Princeton scientists talk about the tough going *before* their big successes." At that point, I hadn't seen the topic of failure and success on the cover of any magazine, and the timing was surreal. It gave me a shot of encouragement and confidence.

The second was about two weeks later. It was the *Wine Spectator* magazine with Thomas Keller on the front that I saw in my local grocery store the weekend before I defended my dissertation. I couldn't believe the timing. Again. Another shot of encouragement.

The life of this book since I was encouraged by these two

magazine covers has entailed victories, defeats, stall-outs, and long stretches of time when I could not carve out time to work on it. The interview with Dr. Maya Angelou marked the beginning of a magical time—a full year in which I could write this book completely. When Dr. Angelou and I met, I was coming off a hard year—one of the hardest of my life. At any point in my life, spending time with Dr. Angelou would have put a rainbow in my sky. But at that juncture, without knowing it, she put a rainbow in my clouds. On that same trip, friends—a former high school history teacher, and lifelong mentor, and his wife—offered to let me use their magical house in the woods in Durham, North Carolina, to write this book. It became my year-long writer's retreat, without which there would be no book.

To wrap up, my hope is that this book is a conversation starter rather than conversation stopper. I feel like I am in a big class and just raised my hand and talked for a very long time. I am now eager to listen to what you have to say.

ACKNOWLEDGMENTS

When a stranger contacts you and says, "I'm really interested in the connection between failure and success and I want to talk to you," it must take a special kind of courage to say yes. Even though I chose the people I contacted because their work inspired me, and told them that when I reached out, I imagine that it would feel like a risk in ways to agree to an interview on this topic. I want to thank the seven phenomenal individuals who did. Our conversations contributed enormously to this book, and they made lasting imprints on me personally. Thank you to Dr. Maya Angelou, Senator Cory Booker, Mr. Carl Hayden, Mayor Pam Iorio, Coach Mike Krzyzewski, Mrs. Libby Leffler Hoaglin, and Dr. James McPherson. Without your courage, candor, and insights, there would be no book.

Also, thank you to the many people who helped make these interviews possible. Some of you are family and friends; a special thank-you to Angie North Marshall, Dr. Bob Bast, Catherine North Hounfodji, Dr. Caryn Carlson, Dad, Dave Gould, Rachel Meyerson, and Aunt Molly. Aunt Molly Margaret North: your bold, courageous, loving, and generous gesture had a huge impact on this book and for me personally. I am deeply grateful. Some people who played central roles in making the interviews possible were strangers whom I now have met. Joshua Raymond: you so generously gave of your efforts and time to help someone you had never met. The endeavor ended up requiring dogged persistence, otherworldly patience, and sheer determination; you offered all three. What a profoundly kind series of deeds. Thank you. It was such a treat to meet you and your wife, and I hope that I get another opportunity to thank you in person. Dr. Ed Wilson and Mrs. Emily Wilson: you brought about an opportunity of a lifetime for a stranger. It would have been very easy, and understandable, for you to decline politely, but you took a risk and gave me a chance. The experience will be a part of me forever. It has been an honor and a pleasure to get to know you both, and I so deeply appreciate your enormous kindness. Some people who played central roles in making the interviews possible I have never met. Thank you, in particular, to Elnardo Webster. And thank you to April Rogers for transcribing all the interviews. I am in awe of your skills; your expertise and fast turnaround have benefited this book greatly. I also know that there are people whose names I don't know who helped in big and small ways to make these interviews possible. Thank you.

Finally, there are people who generously offered their time to talk with me in more informal conversations. In all cases, their insights informed my thinking. I am grateful. Thank you, Ryan Hill, the cofounder and CEO of KIPP New Jersey in Newark. Thank you also to my sister, Catherine North Hounfodji, for enabling that conversation. Thank you also to the many people whose stories—through their speeches, biographies, role in a television series, etc.—are part of the fabric of this book.

Shifting focus to the research side, I want to thank the many research assistants who contributed to my dissertation studies.

Together, you saw these projects from the idea stage to the publication stage, and you made vital contributions. I could not have carried out these projects without you. A special thank-you to two research assistants who were there at the very beginning of these studies and involved through all phases, recruiting participants, collecting and entering data, and training new research assistants; you two also were there when the book idea came about and have encouraged and helped me throughout the whole process in more ways than you know. Very appropriately, you were the last two to read the book and provide editing feedback before I shipped it off to sea. You blow me away with your remarkable talent, myriad strengths, commitment to excellence, work ethic, and sense of humor and fun. You are amazing human beings. I am grateful for all you have contributed to this book and most grateful to have you as friends. Thank you, Rachel Meyerson Jamail and Danielle Brown Becka. Also, a very special thank-you to a research assistant who didn't work on these studies but did collaborate on others and contributed enormously to the book through incredibly instructive guidance on early versions and nearly finished versions: Brittany Sherrill. Brittany, your astute insights and encouragement have been instrumental. You are phenomenally talented—and a phenomenal person—and I am grateful that you shared your talents with me. I also want to thank the five members of my dissertation committee who helped shape and refine these studies: my adviser, Dr. Charles J. Holahan, Dr. Caryn Carlson, Dr. James Pennebaker, Dr. William Swann, and Dr. Patrick Wong. I am deeply grateful for your significant contributions. I want to thank three stellar research assistants who helped me in the final stages of the book in myriad ways, including vetting research-related parts of the book and checking and citing research articles: Kayleigh Thomas, Justin White, and Maddy Schmitt. Your contributions strengthened the book significantly. And thank you to the Southwestern University Psychology Department for your support. I also want to thank the many researchers whose work I drew upon for this book. Your scientific contributions are a valued part of this book.

Several brave individuals offered to read parts of this book in the more beginning stages. What a challenging task in so many ways. Thank you—Dave Gould, Angie, Anna Larson, Rachel, Danielle, Nelia Robbi, Brittany, Jonathan Paliwal, and Keira Gould. And Dave Gould three more times. And many people also bravely, lovingly, and generously offered to provide feedback on various versions of the "whole book." A huge thank-you to the first of those readers: Dad. Thank you also to Anna, Brittany, Anushka Pai, Dave Gould, Lindsay Vest, Amy Emerson, Mehul Patel, and Rachel and Danielle. Your contributions have improved the book enormously, both in ways you can see and many others that are less visible. An added thank-you to Mehul for creating the two graphics of pathways from failure to greater success. And thank you, Mom, for your enormous help with the pictures.

To Caryl Phillips, your interest in my book in our first communication had an immediate and lasting impact. Your belief in my idea strengthened my belief in my idea. Also, your willingness to help was extraordinary; you went above and beyond to help someone who was not in a position to return any kind of favor to you. That means a lot. And the conversation we had over coffee was one of the most helpful, influential conversations I have had about the process of writing this book and trying to get it out there for others to read. The conversation shifted the course I was on in a powerful way. Your combination of candor, encouragement, and vast experience and wisdom was invaluable in this process. Thank you. Thank you also to my courageous, caring cousin, Megan North Shuford, who made that communication possible. Janie Fleming Fransson, you offered your time, expertise, guidance, and support generously. Thank you. Your insights and efforts informed my thinking and improved the book.

Thank you to Andrew Watts and the team at Severn River Publishing. Your offer lifted this book from my desktop and carried it into people's hands, and I am extremely grateful. Thank you for your vision, courage, initiative, ingenuity, interest, energy, hard work, and freedom you offered me. And thank you to my spectacular editor, Christina Roth, whose keen insights and sharp eye refined and elevated the book.

Thank you to my extended family and dear friends. You all have supported, encouraged, housed, listened, fed, held, and helped me throughout the entire time I've worked on this book. I can think of many occasions when your words of encouragement came at just the right time and provided a needed boost to keep going. The conversations we have had about the book—around dinner tables, on runs or walks, in the car, on the phone, over a glass of wine or cup of coffee, or on a dock at a lake—informed and clarified my thinking. I greatly appreciate all the very big and small things you have done to make this book possible. Aunt Janie, you fall into almost all these categories, including dinner-table talks where you provided a delicious meal, and categories that aren't even listed here, like gifting me relevant books and helping me find a path for this book into the world. Thank you. Anna, your generosity in opening up your home to me for the better part of a year made this book possible. I am so deeply grateful. The other roles you played during that time, including supplier of innumerable laughs, running partner, and sounding board, also contributed to this book, and my life, in very meaningful ways. To Dave and Lyn Gould, there are no words. No way of saying thank you that would reflect the depth and scope of my gratitude or illuminate the magnitude of your contribution to this book. This book quite simply would not exist if it weren't for you. An unplanned, forty-five-minute visit on the way to the airport resulted in a game-changer for the book and a life-changer for me. Your enormously generous, seemingly off-the-wall offer to let me write in your magical home in the woods enabled this book to be. Over the course of almost a year, you offered a quiet, inspiring, private space to write. The enormity of the gift of your space was only matched by the pleasure of your company. What a great way to start and end my days by chatting with you. And the myriad special experiences that came about—Scrabble games, an evening sing-along and jam session, tea in the midst of a lightning storm, a lesson on the beehive, hauling wood up to the house in a wheelbarrow in the winter for the woodstove, picking cherries from your cherry tree in the spring, unplanned and planned shared dinners, etc. What a delightful time. You gave me all of that, and in return, I gave you a latte and a croissant (Lyn), a defeat at shuffleboard (Gould), and okay, fine, many victories over me in Scrabble (Gould). Point is: you gave me one of the greatest gifts of my life, and because of that gift, there is this book. Thank you.

Finally, to my family, to whom this book is dedicated, thank you for all that you are. This book exists because of your love.

ABOUT THE AUTHOR

Becca North is a researcher and teacher in the field of psychology. She is currently a Visiting Assistant Professor in Psychology at Southwestern University in Georgetown, Texas. Her research is in the area of happiness and well-being. A big question in her research is: How can negative experiences foster positive psychological change? She has an interdisciplinary background—with a PhD in Psychology from the University of Texas, a Master's in Public Affairs from the Lyndon B. Johnson School of Public Affairs, and an AB in History from Princeton University. After graduating from college, she taught first grade in Compton, California, for three years as a corps member of Teach For America. She grew up in North Carolina and Texas and currently lives in Austin, Texas.

Find out more at beccanorth.com

facebook.com/beccajnorth

twitter.com/BeccaNorth

NOTES

Opening Quotations

"We delight in the beauty of the butterfly...": Dr. Maya Angelou's quotation is from a Facebook post from May 15, 2014.

"I want you to first think about...": The late Reverend Peter Gomes's quotation is from a baccalaureate address he gave at Stanford University on June 18, 2008, available at http://news.stanford.edu/news/2008/june18/bacgomes-061808.html, accessed August 10, 2014.

"It is impossible to live without failing...": J. K. Rowling's comment is an excerpt from her commencement address at Harvard University on June 5, 2008, available at https://news.harvard.edu/gazette/story/2008/06/text-of-j-k-rowling-speech/.

"Last night, as I was sleeping...": Antonio Machado's poem is from "Last Night, as I Was Sleeping," in *Times Alone: Selected Poems of Antonio Machado*, trans. Robert Bly (Middletown, CT: Wesleyan University Press, 1983).

"O my friends, there are resources...": This quotation from Ralph Waldo Emerson is from "The Divinity School Address," a speech he gave at Harvard Divinity School in 1838. *Selections from Ralph Waldo Emerson: An Organic Anthology*, ed. Stephen E. Whicher (Boston: Houghton Mifflin, 1957), 114.

Introduction

(p. 4) The Lincoln billboard, according to information on the bottom of the billboard itself, was the work of the Foundation for a Better Life: www.values.com (currently www.passiton.com) and can be found on that website.

(p. 7) "Libby Leffler Hoaglin...": When Libby Leffler Hoaglin and I spoke, her name was Libby Leffler, but since then, she has changed her name, as is indicated on her LinkedIn page, https://www.linkedin.com/in/libbylh, accessed August 4, 2018.

(p. 7) The quotation describing SoFi, the finance company where Libby Leffler Hoaglin currently works, comes from the company's website, https://www.sofi.com/our-story/, accessed August 4, 2018.

(p. 10) "The poet and philosopher Ralph Waldo Emerson wrote that if a person 'harvests his losses,' then he 'turns the dust of his shoes to gems.'": *Selections from Ralph Waldo Emerson*, ed. S. E. Whicher (Boston: Houghton Mifflin, 1957), 81.

(p. 12) "There is subjectivity in what people call a failure, but the dictionary definition...": The dictionary definition of *fail* is from *Oxford American Dictionary* (New York: Oxford University Press, 1980).

Chapter 1: The Way We Think about Failure

(p. 15) "In January 2012, Bronnie Ware, who worked in palliative care for many years, wrote an article...": Bronnie Ware's article can be found online at "Top 5 Regrets of the Dying," *Huffington Post*, January 21, 2012, http://www.huffingtonpost.com/bronnie-ware/top-5-regrets-of-the-dyin_b_1220965.html. Ware also published a book called *The Top Five Regrets of the Dying: A Life Transformed by the Dearly Departing*.

(p. 16) "It is only a slice of the truth based on a single story about failure.": Thank you to Chimamanda Ngozi Adichie for her TED Talk, "The Danger of a Single Story," given in July 2009, which gave me additional, meaningful language, the notion of "a single story," for describing how our view of failure is a partial truth. Her talk can be found here: https://www.ted.com/talks/chimamanda_adichie_the_danger_of_a_single_story.

Chapter 2: Failure and Success

(p. 25) I interviewed Dr. James McPherson in his office at Princeton University in Princeton, New Jersey, on October 21, 2010.

(p. 26) "When I asked Dr. McPherson what he thought Lincoln considered to be... he said losing the election for US Senate in 1854.": To clarify a minor point, the election itself was in January 1855.

(p. 33) I interviewed Coach Mike Krzyzewski in his office

at Duke University in Durham, North Carolina, on November 7, 2011. Detailed information about Coach Mike Krzyzewski was found at www.coachk.com, accessed October 3, 2013.

(p. 49) I interviewed Carl Hayden in his home office in Elmira, New York, on August 7, 2012.

(p. 49) "SUNY is the largest comprehensive higher education system...": This information about SUNY came from www.suny.edu/about/, accessed August 13, 2018.

(p. 49) "Hayden served in this position under the leadership of a few governors and during a recession, and according to an NBC news report from December 2011...": https://www.nbcnewyork.com/news/local/SUNY-Carl-Hayden-Board-Trustees-Resigned-Cuomo-Carl-McCall-Chairman-135101153.html, accessed August 13, 2018.

(p. 49) "The same NBC news report referred to him as...": This quote and others from the NBC news report mentioned in this section can be found at: https://www.nbcnewyork.com/news/local/SUNY-Carl-Hayden-Board-Trustees-Resigned-Cuomo-Carl-McCall-Chairman-135101153.html.

(p. 49) "He served as chancellor of the Board of Regents, also called "schools chancellor....": The term "schools chancellor" was used in the previously mentioned NBC news report about Hayden.

(p. 49) "The 2011 NBC news report, which reflected on Hayden's career, commented...": Ibid.

(p. 50) "And when Hayden left the Board of Regents, he...": The following quotation from the 2011 NBC news report indicated that the title of chancellor emeritus Hayden received was rare: "He left the regents with the uncommon title of chancellor emeritus."

(p. 58) I interviewed then mayor Cory Booker in his office in City Hall in Newark, New Jersey, on February 17, 2011.

Detailed information about Senator Booker was found at www.-corybooker.com, accessed October 3, 2013. Information about Newark Now, the nonprofit organization that Mayor Booker started, came from my interview with Mayor Booker and from http://brickcityserves.org/organizations/260, accessed August 28, 2012.

(p. 65) I interviewed Mayor Pam Iorio in her home in Tampa, Florida, on April 23, 2011. Detailed information about Mayor Pam Iorio was found in Mike Salinero, "Iorio Honored by County Commissioners," *The Tribune*, April 4, 2013.

(p. 73) "The chef and restaurateur Thomas Keller...": The information about Thomas Keller comes mainly from the *Wine Spectator* article I refer to throughout this book: Harvey Steiman, "The Phoenix and The French Laundry: Thomas Keller's Rise from the Ashes of Failure to Create America's Greatest Restaurant," *Wine Spectator*, April 30, 2010. Supplemental information about Keller came from the Wikipedia page on him, http://en.wikipedia.org/wiki/Thomas_Keller, and the Wikipedia page on The French Laundry, http://en.wikipedia.org/wiki/French_Laundry, both accessed August 2013.

(p. 75) "Dr. Brené Brown, researcher and storyteller, gave a TED Talk in March 2012...": The quotation from Dr. Brown's talk begins about eleven minutes and forty-five seconds into her talk.

(p. 75) "He told Oprah in the discussion after the show that he celebrates failures at Facebook.": Zuckerberg's comments came from a discussion after the show, "Education Panel Continues the Discussion after the Show," accessed August 10, 2014, http://www.oprah.com/oprahshow/The-Panel-Continues-the-Discussion-After-the-Show-Video. The part of the discussion that I refer to goes from about 11:42 to 12:40.

(p. 76) "This could be a defining moment for the company,

and it reminds me of a story I read about an interview with John T. Chambers, who was CEO of Cisco...": The interview that I am referring to here, and quote later, is from A. Bryant, "Corner Office: John T. Chambers," *New York Times*, August 2, 2009.

(p. 77) "A few years ago, I saw this idea written on a bathroom wall in a coffee shop...": The coffee shop where I found this message is Cherry Street Coffee House in Seattle.

(p. 79) "For example, failures promote reflection and reevaluation...": P. T. P. Wong and B. Weiner, "When People Ask 'Why' Questions, and the Heuristics of Attributional Search," *Journal of Personality and Social Psychology* 40 (1981): 650–63.

(p. 79) "One study found that managers in various business settings... 'doing nothing' after successful outcomes than after negative ones": D. Zakay, S. Ellis, and M. Shevalsky, "Outcome Value and Early Warning Indications as Determinants of Willingness to Learn from Experience," *Experimental Psychology* 51 (2004): 150–57; the quotation is from p. 155.

(p. 80) "Other research has shown that, more generally, failures motivate more of a response overall than positive events...": S. E. Taylor, "Asymmetrical Effects of Positive and Negative Events: The Mobilization-Minimization Hypothesis," *Psychological Bulletin* 110 (1991): 67–85.

(p. 80) "Failure is a better impetus for learning than success": R. Hastie, "Causes and Effects of Causal Attribution," *Journal of Personality and Social Psychology* 46 (1984): 44–56.

(p. 80) "Reverend Peter Gomes...": Rev. Gomes's baccalaureate address.

(p. 80) "Perhaps most importantly, research shows that failures are better catalysts for change and growth than success": Research regarding change in this context can be seen in S. Ellis, R. Mendel, and M. Nir, "Learning from Successful and

Failed Experience: The Moderating Role of Kind of After-Event Review," *Journal of Applied Psychology* 91 (2006): 669–80; research regarding failure as a catalyst for growth can be seen in L. A. King and J. A. Hicks, "Whatever Happened to 'What Might Have Been'?: Regrets, Happiness, and Maturity," *American Psychologist* 62 (2007): 625–36.

Chapter 3: A Secret Pathway

(p. 84) "Individuality is an aspect of originality; in fact, the word *individual* is embedded in the dictionary definition of *originality*...": This definition is from *The Random House Dictionary of the English Language, the Unabridged Edition* (New York: Random House, 1966).

(p. 84) "Two dictionary definitions of originality reflect the similarities between the two: 'creative ability' and 'freshness'...": Ibid.

(p. 84) "This definition of *original* sheds light on the twist...": *Oxford American Dictionary*.

(p. 85) "In referring to success in this pathway... which are two dictionary definitions of success.": Ibid.

(p. 86) "Let's go back in time to 1901....": Einstein's story comes from Walter Isaacson, *Einstein: His Life and Universe* (New York: Simon & Schuster, 2007). Specifically, most of what I wrote about comes from pp. 54–79.

(p. 86) "'I will soon have graced every physicist... with my offer.'": This quotation comes from a letter from Einstein to Mileva Marić written on April 4, 1901; ibid., 59.

(p. 86) "But, as Isaacson wrote, 'Einstein did not even get the courtesy of a rejection.'": Ibid, 59.

(p. 86) "In one letter to chemistry professor Wilhelm Ostwald, Einstein's desperation seeped out....": The quotation cited in this sentence is from pp. 59–60 of *Einstein*.

(pp. 86-87) "'Since then [graduating from the Zurich Poly-technic] he has been trying unsuccessfully to get a position as a teaching assistant. . .'": This quotation is from a letter from Einstein's father (ibid., 60); the letter, written on April 13, 1901, is quoted in full in Isaacson's book.

(p. 87) "Isaacson commented in *Einstein*: 'Among the many surprising things about the life of Albert Einstein was the trouble he had getting an academic job.'": Ibid, 54.

(p. 88) "'I was deeply moved by your devotion... your luck-less friend.'": This quotation is from a letter from Einstein to Marcel Grossman, written on April 14, 1901; ibid., 63.

(p. 88) "Had he been consigned instead to the job of an assistant to a professor, he might have felt compelled to churn out safe publications....": Ibid, 79.

(p. 88) "Isaacson wrote that Einstein himself came to believe... saying that it was in 'that worldly cloister where I hatched my most beautiful ideas'": This quotation from Einstein is from a correspondence to Michele Besso on December 12, 1919; ibid.

(p. 89) "J. K. Rowling, author of the bestselling Harry Potter series...": The story of J. K. Rowling presented here, including specific quotations, comes from the commencement address she delivered at Harvard University in 2008.

(p. 92) "Steve Jobs delivered a popular...": The story of Steve Jobs presented here, including specific quotations, comes from his commencement address at Stanford University on June 12, 2005.

Chapter 4: Failure and Your Freak Flag

(p. 98) "He suggests that she stop trying to play a part and just be herself: 'Maybe you should stop... You have a freak flag.

You just don't fly it.'": This quotation from *The Family Stone* comes about fifty-two minutes into the film.

(p. 100) "I later found a monster jawbreaker at a candy store, and a close friend's son volunteered to throw it on a stone...": Thank you to Carson Diehl for your work with the monster jawbreaker.

(p. 101) "In October 2010, *New York Times* columnist David Brooks...": D. Brooks, "The Soft Side," *New York Times*, October 5, 2010.

(p. 103) "The classic 'shock experiments' conducted by Stanley Milgram at Yale University. . .": S. Milgram, "Behavioral Study of Obedience," *Journal of Abnormal and Social Psychology* 67 (1963): 371–78.

(p. 105) "In 1955, Solomon Asch, another influential researcher in psychology...": S. E. Asch, "Opinions and Social Pressure," *Scientific American* 193 (1955): 31–35.

(pp. 107-108) "Operant conditioning is...": B. F. Skinner's work is fundamental to our understanding of operant conditioning; one of his seminal publications is B. F. Skinner, *Science and Human Behavior* (New York: Macmillan, 1953).

(p. 108) "Modeling describes another way...": A. Bandura, *Principles of Behavior Modification* (New York: Holt, Rinehart, & Winston, 1969).

(p. 109) "In October 2005, *Newsweek* magazine ran a cover story...": Marin Alsop's comments in *Newsweek* can be found with this information: "Marin Alsop: Conductor" in Holly Peterson, "How I Got There," *Newsweek*, October 24, 2005, 60.

(pp. 110-111) "Without using the word *modeling*, Oprah Winfrey described...": This story, including quotations, is from Oprah's commencement address at Stanford University on June 15, 2008.

(p. 113) I interviewed Libby Leffler Hoaglin in a conference room at Facebook Headquarters in Menlo Park, California, on August 29, 2013.

(p. 113) "My friend had seen a talk Leffler Hoaglin gave at the Digital-Life-Design (DLD) Women Conference in Munich about how to increase the presence of women in leadership positions...": The link to Leffler Hoaglin's talk at the DLD Women Conference in 2011 is here: https://www.dld-conference.com/DLDwomen11, accessed August 13, 2018.

(p. 113) Information about Ms. Leffler Hoaglin being named the "Most Important Woman Under 30 in Tech" by *Business Insider* can be found here: http://www.businessinsider.com/30-important-women-30-or-under-in-tech-2013-4#1-libby-leffler-30, accessed December 5, 2013. Information about her being on the "FORBES 30 Under 30" is here: http://www.forbes.com/pictures/eeji45ejikf/libby-leffler-28/, accessed March 5, 2015. The quotation "brightest stars" is from a *Forbes* article about the "30 Under 30" 2014 group: Caroline Howard, "30 Under 30 Who Are Changing the World," *Forbes,* January 6, 2014, http://www.forbes.com/sites/carolinehoward/2014/01/06/30-under-30-who-are-changing-the-world-2014/.

(p. 114) "In 2017, she was an invited speaker to the *Fortune* Most Powerful Women Next Gen...": (1) Leffler Hoaglin's attendance as a speaker in 2017 is listed here: https://www.fortuneconferences.com/fortune-mpw-next-gen-2018/2017-speakers/, accessed August 6, 2018; (2) the quotation about the aim of the conference is on the website for the inaugural conference, https://www.fortuneconferences.com/mpw-next-gen-2014/, accessed August 6, 2018.

(p. 122) "Research shows that people who are in emotional pain use more...": S. Rude, E. M. Gortner, and J. Pennebaker,

"Language Use of Depressed and Depression-Vulnerable College Students," *Cognition & Emotion* 18 (2004): 1121–33.

(p. 124) "Consider this quotation about self-trust and originality from Emerson's essay "Self-Reliance": 'We but half express ourselves, and are ashamed of that divine idea which each of us represents....'": Whicher, *Selections from Ralph Waldo Emerson*, 148.

(p. 125) "In 2007, the writer Joan Acocella published...": J. Acocella, *Twenty-Eight Artists and Two Saints* (New York: Pantheon Books, 2007); the quotations arc from the introduction, xiii.

(p. 126) "When the writer Kathryn Harrison reviewed the book...": Harrison's book review was entitled "Lives in the Arts" and appeared in the *New York Times Book Review* on February 18, 2007.

Chapter 5: Your Freak Flag and Success

(p. 127) "And in a one-minute television advertisement...": The commercial is available here: https://www.youtube.com/watch?v=D9T_5MeFA1M, accessed August 6, 2018.

(p. 128) "Consider how the MacArthur Foundation...": Information about the "genius grants," including quotations from the website, were found here: http://www.macfound.org/programs/fellows/strategy/, accessed August 11, 2014.

(p. 128) "A current definition of *genius*...": The definition can be found in the *Oxford American Dictionary*. The author Elizabeth Gilbert brought this antiquated definition of genius to my attention in her powerful TED Talk entitled "Your Elusive Creative Genius" from February 2009. Her talk can be found

here: http://www.ted.com/talks/elizabeth_gilbert_on_genius?
language=en, accessed February 25, 2015.

(p. 129) "Thomas Friedman, columnist for the *New York Times* and Pulitzer Prize–winning author...": Friedman's commencement address at Williams College in 2005 is available here: http://www.humanity.org/voices/commencements/tom-friedman-williams-college-speech-2005?
page=friedman_at_williams, accessed December 2, 2013.

(p. 130) "Years later, in an op-ed in the *New York Times*...": T. Friedman, "Broadway and the Mosque," *New York Times*, August 3, 2010.

(p. 130) "Economist Alan Blinder... argued that creativity and inventiveness are among the most...": Alan S. Blinder, "Education for the Third Industrial Revolution," in *Creating a New Teaching Profession,* ed. J. Hannaway and D. Goldhaber (Washington, DC: Urban Institute Press, 2009), 22.

(p. 130) "Walter Isaacson wrote: 'For this new century of globalization... our success will depend on our creativity.'": Isaacson, 7.

(p. 130) "And the writer Daniel Pink argued...": D. H. Pink, *A Whole New Mind: Why Right-Brainers Will Rule the Future* (New York: Riverhead Books, 2005), 130.

(p. 130) "A 2011 article in the *New York Times*...": Steve Lohr, "Reaping the Rewards of Risk-Taking," *New York Times*, August 28, 2011.

(pp. 130-131) "As Einstein said, 'It is important to foster individuality...'": Isaacson, 7.

(p. 131) "Thomas Friedman spoke about his belief that innovation is actually essential...": This section about Thomas Friedman is from the transcript and video of his interview with Walter Isaacson, both accessed November 13, 2013 at the following: Aspen Ideas, July 1, 2011, http://www.aspenideas.org/sites/default/files/transcripts/AIF11_088_That_Used_to_be_us.pdf (transcript) and "Thomas Friedman Remarks," C-Span, June 30, 2011, http://www.c-spanvideo.org/program/300299-1 (video).

(p. 132) "Consider the words of poet and philosopher Ralph Waldo Emerson...": *Selections from Ralph Waldo Emerson*, ed. S. E. Whicher (Boston: Houghton Mifflin, 1957), 8–9.

(p. 133) "In the mid-twentieth century, influential psychologists Abraham Maslow and Carl Rogers argued that expressing...": A. H. Maslow, *Motivation and Personality, Second Edition* (New York: Harper & Row, 1970); C. R. Rogers, "The Actualizing Tendency in Relation to 'Motives' and to Consciousness," in *Nebraska Symposium on Motivation*, ed. M. R. Jones (Lincoln: University of Nebraska Press, 1963), vol. 11, 1–24.

(p. 133) "Emerging research in psychology on the 'true self'...": R. Schlegel, J. Hicks, L. King, and J. Arndt, "Feeling Like You Know Who You Are: Perceived True Self-Knowledge and Meaning in Life," *Personality and Social Psychology Bulletin* 37 (2011): 745–56.

(p. 133) "Other research has shown...": Two examples of this research are K. M. Sheldon, "The Self-Concordance Model of Healthy Goal Striving: When Personal Goals Correctly Represent the Person," in E. L. Deci and R. M. Ryan, eds., *Handbook of Self-Determination Research* (Rochester, NY: University of Rochester Press, 2002), 65–86; K. M. Sheldon, "The Self-Concordance Model of Healthy Goal Striving: When Personal Goals Correctly Represent the Person," in P. Schmuck and K. M. Sheldon, eds., *Life Goals and Well-Being: Towards a Positive Psychology of Human Striving* (Seattle, WA: Hogrefe & Huber Publishers, 2001), 18–36. Related research shows that engaging with meaningful goals gives purpose to life (Ryff 1989; Scheier and Carver 2001) and that a sense of purpose fosters personal development (Ryff 1989): C. D. Ryff, "Happiness Is Everything, or Is It? Explorations on the Meaning of Psychological Well-Being," *Journal of Personality and Social Psychology* 57 (1989): 1069–81; M. F. Scheier and C. S. Carver, "Adapting to Cancer: The Importance of Hope and Purpose," in A. Baum and B. L. Andersen, eds., *Psychological Interventions for Cancer* (Washington, DC: American Psychological Association, 2001), 15–36.

(pp. 133-134) "Psychologists Ed Deci and Richard Ryan have written extensively about the benefits of living one's life according to internal values... psychological well-being is enhanced.": E. L. Deci and R. M. Ryan, *Intrinsic Motivation and Self-Determination in Human Behavior* (New York: Plenum, 1985); Deci and Ryan, "A Motivational Approach to Self: Integration in Personality," in *Nebraska Symposium on Motivation,* vol. 38, *Perspectives on Motivation*, ed. R. Dienstbier (Lincoln: University of Nebraska Press, 1991), 237–88; Deci and Ryan, "Human Autonomy: The Basis for True Self-Esteem," in M. H. Kernis, ed., *Efficacy, Agency, and Self-Esteem* (New York: Plenum, 1995), 31–46.

(p. 134) "Relatedly, psychologist Martin Seligman and colleagues have found that drawing on one's signature strengths...": M. E. P. Seligman, T. Rashid, and A. C. Parks, "Positive Psychotherapy," *American Psychologist* 61 (2006): 774–88; N. Park, C. Peterson, and M. E. P. Seligman, "Strengths of Character and Well-Being," *Journal of Social and Clinical Psychology* 23 (2004): 603–19; Seligman, *Authentic Happiness* (New York: Free Press, 2002).

(p. 134) "And, in the job context, workers who pursued goals that employed their greatest...": A. Wrzesniewski, C. R. McCauley, P. Rozin, and B. Schwartz, "Jobs, Careers, and Callings: People's Relations to Their Work," *Journal of Research in Personality* 31 (1997): 21–33.

(p. 134) "There is a chapter in *On Liberty*, an essay by the philosopher John Stuart Mill published in 1859...": The quotation "one of the principal ingredients of human happiness" comes from John Stuart Mill, *On Liberty* (Mineola, NY: Dover Publications, 2002), p. 47. First published 1859 by J. W. Parker and Son (London).

(p. 134) "Emerson conveys a similar sentiment...": The poem is from Whicher, *Selections from Ralph Waldo Emerson*, 11.

(p. 135) Mill argued that originality is "quite the chief ingredient of individual and social progress": Mill, p. 47.

(p. 135) "'It will not be denied by anybody, that originality is a...'": Ibid., pp. 53–54.

(p. 136) "Einstein alluded to the idea that originality drives progress... Isaacson noted: 'Einstein fits into that category.'": Isaacson, 7.

(p. 136) "He describes how expressing originality—'cultivating it and calling it forth'...": Mill, p. 52.

(pp. 136-137) "'It is not by wearing down into uniformity all that is individual . . .'": Ibid., pp. 52–53.

Chapter 6: "Failure Sucks"

(p. 141) "In late October 2009, Max Levchin, cofounder of the online payment service PayPal...": This story about Levchin, including the quotation, is from an NPR piece called "FailCon: Failing Forward to Success." The transcript is here: *Morning Edition*, October 29, 2009, http://www.npr.org/templates/story/story.php?storyId=114271856.

(p. 141) "When Levchin appeared on *Morning Edition*, he had recently spoken at the first FailCon...": Information about

FailCon is from http://thefailcon.com/about.html, accessed September 10, 2013.

(p. 142) "He put it bluntly: 'Failure sucks'": This quotation comes from an article on wired.com by Ryan Singel, "A Silicon Valley Conference on Failing Is Big Success," accessed September 11, 2013, http://www.wired.com/epicenter/2009/10/failcon-succeeds/.

(p. 142) The comedian Conan O'Brien had a similar message in a commencement address he gave at Dartmouth College...": Conan O'Brien's commencement speech at Dartmouth was on June 12, 2011.

(p. 143) "In one experiment, William Swann...": W. B. Swann, J. J. Griffin, S. Predmore, and B. Gaines, "The Cognitive-Affective Crossfire: When Self-Consistency Confronts Self-Enhancement," *Journal of Personality and Social Psychology* 52 (1987): 881–89.

(p. 144) "Mark Leary, professor of psychology...": M. R. Leary, K. L. Haupt, K. S. Strausser, and J. T. Chokel, "Calibrating the Sociometer: The Relationship between Interpersonal Appraisals and State Self-Esteem," *Journal of Personality and Social Psychology* 74 (1998): 1290–99; M. R. Leary, B. Gallagher, E. Fors, N. Buttermore, E. Baldwin, K. Kennedy, and A. Mills, "The Invalidity of Disclaimers about the Effects of Social Feedback on Self-Esteem," *Personality and Social Psychology Bulletin* 29 (2003): 623–36.

(p. 146) "For example, people experiencing social rejection had a cardiovascular response...": W. B. Mendes, B. Major, S. McCoy, and J. Blascovich, "How Attributional Ambiguity Shapes Physiological and Emotional Responses to Social Rejection and Acceptance," *Journal of Personality and Social Psychology* 94 (2008): 278–91.

(p. 146) "And at a hormonal level, rejection produces more cortisol...": S. S. Dickerson, T. L. Gruenewald, and M. E.

Kemeny, "When the Social Self Is Threatened: Shame, Physiology, and Health," *Journal of Personality* 72 (2004): 1191–216.

(p. 146) "Research using functional Magnetic Resonance Imaging (fMRI)...": E. Kross, M. G. Berman, W. Mischel, E. E. Smith, and T. D. Wager, "Social Rejection Shares Somatosensory Representations with Physical Pain," *Proceedings of the National Academy of Sciences* 108 (2011): 6270–75.

Chapter 7: "The Great American Taboo"

(p. 150) "Philip Schultz, author of a Pulitzer Prize–winning collection of poems...": I read about Schultz in an article in *Psychology Today* written by Bruce Grierson in May 2009; Schultz's phrase "the great American taboo" is on p. 66 of the article, available at https://www.psychologytoday.com/articles/200904/weathering-the-storm, accessed February 25, 2015. His book of poems: P. Schultz, *Failure* (Harcourt: New York, 2007).

(p. 150) "In a July 2006 *Bloomberg Businessweek* article...": T. Kuczmarski, "How Failure Breeds Success," *Bloomberg Businessweek,* July 9, 2006, http://www.businessweek.com/stories/2006-07-09/how-failure-breeds-success.

(p. 151) "In his baccalaureate address at Stanford in 2008, Reverend Peter Gomes...": http://news.stanford.edu/news/2008/june18/bacgomes-061808.html.

(p. 152) "Ralph Waldo Emerson wrote that if a person 'harvests his losses,' then he 'turns the dust of his shoes to gems'": Whicher, *Selections from Ralph Waldo Emerson*, 81.

Part 3: Turning the Dust of Our Shoes to Gems

(p. 153) The title of part 3, "Turning the Dust of Our Shoes to Gems," is an adaptation of a phrase Ralph Waldo Emerson used in a journal entry, "Thus he harvests his losses, and turns the dust of his shoes to gems," from Whicher, *Selections from Ralph Waldo Emerson*, 81.

Chapter 8: How to Grow from Failure: A Primer

(p. 155) "Resilience entails bouncing back readily... as is reflected in the dictionary definition...": This definition comes from *Oxford American Dictionary*.

(p. 156) "Traditionally, research on responding to negative events, like failure...": Here are some studies from this line of research: M. E. P. Seligman, S. F. Maier, and R. L. Solomon, "Unpredictable and Uncontrollable Aversive Events," in F. R. Brush, ed., *Aversive Conditioning and Learning* (New York: Academic Press, 1971), 347–400; Seligman, "Learned Helplessness," *Annual Review of Medicine* 23 (1972): 407–12; C. S. Dweck, "The Role of Expectations and Attributions in the Alleviation of Learned Helplessness," *Journal of Personality and Social Psychology* 31 (1975): 674–85; Dweck, T. E. Goetz, and N. L. Strauss, "Sex Differences in Learned Helplessness: IV. An Experimental and Naturalistic Study of Failure Generalization and Its Mediators," *Journal of Personality and Social Psychology* 38 (1980): 441–52; C. Peterson and Seligman, "Causal Explanations as a Risk Factor for Depression: Theory and Evidence," *Psychological Review* 91 (1984): 347–74; Dweck and E. L. Leggett, "A Social-Cognitive Approach to Motivation and Personality," *Psychological Review* 95 (1988): 256–73; G. M. Buchanan and Seligman, eds., *Explanatory Style* (Hillsdale, NJ: Erlbaum, 1995); K. K. Burhans and Dweck, "Helplessness in Early Childhood: The Role of Contingent Worth," *Child Development* 66

(1995): 1719–38; M. L. Kamins and Dweck, "Person versus Process Praise and Criticism: Implications for Contingent Self-Worth and Coping," *Developmental Psychology* 35 (1999): 835–47.

(p. 158) "Diverse research from many areas cutting across a wide range of negative experiences—including failure, relationship problems, trauma, and disease—provides converging evidence....": Two pioneering and leading researchers in the area of posttraumatic growth are Richard Tedeschi and Lawrence Calhoun; one of their many publications on this topic is: R. G. Tedeschi and L. G. Calhoun, "Posttraumatic Growth: Conceptual Foundations and Empirical Evidence," *Psychological Inquiry* 15 (2004): 1–18.

Chapter 9: "Embrace the Suck"

(p. 161) "As part of the training, Ducard instructed Bruce to breathe in a toxin...": This scene takes place approximately thirty-two minutes into the movie *Batman Begins*.

(p. 161) "Later, when he returned to Gotham City...": This scene is approximately forty-five minutes into the movie.

(p. 162) "It involves allowing yourself to experience negative emotions...": As a note, the term commonly used in research is *psychological acceptance*. Psychological acceptance is defined as a willingness to experience all emotions—including the negative ones—without trying to change, avoid, or control them. Since positive emotions are typically easier to embrace, the concept of embracing all emotions—psychological acceptance—is roughly equivalent to embracing negative emotions. Psychological acceptance is described here: S. C. Hayes, "Content, Context, and the Types of Psychological Acceptance," in S. C. Hayes, N. S. Jacobson, V. M. Follette, and M. J. Dougher, eds., *Acceptance and Change: Content and*

Context in Psychotherapy (Reno, NV: Context Press, 1994), 13–32.

(p. 162) "*Acceptance of negative emotions* is a term that has been used in research to describe this phenomenon; in line with the dictionary definition...": This definition is from *Oxford American Dictionary*.

(p. 162) "Dwelling on negative emotions... inhibits action required to effect positive change.": Dr. Susan Nolen-Hoeksema researched rumination extensively. Here are two studies: S. Nolen-Hoeksema, "The Role of Rumination in Depressive Disorders and Mixed Anxiety/Depressive Symptoms," *Journal of Abnormal Psychology* 109 (2000): 504–11; Nolen-Hoeksema, "Responses to Depression and Their Effects on the Duration of Depressive Episodes," *Journal of Abnormal Psychology* 100 (1991): 569–82.

(p. 163) The quotation "For an angel went down at a certain season into the pool, and troubled the water: whosoever then first after the troubling of the water stepped in was made whole of whatsoever disease he had" is from John 5:4 in the King James Version of the Bible.

(p. 163) "Dr. Cornel West, author, philosopher...": The quotation of Dr. West is from one of his books: C. West, *Hope on a Tightrope: Words and Wisdom* (New York: Smiley Books, 2008), 85–86.

(p. 163) "John Steinbeck wrote that this kind of thinking...": This Steinbeck quotation comes from J. Steinbeck, *The Log from the Sea of Cortez* (New York: The Viking Press, 1951).

(p. 163) "This philosophy encourages an acceptance of things as...": S. Shillinglaw, introduction to *Of Mice and Men* by J. Steinbeck (New York: Penguin, 1994).

(p. 163) "The working title of his novel *Of Mice and Men*, 'Something That Happened,' reflects his approach" comes from Shillinglaw.

(p. 164) "He believed that seeing life as it is...": The quotation of Steinbeck at the end of this sentence, beginning "In their sometimes intolerant refusal to face facts as they are," comes from Steinbeck, 138.

(p. 165) "'In surgery, the healing process begins with a cut...'": *Grey's Anatomy*, season 6, episode 12, "I Like You So Much Better When You're Naked," aired January 21, 2010, on ABC, accessed August 12, 2014, http://en.wikiquote.org/wiki/Grey%27s_Anatomy_(Season_6)#I_Like_You_So_Much_Better_When_You.27re_-Naked_.5B6.12.5D.

(p. 166) "Later, I learned that 'embrace the suck'...": The definition of the military term "embrace the suck" is from Austin Bay talking about his book, *Embrace the Suck: A Pocket Guide to Milspeak*, on NPR's *Morning Edition*, March 8, 2007, http://www.npr.org/2007/03/08/7458809/embrace-the-suck-and-more-military-speak.

(p. 166) "Accepting negative emotions cultivates positive...": S. C. Hayes et al., "Measuring Experiential Avoidance: A Preliminary Test of a Working Model," *Psychological Record* 54 (2004): 553–78.

(p. 167) "One study from research on couples' therapy pitted...": N. S. Jacobson, A. Christensen, S. E. Prince, J. Cordova, and K. Eldridge, "Integrative Behavioral Couple Therapy: An Acceptance-Based, Promising New Treatment for Couple Discord," *Journal of Consulting and Clinical Psychology* 68 (2000): 351–55.

(p. 167) "The researchers, in reflecting on what could explain the results, wrote: 'Paradoxically, acceptance interventions are also predicted to produce change...'": The quotation is from pp. 351–52 of the journal article.

(p. 167) "In addition, two established therapies for treating people with posttraumatic stress disorder (PTSD), prolonged exposure therapy and cognitive processing therapy...": N. Resick, A. Weaver, and C. A. Feuer, "A Comparison of Cognitive-Processing Therapy with Prolonged Exposure and a Waiting Condition for the Treatment of Chronic Posttraumatic Stress Disorder in Female Rape Victims," *Journal of Consulting and Clinical Psychology* 70 (2002): 867–79.

(p. 167) "More generally, acceptance-based strategies have been associated with positive change in a range of psychological conditions...": S. C. Hayes, J. B. Luoma, F. W. Bond, A. Masuda, and J. Lillis, "Acceptance and Commitment Therapy: Model, Processes, and Outcomes," *Behaviour Research and Therapy* 44 (2006): 1–25; Hayes, "Content, Context, and the Types of Psychological Acceptance."

(pp. 167-168) "Mindfulness involves... in several therapies and studies.": The quotation about mindfulness and the finding that mindfulness has been found to have a positive impact on psychological well-being is from J. D. Teasdale, Z. V. Segal, and J. M. G. Williams, "Mindfulness Training and Problem Formulation," *Clinical Psychology: Science and Practice* 10 (2003): 157–60; and the following is research indicating that mindfulness "has led to improved psychological well-being in several therapies (e.g., Segal, Williams, and Teasdale 2013) and empirical studies (Bränström et al. 2010): Z. V. Segal, J. M. G. Williams, and J. D. Teasdale, *Mindfulness-Based Cognitive Therapy for Depression, Second Edition* (New York: Guilford, 2013); R. Bränström, P. Kvillemo, Y. Brandberg, and J. T. Moskowitz, "Self-Report Mindfulness as a Mediator of Psychological Well-Being in a Stress Reduction Intervention for Cancer Patients—A Randomized Study," *Annals of Behavioral Medicine* 39 (2010): 151–61.

(p. 168) "Research outside of the therapy setting also shows that openly expressing emotions...": J. Frattaroli, "Experimental

Disclosure and Its Moderators: A Meta-Analysis," *Psychological Bulletin* 132 (2006): 823–65.

(p. 168) "James Pennebaker, a psychology professor at the University of Texas...": e.g., J. W. Pennebaker, "Writing about Emotional Experiences as a Therapeutic Process," *Psychological Science* 8 (1997): 162–66.

(p. 168) "Similarly, Annette Stanton, a psychology professor at UCLA...": A. L. Stanton et al., "Emotionally Expressive Coping Predicts Psychological and Physical Adjustment to Breast Cancer," *Journal of Counseling and Clinical Psychology* 68 (2000): 875–82.

(p. 168) "Carl Rogers, an influential psychologist in the twentieth century...": The description about Rogers's work is based on his book: C. Rogers, *On Becoming a Person: A Therapist's View of Psychotherapy* (New York: Houghton Mifflin, 1961).

(p. 168) "Rogers argued that therapists best foster growth...": The Rogers quotation at the end of this sentence, beginning "So I find that when I can accept," is from Rogers, *On Becoming a Person*, 21.

(pp. 168-169) "Rogers contended that when people...": The Rogers quotation at the end of this sentence, beginning ". . . the curious paradox is that when I accept myself as I am, then I change," is from ibid., 17.

(p. 169) "In a scene that takes place in a coffee shop...": This *Parenthood* clip is from season 4, episode 3, "Everything Is Not Okay," aired fall 2012 (from about 32:30 to 33:30).

(p. 170) "Later in the same episode, Kristina and Adam are talking in bed...": Ibid. (from 40:50 to 42:19).

(p. 171) "Research on how people show support for a loved one who is a victim of trauma...": C. B. Wortman and C. Dunkel-Schetter, "Interpersonal Relationships and Cancer: A Theoretical Analysis," *Journal of Social Issues* 35 (1979): 120–

55; Wortman and Dunkel-Schetter, "Conceptual and Methodological Issues in the Study of Social Support," in A. Baum and J. Singer, eds., *Handbook of Psychology and Health* (Hillsdale, NJ: Erlbaum, 1987), 63–108.

(p. 171) "It is associated with more depressive symptoms... is described by victims to be one of the most common and least supportive responses.": K. M. Ingram, N. E. Betz, E. J. Mindes, M. M. Schmitt, and N. G. Smith, "Unsupportive Responses from Others Concerning a Stressful Life Event: Development of the Unsupportive Social Interactions Inventory," *Journal of Social and Clinical Psychology* 20 (2001): 173–207.

(p. 171) "Similarly, research on cancer victims' perceptions of social support...": G. A. Dakof and S. E. Taylor, "Victims' Perceptions of Social Support: What Is Helpful from Whom?," *Journal of Personality and Social Psychology* 58 (1990): 80–89.

(p. 172) "This idea is reflected in the motto of FailCon, the conference on failure: 'Embrace your mistakes. Build your success'": The FailCon motto is on their website: http://thefailcon.com/, accessed August 8, 2018.

(p. 173) "Psychologists have observed that there is societal pressure to be positive...": e.g., K. Werner and J. J. Gross, "Emotion Regulation and Psychopathology: A Conceptual Framework," in *Emotion Regulation and Psychopathology: A Transdiagnostic Approach to Etiology and Treatment*, ed. A. M. Kring and D. M. Sloan (New York: Guilford Press, 2009), 13–37.

(p. 173) "As a result, we tend to resist negative emotions as soon as they appear.": Werner and Gross, "Emotion Regulation and Psychopathology."

(p. 173) "In his book *Happier: Learn the Secrets to Daily Joy and Lasting Fulfillment*, Ben-Shahar...": T. Ben-Shahar,

"Happier: Learn the Secrets to Daily Joy and Lasting Fulfillment (New York: McGraw-Hill, 2007).

Chapter 10: "Does This Path Have a Heart?"

(p. 175) "He was known there as a 'genius': 'Surely, if ever a man had the magic word in his finger tips... its holiest secret.'" Willa Cather, "The Sculptor's Funeral," in *Coming, Aphrodite! and Other Stories*, ed. Margaret Anne O'Connor (New York: Penguin, 1999), 152.

(pp. 175-176) "One man recalled how Merrick was absentminded... once killing a cow that way: 'Harve, he was watchin' the sun set... got way.'": Ibid, 154.

(p. 176) "Another person commenting on Merrick's ineptitude said: 'Harve never was much account for anything practical, and he shore was never fond of work.'": Ibid, 154.

(p. 176) "Recently, research has punctured the conventional assumption that persistence is always optimal... can be detrimental.": C. Wrosch, M. Scheier, G. Miller, R. Schulz, and C. Carver, "Adaptive Self-Regulation of Unattainable Goals: Goal Disengagement, Goal Reengagement, and Subjective Well-Being," *Personality and Social Psychology Bulletin* 29 (2003): 1494–508.

(p. 176) "In one study, psychology professors Gregory Miller and Carsten Wrosch found that people who had more difficulty disengaging from unattainable goals (i.e., quitting)...": G. Miller and C. Wrosch, "You've Gotta Know When to Fold 'Em: Goal Disengagement and Systemic Inflammation in Adolescence," *Psychological Science* 18 (2007): 773–77.

(p. 176) "Inflammation is thought to underlie many diseases...": S. Taylor, *Health Psychology,* 9th ed. (New York: McGraw-Hill, 2015).

(p. 176) "Other studies have shown that individuals who

disengage from unattainable goals—who quit—have better well-being...": C. Wrosch et al., "Adaptive Self-Regulation"; C. Wrosch, G., E. Miller, C. S. Scheier, and S. B. de Pontet, "Giving Up on Unattainable Goals: Benefits for Health?," *Personality and Social Psychology Bulletin* 33 (2007): 251–65.

(p. 176) "Sometimes people persist with a strategy that has failed many times just to convince themselves or others that their resources have not been spent in vain...": J. Ross and B. M. Staw, "Expo 86: An Escalation Prototype," *Administrative Science Quarterly* 31 (1986): 274–97; Staw, "The Escalation of Commitment to a Course of Action," *Academy of Management Review* 6 (1981): 577–87; "...they persist with a failed strategy even when viable, possibly more fruitful, alternatives exist.": C. I. Diener and C. S. Dweck, "An Analysis of Learned Helplessness: Continuous Changes in Performance, Strategy, and Achievement Cognitions Following Failure," *Journal of Personality and Social Psychology* 36 (1978): 451–62.

(p. 176) "Sometimes quitting is best.": Another article that demonstrates this finding is C. Wrosch, M. F. Scheier, C. S. Carver, and R. Schulz, "The Importance of Goal Disengagement in Adaptive Self-Regulation: When Giving Up Is Beneficial," *Self and Identity* 2 (2003): 1–20.

(pp. 176-177) "Furthermore, recent research indicates that focusing on just these two responses...": R. F. Baumeister, J. D. Campbell, J. I. Krueger, and K. D. Vohs, "Doesn't High Self-Esteem Cause Better Performance, Interpersonal Success, Happiness, or Healthier Lifestyles?," *Psychological Science in the Public Interest* 4 (2003): 1–44.

(p. 177) "*Goal reengagement* is a term that has been used...": C. Wrosch et al., "Adaptive Self-Regulation."

(p. 177) "Research shows that when people confront unattainable goals, reengaging with new, intrinsically...": Ibid.

(p. 177) "Relatedly, research on responding well to crises in early adulthood...": O. C. Robinson, G. R. T. Wright, and J. A. Smith, "The Holistic Phase Model of Early Adult Crisis," *Journal of Adult Development* 20 (2013): 27–37.

(pp. 177-178) "Research on goal reengagement challenges accepted notions of how to respond well to negative events... Previous research indicates, for example, that when people's goals are in step with their deeper needs and values, psychological well-being is enhanced...": Deci and Ryan, "Human Autonomy"; K. M. Sheldon, "The Self-Concordance Model of Healthy Goal Striving: When Personal Goals Correctly Represent the Person," in Deci and Ryan, *Handbook of Self-Determination Research*, 65–86; ". . . research also demonstrates that engaging with new, meaningful goals gives purpose to life...": Ryff, "Happiness Is Everything, or Is It?"; Scheier and Carver, "Adapting to Cancer"; "...and that a sense of purpose fosters long-term personal development.": Ryff, "Happiness Is Everything, or Is It?"

(p. 178) "The author Carlos Castaneda wrote: 'Look at every path closely and deliberately...'" Carlos Castaneda, *The Teachings of Don Juan: A Yaqui Way of Knowledge* (New York: Pocket Books, 1968).

(p. 180) "But it can be a limitation because it is hard to generalize findings of tightly controlled experiments...": The scientific term used to describe this phenomenon is *ecological validity*. Ecological validity is an indicator of the extent to which behaviors in a laboratory setting represent behaviors in real-world settings. The following article documents how studies highlighting the benefit of persistence lack ecological validity: Baumeister et al., "Doesn't High Self-Esteem Cause Better Performance, Interpersonal Success, Happiness, or Healthier Lifestyles?"

(p. 181) "This approach doesn't take into account the possibility that growth...": Considering a long-term temporal component in responding to failure is consistent with research showing that responding adaptively to developmental crises is a process that evolves across time: Robinson, Wright, and Smith, "The Holistic Phase Model of Early Adult Crisis."

Chapter 11: Tender and Tough

(p. 183) "I conducted two studies using different methods and different participant samples...": Detailed information about these studies can be found in the research article R. J. North, C. J. Holahan, C. L. Carlson, and S. A. Pahl, "From Failure to Flourishing: The Roles of Acceptance and Goal Reengagement," *Journal of Adult Development* 21 (2014): 239–50.

(p. 190) "These two studies are a small part of a large, growing body of research suggesting that accepting the negative and taking action...": I, along with collaborators, have contributed to this literature and developed ideas discussed here through other publications. The following are articles and chapters that fall into this category and are not discussed specifically elsewhere in this book: R. J North and W. B. Swann, Jr., "What's Positive about Self-Verification?" in C. R. Snyder, S. J. Lopez, L. M. Edwards, and S. C. Marques (eds.), *Handbook of Positive Psychology,* 3rd edition (New York: Oxford University Press, 2016); R. J. North and W. B. Swann, Jr., "Self-Verification 360°: Illuminating the Light and Dark Sides," *Self and Identity*, 8 (2009): 131–46; R. J. North and W. B. Swann, Jr., "What's Positive about Self-Verification?" in C. R. Snyder and Shane J. Lopez (eds.), *Handbook of Positive Psychology*, 2nd edition (New York: Oxford University Press, 2009), 465–82; C. J. Holahan, R. J. North, and R. H. Moos, "Stress," in A. Wenzel (ed.), *The SAGE Encyclopedia of Abnormal and Clinical Psychology*, Thousand Oaks, CA: Sage, 2017), 3339–43.

(p. 190): "Research on posttraumatic growth—growth after

trauma—indicates that...": T. B. Kashdan and J. Q. Kane, "Post-Traumatic Distress and the Presence of Post-Traumatic Growth and Meaning in Life: Experiential Avoidance as a Moderator," *Personality and Individual Differences* 50 (2011): 84–89.

(p. 191) "Acceptance and commitment therapy (ACT), which has been effective...": S. C. Hayes and K. G. Wilson, "Acceptance and Commitment Therapy: Altering the Verbal Support for Experiential Avoidance," *The Behavior Analyst* 17 (1994): 289–303.

(p. 191) "Dialectical behavior therapy (DBT), which has been effective in treating people...": M. M. Linehan, *Cognitive-Behavioral Treatment of Borderline Personality Disorder* (New York: Guilford Press, 1993).

(p. 191) "In a writing experiment, colleagues and I tested a similar strategy in a non-therapy situation...": R. J. North, A. V. Pai, J. G. Hixon, and C. J. Holahan, "Finding Happiness in Negative Emotions: An Experimental Test of a Novel Expressive Writing Paradigm," *Journal of Positive Psychology* 6 (2011): 192–203.

(p. 191) "In a subsequent study, researchers and I analyzed the language...": R. J. North, R. L. Meyerson, D. N. Brown, and C. J. Holahan, "The Language of Psychological Change: Decoding an Expressive Writing Paradigm," *Journal of Language and Social Psychology* 32 (2013): 142–61; "...because research has shown that linguistic analysis can be like an x-ray illuminating people's cognitive processes.": James Pennebaker has pioneered research on how language is a tool for providing insights into psychological processes. He wrote a book about his research: J. W. Pennebaker, *The Secret Life of Pronouns: What Our Words Say about Us* (New York: Bloomsbury Press, 2012). Also, here is a journal article that explains how language provides clues about we think: Y. R. Tausczik and J. W. Pennebaker, "The Psychological Meaning of Words:

LIWC and Computerized Text Analysis Methods," *Journal of Language and Social Psychology* 29 (2010): 24–54.

(p. 191) "Our findings revealed that over the course of writing about their problem, participants who used the strategy..." North et al., "The Language of Psychological Change."

(p. 192) "Mayor Booker said, 'What is so urgently necessary...'": This quotation of Senator Booker is from lecture three of The Unfinished Journey of America's Spirit, "The Future: Humble Hopes and Insane Idealism," from around 43:00–43:25, October 3, 2009, accessed August 6, 2014, http://aas.princeton.edu/event/the-future-humble-hopes-and-insane-idealism/.

(p. 192) "Mayor Booker underscored his point by drawing on a quotation about how optimists...": Ibid., around 43:30–44:25.

Chapter 12: The Way We Think about Success

(p. 199) "Not that it would take research to convince you of success's upside...": Research showing that successes provide people with a sense of competence, confidence, and self-efficacy comes from the following publications: D. T. Hall and L. W. Forster, "A Psychological Success Cycle and Goal Setting: Goals, Performance, and Attitudes," *Academy of Management Journal* 20 (1977): 282–90; D. T. Hall and F. S. Hall, "The Relationship between Goals, Performance, Success, Self-Image, and Involvement under Different Organization Climates," *Journal of Vocational Behavior* 9 (1976): 267–78; A. Bandura, "Self-Efficacy: Toward a Unifying Theory of Behavioral Change," *Psychological Review* 84 (1977): 191–215; Bandura, "Self-Regulation of Motivation and Action through Internal Standards and Goal Systems," in *Goal Concepts in Personality and Social Psychology* (Hillsdale, NJ: Erlbaum, 1989), 19–85.

(p. 200) "Successes do not promote much reflection or reevaluation...": Taylor, "Asymmetrical Effects of Positive and Negative Events"; Wong and Weiner, "When People Ask 'Why' Questions."

(p. 200) "Successes encourage stability and provide momentum...": Ellis, Mendel, and Nir, "Learning from Successful and Failed Experience."

(p. 200) "Successes tend to impede change and growth.": Ibid.

(p. 200) "Successes make us more risk averse and foster complacency.": Ibid.; S. B. Sitkin, "Learning through Failure: The Strategy of Small Losses," *Research in Organizational Behavior* 14 (1992): 231–66.

(p. 200) "The comedian Conan O'Brien used an analogy of a white tuxedo...": This quotation from Conan O'Brien is from his speech at Harvard University's Class Day; the speech was given to Harvard's class of 2000 on June 7, 2000.

(p. 203) "Much research on the connection between money and happiness has shown that there is a small, positive relationship...": E. Diener and R. Biswas-Diener, "Will Money Increase Subjective Well-Being? A Literature Review and Guide to Needed Research," *Social Indicators Research* 57 (2002): 119–69; R. A. Easterlin, "The Economics of Happiness," *Daedalus* 133, no. 2 (2004), 26–33.

(p. 203) "Furthermore, longitudinal studies exploring the connection... with any increase in happiness.": R. J. North, C. J. Holahan, R. H. Moos, and R. C. Cronkite, "Family Support, Family Income, and Happiness: A 10-Year Perspective," *Journal of Family Psychology* 22, no. 3 (2008), 475–83; R. A. Easterlin, "Diminishing Marginal Utility of Income? Caveat Emptor," *Social Indicators Research* 70 (2005): 243–55.

(p. 204) "Steve Jobs articulated a similar idea back in 1994 when he was interviewed by John McClaughlin of the Santa

Clara Valley Historical...": I bought and downloaded this interview on August 6, 2014. The interview took place at NeXT Computer Headquarters in Redwood City, California, in November 1994.

(pp. 204-205) "'So, the thing I would say is, when you grow up, you tend to get told that...'": Ibid., around 10:25–11:57.

Chapter 13: A Simple, Revolutionary Shift in the Way We Lead Our Lives

(pp. 207-208) I interviewed Dr. Maya Angelou in her home in Winston-Salem, North Carolina, on June 17, 2013. Detailed information about Dr. Maya Angelou was found at http://mayaangelou.com/bio/, accessed October 3, 2013.

(p. 222) "When Mark Zuckerberg, CEO and founder of Facebook, was a guest on *The Oprah Winfrey Show* in 2010, a short video was shown about daily life at Facebook...": "Inside Mark Zuckerberg's Home and Facebook Headquarters," aired September 24, 2010, on ABC, http://www.oprah.com/oprahshow/Take-a-Look-into-the-Life-of-Mark-Zuckerberg-Video_1.

(p. 223) "He distinguishes between two types of freedom: positive and negative.": E. Fromm, *Escape from Freedom* (New York: Avon Books, 1941).

(p. 225) "As you may recall, the number one regret...": Ware, "Top 5 Regrets of the Dying."

(p. 231) "In June 1978, the Mormon church declared that black men could become priests.": These details came from the following article: John Turner, "Why Race Is Still a Problem for Mormons," *New York Times,* August 18, 2012.

Chapter 14: Hidden Magic

(p. 237) "O my friends, there are resources in us...": Emerson, in Whicher, *Selections from Ralph Waldo Emerson*, 114.

Epilogue

(p. 242) "The first, a *Princeton Alumni Weekly* magazine, I found in my mailbox in the beginning of April...": This *Princeton Alumni Weekly* (PAW) was from April 7, 2010.

REFERENCES

Acocella, J. 2007. *Twenty-Eight Artists and Two Saints.* New York: Pantheon Books.

Asch, S. E. 1955. "Opinions and Social Pressure." *Scientific American* 193, no. 5: 31–35. doi:10.1038/scientificamerican1155-31.

Bandura, A. 1969. *Principles of Behavior Modification.* New York: Holt, Rinehart, and Winston.

———. 1989. "Self-Regulation of Motivation and Action through Internal Standards and Goal Systems." In *Goal Concepts in Personality and Social Psychology*, edited by L. A. Pervin, 19–85. Hillsdale, NJ: Lawrence Erlbaum Associates, Inc.

———. 1977. "Self-Efficacy: Toward a Unifying Theory of Behavioral Change." *Psychological Review* 84, no. 2: 191–215. doi:10.1037/0033-295X.84.2.191.

Baumeister, R. F., J. D. Campbell, J. I. Krueger, and K. D. Vohs. 2003. "Doesn't High Self-Esteem Cause Better Performance, Interpersonal Success, Happiness, or Healthier Lifestyles?" *Psychological Science in the Public Interest* 4:1–44.

Ben-Shahar, T. 2007. *Happier: Learn the Secrets to Daily Joy and Lasting Fulfillment*. New York: McGraw-Hill.

Blinder, Alan S. 2009. "Education for the Third Industrial Revolution." In *Creating a New Teaching Profession*, edited by J. Hannaway and D. Goldhaber, 22. Washington, DC: Urban Institute Press.

Bränström, R., P. Kvillemo, Y. Brandberg, and J. T. Moskowitz. 2010. "Self-Report Mindfulness as a Mediator of Psychological Well-Being in a Stress Reduction Intervention for Cancer Patients—A Randomized Study." *Annals of Behavioral Medicine* 39, no. 2: 151–61. doi:10.1007/s12160-010-9168-6.

Brooks, D. "The Soft Side." *New York Times*, October 5, 2010.

Bryant, A. "Corner Office: John T. Chambers." *New York Times*, August 2, 2009.

Buchanan, G. M., and M. P. Seligman, eds. 1995. *Explanatory Style*. Hillsdale, NJ: Lawrence Erlbaum Associates, Inc.

Burhans, K. K., and C. S. Dweck. 1995. "Helplessness in Early Childhood: The Role of Contingent Worth." *Child Development* 66, no. 6: 1719–38. doi:10.2307/1131906.

Castaneda, Carlos. 1968. *The Teachings of Don Juan: A Yaqui Way of Knowledge*. New York: Pocket Books.

Cather, Willa. 1999. "The Sculptor's Funeral." In *Coming, Aphrodite! and Other Stories*, edited by Margaret Anne O'Connor, 152. New York: Penguin.

Dakof, G. A., and S. E. Taylor. 1990. "Victims' Perceptions of Social Support: What Is Helpful from Whom?" *Journal of Personality and Social Psychology* 58, no. 1: 80–89. doi:10.1037/0022-3514.58.1.80.

Deci, E. L., and R. M. Ryan. 1985. *Intrinsic Motivation and Self-Determination in Human Behavior*. New York: Plenum Press.

―――. 1991. "A Motivational Approach to Self: Integration in Personality." In *Nebraska Symposium on Motivation*, vol. 38, *Perspectives on Motivation*, edited by R. A. Dienstbier, 237–88. Lincoln, NE: University of Nebraska Press.

―――. 1995. "Human Autonomy: The Basis for True Self-Esteem." In *Efficacy, Agency, and Self-Esteem*, edited by M. H. Kernis, 31–49. New York: Plenum Press.

Dickerson, S. S., T. L. Gruenewald, and M. E. Kemeny. 2004. "When the Social Self Is Threatened: Shame, Physiology, and Health." *Journal of Personality* 72, no. 6: 1191–216. doi:10.1111/j.1467-6494.2004.00295.x.

Diener, C. I., and C. S. Dweck. 1978. "An Analysis of Learned Helplessness: Continuous Changes in Performance, Strategy, and Achievement Cognitions Following Failure." *Journal of Personality and Social Psychology* 36, no. 5: 451–62. doi:10.1037//0022-3514.36.5.451.

Diener, E., and R. Biswas-Diener. 2002. "Will Money Increase Subjective Well-Being? A Literature Review and Guide to Needed Research." *Social Indicators Research* 57, no. 2: 119–69.

Dweck, C. S. 1975. "The Role of Expectations and Attributions in the Alleviation of Learned Helplessness." *Journal of Personality and Social Psychology* 31, no. 4: 674–85. doi:10.1037/h0077149.

Dweck, C. S., T. E. Goetz, and N. L. Strauss. 1980. "Sex Differences in Learned Helplessness: IV. An Experimental and Naturalistic Study of Failure Generalization and Its Mediators." *Journal of Personality and Social Psychology* 38, no. 3: 441–52. doi:10.1037/0022-3514.38.3.441.

Dweck, C. S., and E. L. Leggett. 1988. "A Social-Cognitive Approach to Motivation and Personality." *Psychological Review* 95, no. 2: 256–73. doi:10.1037/0033-295X.95.2.256.

Easterlin, R. A. 2004. "The Economics of Happiness." *Daedalus* 133, no. 2: 26–33.

———. 2005. "Diminishing Marginal Utility of Income? Caveat Emptor." *Social Indicators Research* 70:243–55.

Ellis, S., R. Mendel, and M. Nir. 2006. "Learning from Successful and Failed Experience: The Moderating Role of Kind of After-Event Review." *Journal of Applied Psychology* 91, no. 3: 669–80. doi:10.1037/0021-9010.91.3.669.

Frattaroli, J. 2006. "Experimental Disclosure and Its Moderators: A Meta-Analysis." *Psychological Bulletin* 132, no. 6: 823–65. doi:10.1037/0033-2909.132.6.823.

Friedman, T. "Broadway and the Mosque." *New York Times*, August 3, 2010.

Fromm, E. 1941. *Escape from Freedom*. New York: Avon Books.

Hall, D. T., and L. W. Foster. 1977. "A Psychological Success Cycle and Goal Setting: Goals, Performance, and Attitudes." *Academy of Management Journal* 20, no. 2: 282–90. doi:10.2307/255401.

Hall, D. T., and F. S. Hall. 1976. "The Relationship between Goals, Performance, Success, Self-Image, and Involvement under Different Organization Climates." *Journal of Vocational Behavior* 9, no. 3: 267–78. doi:10.1016/0001-8791(76)90055-5.

Harrison, K. "Lives in the Arts." *New York Times*, February 18, 2007.

Hastie, R. 1984. "Causes and Effects of Causal Attribution." *Journal of Personality and Social Psychology* 46, no. 1: 44–56. doi:10.1037/0022-3514.46.1.44.

Hayes, S. C., 1994. "Content, Context, and the Types of Psychological Acceptance." In *Acceptance and Change: Content and Context in Psychotherapy*, edited by S. C. Hayes, N. S. Jacobson, V. M. Follette, and M. J. Dougher, 13–32. Reno, NV: Context Press.

Hayes, S. C., J. B. Luoma, F. W. Bond, A. Masuda, and J. Lillis. 2006. "Acceptance and Commitment Therapy: Model, Processes, and Outcomes." *Behaviour Research and Therapy* 44, no. 1: 1–25. doi:10.1016/j.brat.2005.06.006.

Hayes, S. C., K. Strosahl, K. G. Wilson, R. T. Bissett, J. Pistorello, D. Toarmino... and S. M. McCurry. 2004. "Measuring Experiential Avoidance: A Preliminary Test of a Working Model." *Psychological Record* 54, no. 4: 553–78.

Hayes, S. C., and K. G. Wilson. 1994. "Acceptance and Commitment Therapy: Altering the Verbal Support for Experiential Avoidance." *Behavior Analyst* 17, no. 2: 289–303.

Holahan, C. J., North, R. J., and Moos, R. H. 2017. "Stress." In *The SAGE Encyclopedia of Abnormal and Clinical Psychology*, edited by A. Wenzel, 3339–43. Thousand Oaks, CA: Sage.

Ingram, K. M., N. E. Betz, E. J. Mindes, M. M. Schmitt, and N. G. Smith. 2001. "Unsupportive Responses from Others Concerning a Stressful Life Event: Development of the Unsupportive Social Interactions Inventory." *Journal of Social and Clinical Psychology* 20, no. 2: 173–207. doi:10.1521/jscp.20.2.173.22265.

Jacobson, N. S., A. Christensen, S. E. Prince, J. Cordova, and K. Eldridge. 2000. "Integrative Behavioral Couple Therapy: An Acceptance-Based, Promising New Treatment for Couple Discord." *Journal of Consulting and Clinical Psychology* 68, no. 2: 351–55. doi:10.1037/0022-006X.68.2.351.

Kamins, M. L., and C. S. Dweck. 1999. "Person versus Process Praise and Criticism: Implications for Contingent Self-Worth and Coping." *Developmental Psychology* 3, no. 3: 835–47. doi:10.1037/0012-1649.35.3.835.

Kashdan, T. B., and J. Q. Kane. 2011. "Post-Traumatic Distress and the Presence of Post-Traumatic Growth and

Meaning in Life: Experiential Avoidance as a Moderator." *Personality and Individual Differences* 50, no. 1: 84–89. doi:10.1016/j.paid.2010.08.028.

King, L. A., and J. A. Hicks. 2007. "Whatever Happened to 'What Might Have Been'?: Regrets, Happiness, and Maturity." *American Psychologist* 62, no. 7: 625–36. doi:10.1037/0003-066X.62.7.625.

Kross, E., M. G. Berman, W. Mischel, E. E. Smith, and T. D. Wager. 2011. "Social Rejection Shares Somatosensory Representations with Physical Pain." *PNAS Proceedings of the National Academy of Sciences of the United States of America* 108, no. 15: 6270–75. doi:10.1073/pnas.1102693108.

Kuczmarski, T. "How Failure Breeds Success." *Bloomberg Businessweek,* July 9, 2006.

Leary, M. R., B. Gallagher, E. Fors, N. Buttermore, E. Baldwin, K. Kennedy, and A. Mills. 2003. "The Invalidity of Disclaimers about the Effects of Social Feedback on Self-Esteem." *Personality and Social Psychology Bulletin* 29, no. 5: 623–36. doi:10.1177/0146167203029005007.

Leary, M. R., A. L. Haupt, K. S. Strausser, and J. T. Chokel. 1998. "Calibrating the Sociometer: The Relationship between Interpersonal Appraisals and State Self-Esteem." *Journal of Personality and Social Psychology* 74, no. 5: 1290–99. doi:10.1037/0022-3514.74.5.1290.

Linehan, M. M. 1993. *Cognitive-Behavioral Treatment of Borderline Personality Disorder*. New York: Guilford Press.

Lohr, S. "Reaping the Rewards of Risk-Taking." *New York Times*, August 28, 2011.

Maslow, A. H. 1970. *Motivation and Personality*. Second edition. New York: Harper & Row.

Mendes, W. B., B. Major, S. McCoy, and J. Blascovich. 2008. "How Attributional Ambiguity Shapes Physiological and Emotional Responses to Social Rejection and Acceptance."

Journal of Personality and Social Psychology 94, no. 2: 278–91. doi:10.1037/0022-3514.94.2.278.

Milgram, S. 1963. "Behavioral Study of Obedience." *Journal of Abnormal and Social Psychology* 6, no. 4: 371–78. doi:10.1037/h0040525.

Mill, J. S. 2002. *On Liberty.* Mineola, NY: Dover Publications. First published 1859 by J. W. Parker and Son (London).

Miller, G. E., and C. Wrosch. 2007. "You've Gotta Know When to Fold 'Em: Goal Disengagement and Systemic Inflammation in Adolescence." *Psychological Science* 18, no. 9: 773–77. doi:10.1111/j.1467-9280.2007.01977.x.

Nolen-Hoeksema, S. 1991. "Responses to Depression and Their Effects on the Duration of Depressive Episodes." *Journal of Abnormal Psychology* 100, no. 4: 569–82. doi:10.1037/0021-843X.100.4.569.

———. 2000. "The Role of Rumination in Depressive Disorders and Mixed Anxiety/Depressive Symptoms." *Journal of Abnormal Psychology* 109, no. 3: 504–11. doi:10.1037/0021-843X.109.3.504.

North, R. J., C. J. Holahan, C. L. Carlson, and S. A. Pahl. 2014. "From Failure to Flourishing: The Roles of Acceptance and Goal Reengagement." *Journal of Adult Development* 21, no. 4: 239–50. doi:10.1007/s10804-014-9195-9.

North, R. J., C. J. Holahan, R. H. Moos, and R. C. Cronkite. 2008. "Family Support, Family Income, and Happiness: A 10-Year Perspective." *Journal of Family Psychology* 22, no. 3: 475–83. doi:10.1037/0893-3200.22.3.475.

North, R. J., R. L. Meyerson, D. N. Brown, and C. J. Holahan. 2013. "The Language of Psychological Change: Decoding an Expressive Writing Paradigm." *Journal of Language and Social Psychology* 32, no. 2: 142–61. doi:10.1177/0261927X12456381.

North, R. J., A. V. Pai, J. G. Hixon, and C. J. Holahan. 2011.

"Finding Happiness in Negative Emotions: An Experimental Test of a Novel Expressive Writing Paradigm." *Journal of Positive Psychology* 6, no. 3: 192–203. doi:10.1080/17439760.2011.570365.

North, R. J., and W. B. Swann, Jr. 2016. "What's Positive about Self-Verification?" In *Handbook of Positive Psychology*, third edition, edited by C. R. Snyder, S. J. Lopez, L. M. Edwards, and S. C. Marques. New York: Oxford University Press.

———. 2009. "Self-Verification 360°: Illuminating the Light and Dark Sides." *Self and Identity* 8:131–46.

———. 2009. "What's Positive about Self-Verification?" In *Handbook of Positive Psychology*, second edition, edited by C. R. Snyder and Shane J. Lopez, 465–82. New York: Oxford University Press.

Park, N., C. Peterson, and M. E. P. Seligman. 2004. "Strengths of Character and Well-Being." *Journal of Social and Clinical Psychology* 23:603–19.

Pennebaker, J. W. 1997. "Writing about Emotional Experiences as a Therapeutic Process." *Psychological Science* 8, no. 3: 162–66. doi:10.1111/j.1467-9280.1997.tb00403.x.

———. 2011. *The Secret Life of Pronouns: What Our Words Say about Us*. New York: Bloomsbury Press.

Peterson, C., and M. E. Seligman. 1984. "Causal Explanations as a Risk Factor for Depression: Theory and Evidence." *Psychological Review* 91, no. 3: 347–74. doi:10.1037/0033-295X.91.3.347.

Pink, D. H. 2006. *A Whole New Mind: Why Right-Brainers Will Rule the Future*. New York: Riverhead Books.

Resick, P. A., P. Nishith, T. L. Weaver, M. C. Astin, and C. A. Feuer. 2002. "A Comparison of Cognitive-Processing Therapy with Prolonged Exposure and a Waiting Condition for the Treatment of Chronic Posttraumatic Stress Disorder in Female Rape Victims." *Journal of Consulting and Clinical Psychology* 70, no. 4: 867–79. doi:10.1037/0022-006X.70.4.867.

Robinson, O. C., G. R. T. Wright, and J. A. Smith. 2013. "The Holistic Phase Model of Early Adult Crisis." *Journal of Adult Development* 20, no. 1: 27–37. doi:10.1007/s10804-013-9153-y.

Rogers, C. R. 1961. *On Becoming a Person: A Therapist's View of Psychotherapy*. Boston: Houghton Mifflin.

———. 1963. "The Actualizing Tendency in Relation to 'Motives' and to Consciousness." In M. R. Jones, *Nebraska Symposium on Motivation*, vol. 11, edited by M. R. Jones, 1–24. Lincoln, NE: University of Nebraska Press.

Ross, J., and B. M. Staw. 1986. "Expo 86: An Escalation Prototype." *Administrative Science Quarterly* 31, no. 2: 274–97.

Rude, S. S., E. Gortner, and J. W. Pennebaker. 2004. "Language Use of Depressed and Depression-Vulnerable College Students." *Cognition and Emotion* 18, no. 8: 1121–33. doi:10.1080/02699930441000030.

Ryff, C. D. 1989. "Happiness Is Everything, or Is It? Explorations on the Meaning of Psychological Well-Being." *Journal of Personality and Social Psychology* 57, no. 6: 1069–81. doi:10.1037/0022-3514.57.6.1069.

Scheier, M. F., and C. S. Carver. 2001. "Adapting to Cancer: The Importance of Hope and Purpose." In *Psychosocial Interventions for Cancer*, edited by A. Baum and B. L. Andersen, 15–36. Washington, DC: American Psychological Association. doi:10.1037/10402-002.

Schlegel, R. J., J. A. Hicks, L. A. King, and J. Arndt. 2011. "Feeling Like You Know Who You Are: Perceived True Self-Knowledge and Meaning in Life." *Personality and Social*

Psychology Bulletin 37, no. 6: 745–56. doi:10.1177/0146167211400424.

Segal, Z. V., J. G. Williams, and J. D. Teasdale. 2013. *Mindfulness-Based Cognitive Therapy for Depression.* 2nd ed. New York: Guilford Press.

Seligman, M. E. P. 1972. "Learned Helplessness." *Annual Review of Medicine* 23:407–12. New York: Academic Press.

———. 2002. *Authentic Happiness: Using the New Positive Psychology to Realize Your Potential for Lasting Fulfillment.* New York: Free Press.

Seligman, M. E. P., S. F. Maier, and R. L. Solomon. 1971. "Unpredictable and Uncontrollable Aversive Events." In *Aversive Conditioning and Learning,* edited by F. R. Brush, 347–400. New York: Academic Press.

Seligman, M. P., T. Rashid, and A. C. Parks. 2006. "Positive Psychotherapy." *American Psychologist* 61, no. 8: 774–88. doi:10.1037/0003-066X.61.8.774.

Sheldon, K. M. 2001. "The Self-Concordance Model of Healthy Goal Striving: When Personal Goals Correctly Represent the Person." In *Life Goals and Well-Being: Towards a Positive Psychology of Human Striving,* edited by P. Schmuck and K. M. Sheldon, 18–36. Seattle, WA: Hogrefe & Huber Publishers.

———. 2002. "The Self-Concordance Model of Healthy Goal Striving: When Personal Goals Correctly Represent the Person." In *Handbook of Self-Determination Research,* edited by E. L. Deci and R. M. Ryan, 65–86. Rochester, NY: University of Rochester Press.

Shillinglaw, S. 1994. Introduction. In J. Steinbeck, *Of Mice and Men.* New York: Penguin.

Steinbeck, J. 1951. *The Log from the Sea of Cortez.* New York: The Viking Press.

Sitkin, S. B. 1992. "Learning through Failure: The Strategy

of Small Losses." *Research in Organizational Behavior* 14:231–66.

Skinner, B. F. 1953. *Science and Human Behavior*. New York: Macmillan.

Stanton, A. L., S. Danoff-Burg, C. L. Cameron, M. Bishop, C. A. Collins, S. B. Kirk... and R. Twillman. 2000. "Emotionally Expressive Coping Predicts Psychological and Physical Adjustment to Breast Cancer." *Journal of Consulting and Clinical Psychology* 68, no. 5: 875–82. doi:10.1037/0022-006X.68.5.875.

Staw, B. M. 1981. "The Escalation of Commitment to a Course of Action." *Academy of Management Review* 6, no. 4: 577–87. doi:10.5465/AMR.1981.4285694.

Swann, W. B., J. J. Griffin, S. C. Predmore, and B. Gaines. 1987. "The Cognitive-Affective Crossfire: When Self-Consistency Confronts Self-Enhancement." *Journal of Personality and Social Psychology* 52, no. 5, 881–89. doi:10.1037/0022-3514.52.5.881.

Tausczik, Y. R., and J. W. Pennebaker. 2010. "The Psychological Meaning of Words: LIWC and Computerized Text Analysis Methods." *Journal of Language and Social Psychology* 29, no. 1: 24–54. doi:10.1177/0261927X09351676.

Taylor, S. E. 1991. "Asymmetrical Effects of Positive and Negative Events: The Mobilization-Minimization Hypothesis." *Psychological Bulletin* 110, no. 1: 67–85. doi:10.1037/0033-2909.110.1.67.

Teasdale, J. D., Z. V. Segal, and J. G. Williams. 2003. "Mindfulness Training and Problem Formulation." *Clinical Psychology: Science and Practice* 10, no. 2: 157–60. doi:10.1093/clipsy/bpg017.

Tedeschi, R. G., and L. G. Calhoun. 2004. "Posttraumatic Growth: Conceptual Foundations and Empirical Evidence." *Psychological Inquiry* 15:1–18.

Turner, J. "Why Race Is Still a Problem for Mormons." *New York Times,* August 18, 2012.

Werner, K., and J. J. Gross. 2009. "Emotion Regulation and Psychopathology: A Conceptual Framework." In *Emotion Regulation and Psychopathology: A Transdiagnostic Approach to Etiology and Treatment*, edited by A. M. Kring and D. M. Sloan, 13–37. New York: Guilford Press.

West, C. 2008. *Hope on a Tightrope: Words and Wisdom.* New York: Smiley Books.

Whicher, S. E. 1957. *Selections from Ralph Waldo Emerson: An Organic Anthology*. Boston: Houghton Mifflin.

Wong, P. T., and B. Weiner. 1981. "When People Ask 'Why' Questions, and the Heuristics of Attributional Search." *Journal of Personality and Social Psychology* 40, no. 4: 650–63. doi:10.1037/0022-3514.40.4.650.

Wortman, C. B., and C. Dunkel-Schetter. 1979. "Interpersonal Relationships and Cancer: A Theoretical Analysis." *Journal of Social Issues* 35, no. 1: 120–55. doi:10.1111/j.1540-4560.1979.tb00792.x.

———. 1987. "Conceptual and Methodological Issues in the Study of Social Support." In *Handbook of Psychology and Health,* vol. 5, edited by A. Baum and J. E. Singer, 63–108. Hillsdale, NJ: Lawrence Erlbaum Associates, Inc.

Wrosch, C., G. E. Miller, M. F. Scheier, and S. B. de Pontet. 2007. "Giving Up on Unattainable Goals: Benefits for Health?" *Personality and Social Psychology Bulletin* 33, no. 2: 251–65. doi:10.1177/0146167206294905.

Wrosch, C., M. F. Scheier, C. S. Carver, and R. Schulz. 2003. "The Importance of Goal Disengagement in Adaptive Self-Regulation: When Giving Up Is Beneficial." *Self and Identity* 2, no. 1: 1–20. doi:10.1080/15298860309021.

Wrosch, C., M. F. Scheier, G. E. Miller, R. Schulz, and C. S. Carver. 2003. "Adaptive Self-Regulation of Unattainable Goals:

Goal Disengagement, Goal Reengagement, and Subjective Well-Being." *Personality and Social Psychology Bulletin* 29, no. 12: 1494–508. doi:10.1177/0146167203256921.

Wrzesniewski, A., C. McCauley, P. Rozin, and B. Schwartz. 1997. "Jobs, Careers, and Callings: People's Relations to Their Work." *Journal of Research in Personality* 31, no. 1: 21–33. doi:10.1006/jrpe.1997.2162.

Zakay, D., S. Ellis, and M. Shevalsky. 2004. "Outcome Value and Early Warning Indications as Determinants of Willingness to Learn from Experience." *Experimental Psychology* 51, no. 2, 150–57. doi:10.1027/1618-3169.51.2.150.

Made in the USA
Coppell, TX
14 October 2022

84620301R00184